ON SHARING FATE

ETHICS AND ACTION

A series edited by Tom Regan

Norman S. Care

On Sharing Fate

TEMPLE UNIVERSITY PRESS

PHILADELPHIA

Temple University Press, Philadelphia 19122
Copyright © 1987 by Temple University
All rights reserved
Published 1987
Printed in the United States of America

The paper used in this publication meets the minimum requirements of American National Standard for Information Sciences—Permanence of Paper for Printed Library Materials, ANSI Z39.48-1984

Library of Congress Cataloging-in-Publication Data

Care, Norman S.
  On sharing fate.
  (Ethics and Action)
  Includes index.
  1. Ethics.   2. Social ethics.   3. Responsibility.
I. Title.   II. Series.
BJ1012.C32   1987   170   86-32303
ISBN 0-87722-473-0 (alk. paper)

For Barbara

CONTENTS

Preface / xi

CHAPTER 1
CHALLENGES TO INDIVIDUAL RESPONSIBILITY / 3

1. Self-Responsibility and Other-Responsibility / 3
2. "Policies" / 6
3. Questions / 10
4. Troubling Facts / 11
5. Perspective / 19
6. Moral Reaction / 21
7. Fatalism and Pessimism / 24

CHAPTER 2
CAREER CHOICE / 26

1. A Question of Individual Responsibility / 26
2. Common Opinion / 28
3. Careers and Competent Individuals / 29
4. The Problem of Career Choice / 33
5. The Moral Standing of Individual Lives: Three Perspectives / 34
6. The Selection Problem / 41
7. Replies to Two Objections / 45

CHAPTER 3
MEMBERSHIP IN THE MORAL COMMUNITY / 49

1. A Problem of Definition / 49
2. Moral Agency as Membership in the Moral Community / 50
3. On What Membership Includes / 53
4. Full Membership / 55
5. Grounds / 60
6. On the Existence of the Moral Community / 65

CHAPTER 4
PARTICIPATION AND POLICY / 68

1. The Moral Acceptability of Policy / 68
2. A Dilemma / 69
3. Responses to the Dilemma / 70
4. Assumptions About the Participation View / 72
5. Conditions of (Strong) Participation / 77
6. Problems / 84
7. Is (Strong) Participation Practicable? / 86
8. Two Further Problems / 90
9. Observations / 93

CHAPTER 5
FUTURE GENERATIONS, PUBLIC POLICY, AND THE MOTIVATION PROBLEM / 95

1. The Motivation Problem / 95
2. Notes / 98
3. "Concern for Generations to Come" / 99
4. Stipulations / 101
5. Notes About Future People / 106
6. Motivation and Particularity / 107
7. Community Bonding and Reciprocation / 109
8. Extended Shared-Fate Motivation / 111
9. Summary / 115

CHAPTER 6
PUBLIC POLICY AND THE INTERPRETATION OF PERSONS / 117

1. When Public Policy Is Weak / 117
2. Two Limits on Responsibility / 121
3. Two Notes and Two Questions / 126
4. Ordinary Persons and Members of the Moral Community / 130
5. End Note / 139

Contents

CHAPTER 7
THE WEIGHT OF ESTABLISHED LIBERTY / 141

1. A Problem of Justification / 141
2. The Claims of Established Liberty / 148
3. The Subject of Justice / 150
4. World Community and Established Liberty / 157
5. Problems and Obscurities / 160
6. On What to Do / 164

CHAPTER 8
ON THE IMPORTANCE OF ONE'S LIFE / 168

1. The Claims of One's Own Life / 168
2. The Proper Care of Oneself / 169
3. Self-Realization / 173
4. Individuality / 178
5. Is One's Life Important? / 181
6. Reconciliation and the Human Condition / 184
7. On One's Own Importance / 188
8. Feasibility and Reasonableness / 191

Notes / 195
Works Cited / 231
Index / 239

PREFACE

This book concerns our idea of individual responsibility. It is an effort to understand how, in a world like ours, certain main elements in that idea should be interpreted and arranged. In our form of moral life the idea of individual responsibility contains as elements both "self-responsibility" and "other-responsibility." On the one side, we as individuals have "but one life to live," and it seems legitimate (within limits) to "be in life for oneself." On the other side, we are "in life together"—we "share fate" with others to some extent—and it seems legitimate to look to one another for a certain amount of support and help. Both these elements are *within* our idea of individual responsibility. How they are to be interpreted and ordered is a philosophical puzzle with very great practical implications.

My moral intuitions warn me that, when the human condition is the way ours is, it is morally wrong to interpret and order these elements in the idea of individual responsibility in such a way that self-responsibility is considered to be more important than, or even as important as, other-responsibility. The human condition in our time is riddled with destitution, gross inequality in people's life prospects, and efforts at amelioration that are both meager and inefficient. I want to say that, when the human condition is riddled with faults in this way, the form of moral life we share teaches that we are to place other-responsibility before self-responsibility in some of our most important life decisions. I call the view that expresses this teaching "shared-fate individualism." I am not sure it is correct. In the discussion that follows I attempt to clarify it, explore its merits, and, to some extent, defend and support it.

I think of shared-fate individualism as a moral conception that applies to competent individuals who pursue their lives in circumstances like those that obtain in today's world. If the circumstances that obtain in today's world were to change in significant ways, then perhaps the shared-fate conception of individual responsibility would give way to some other moral conception. But this "giving way" would not be a simple rejection of an "old" view in favor of a "new" one. In fact (so I believe), our form of moral life has certain general ideas in it (for example, the idea of individual responsibility), and we have moral conceptions that interpret and relate the elements in those ideas (for example, the notions of self-responsibility and other-responsibility) in different ways according to differences in the circumstances of human life. So in this discussion I think of myself as exploring our form of moral life as it bears on individual responsibility with, so to speak, my eyes fixed on certain facts about the circumstances of life in our time.

Shared-fate individualism is hardly an unfamiliar view. But it is worth emphasizing that its subject is the individual. Recent philosophical discussions of justice have focused on what it is for a society (for example, a national community) to be "well-ordered." Typically, the well-ordered society is thought to be one whose "basic structure" (that is, its chief political, economic, and legal institutions and practices) obeys, and is known by its members to obey, the principles of justice.[1] What these principles are is controversial among theories of justice. But when the well-ordered society obeys these principles (whatever they are), certain inequalities among its members may then be treated as tolerable, and certain sacrifices may be demanded of its members, or certain of its members, without justified complaint. But my discussion does not focus on the basic structure of society—at any rate, not on the basic structure of a society *qua* national community. It focuses on the individual as a part of something much larger—call it "humankind," or perhaps "the moral community"—and in our time there exists no (or at best only a very partial) general basic structure for this larger community. A theory of justice for the basic structure of a national community does not by itself settle the issues of individual responsibility that I wish to discuss. For even if, for example, a national community's basic structure, according to a theory of justice, ought to operate so as to respect individual rights before general utility, it does not follow that *I* ought to operate *my life* so that *I* put the exercise of *my rights* before the good of others. Again, even if, for example, a national community's basic structure, according to a theory of justice, ought to make individual liberty a major value so that self-realizationist projects may flourish, it does not follow that *I* ought to operate *my life* so that *I* put *my self-realization* before the welfare of others. A conception of justice for the basic structure of society leaves open the problem of a conception of responsibility for individuals.[2]

The organization of my discussion is simple. It is possible for some philosophical works to proceed by elaborating upon a "master argument" for a given conclusion. My discussion is not like that. It is much more exploratory and clarificatory than systematic. It moves back and forth between "normative" considerations and "theoretical" considerations. I have come to think that moral conceptions *raise* philosophical issues rather than neatly resolve them. So, in rough terms, my Chapter 1 sets out certain troubling facts about the human condition in our time, and Chapter 2 presents and explains "shared-fate individualism." Then in Chapters 3 through 8 I respond to some philosophical questions that are raised by this moral conception. These questions are different from one another in important ways, so I pay some attention to the questions themselves—how they are to be understood—as well as to how they are to be answered. They concern justification, motivation, moral agency, "membership in the moral community," public policy, future generations, "established" (that is, honest, hard-won) individual liberty, and even the "individuality" that gives one's life substance and, in a sense, importance.

I need to mention at this point that my discussion does not often reach to politics. There are of course major questions concerning how individual responsibility is to be understood when, say, the policies of the government of one's nation state, or those of certain business firms, operate to increase the misfortune of others, in contrast to the situation in which the plight of others is not related to such policies. I recognize that these questions are important; there is some reference to them in my discussion (e.g., in Chapters 6 and 7); but I give no sustained attention to them. As I construe my project I am concerned with a matter that is logically prior to, or at least independent of, some of the much-discussed political aspects of problems of individual responsibility. Shared-fate individualism, as it interests me, is ultimately a mode of orientation to the human condition; it has the effect of assessing the moral standing of one's own life in a certain way—a way that has individualist, egalitarian, and communitarian dimensions to it. My discussion as a whole is an attempt to elaborate and understand these dimensions; to some extent Chapter 8 (perhaps together with Chapter 2) provides an overview. Insofar as the book does not deal with political questions, it may go against what some readers expect, or demand, of a philosophical discussion of individual responsibility. Indeed, the particular separation of morality and politics thus suggested may seem controversial or mistaken. But the question of how one's life is to be understood and assessed in a human condition that is flawed in the ways ours is seems to me prior to at least some of the questions that arise in relatively determinate political contexts. I have come to think that it is only when the prior moral question is given a substantive answer (I distinguish some candidate answers in Chapter 2) that the urgency of the political questions can become apparent.

In the end I find shared-fate individualism to be defensible (in a sense I try to explain) against certain criticisms that might be directed at it. I think it is defensible even though I can see that it is not at all attractive. After all, it enjoins us in the context of certain serious life decisions (for example, career choice) to put other-responsibility (for example, service to others) before self-responsibility (for example, self-realization), and it thus makes us risk important kinds of disappointment, frustration, or lack of fulfillment in our lives. That is not a pleasant prospect. Still, I think shared-fate individualism is plausible as an account of "what morality requires" (not merely "what morality permits") in the circumstances of today's human community, despite its lack of appeal.

Some parts of my discussion draw upon published material, though in all cases there have been revisions. Chapter 2 originally appeared in *Ethics*, 94 (Jan., 1984); Chapter 4 in *Ethics* 88 (July, 1978); Chapter 5 in *Environmental Ethics* 4 (Fall, 1982); and section 42 of Chapter 6 in *Nous* 19 (Sept., 1985). My thanks to the editors of these journals for their cooperation.

Preface

Many people have helped me with early drafts of different parts of this book. My thanks to Lynda V. Mapes, Thomas R. Frieden, Ernest Partridge, Douglas MacLean, Gary M. Ebbs, David Greenbaum, B. J. Diggs, Alisa Carse, William N. Nelson, Louis Lombardi, Kenneth Kipnis, Warner Wick, Harlan Wilson, and Ernest R. House. I am grateful to my colleagues at Oberlin College—Daniel D. Merrill, Robert H. Grimm, Alfred F. MacKay, David A. Love, Peter K. McInerney, and Ira S. Steinberg—for their patience and help over a long time. I much appreciate the encouragement I have received from Brian Barry, Alasdair MacIntyre, Laurence Thomas, and Charles Landesman. Special thanks to my daughter, Jennifer, for some terrific typing at a crucial time, and to Karen Barnes for assistance in the preparation of the final manuscript. The good spirits of Betty Wigginton, and her unflagging support for this project through so many of its ups and downs, have been precious to me. Finally, let me express my appreciation of the treatment I have received at Temple University Press: I am very grateful to Jane Cullen for her warm reception of my work, to the anonymous reviewers for their comments, and to Doris Braendel for her careful attention to my writing.

ON SHARING FATE

1

CHALLENGES

TO INDIVIDUAL

RESPONSIBILITY

1 / Self-Responsibility and Other-Responsibility

A part of being a responsible person is taking oneself seriously. Another part is taking others seriously. The idea of individual responsibility contains, as elements, the ideas of self-responsibility and other-responsibility. Doubtless the general idea of individual responsibility contains other elements as well, but in what follows I focus on just these two main elements and what seems relevant to them.

If one aspires to be a responsible person in today's world, one may very well face a conflict between self-responsibility and other-responsibility. One doesn't have to face the conflict every minute of every day. It may only sometimes seem urgent; much of the time it simmers beneath the surface of thought and experience. But most people who take themselves and others seriously will find themselves troubled by it at certain times in their lives, for example, at those times when career decisions or decisions about manner of life are at stake, or when choices must be made concerning what moral attitudes to press upon children. How one deals with the conflict is important, for it helps determine what kind of person one is to be and what kind of life one is to live.[1]

Here is a brief sketch of the conflict I have in mind.

On the one side, we recognize that an important part of individual responsibility is one's responsibility to oneself. Our recognition of this may show up in different ways in different contexts. We may urge persons who seem to over-subordinate themselves to others to assert themselves, or to take themselves more seriously, and we may even try to help them see themselves as worth more than their subservience suggests they do. We may be made uneasy by persons who seem excessively apathetic or quiescent, and we may want to help them locate challenges, projects, or goals that can stir in them the efforts of self-development. We think that persons have certain duties or obligations to themselves and that action in their own behalf is in general something they owe to themselves, although what exactly one's duties or obligations to oneself may be in particular cases is sometimes (but not always) controversial or hard to make out. It is a familiar theme in our received moral ideology that persons ought to pursue their own interests, though we qualify this theme so that it is understood to refer, not to any interests persons have, but only to those that they have thought through, considered the consequences of fulfilling, distinguished from the fickle impulses of the moment, and so forth. We urge persons to take themselves seriously by encouraging them to make every effort to determine what their considered interests are and then to find and cultivate ways of pursuing those interests. Indeed, the complicated social system in which we live—especially, perhaps, in its political institutions—is supposed to be committed in some general fashion to maximizing personal liberty, and this is thought to be an important commitment because a system that maximizes personal liberty is one that leaves persons free to develop themselves. "You have but one life to live—don't waste it," "Assert yourself," "Develop your potential," 'Realize yourself," such familiar injunctions reflect the important self-directed element in our idea of individual responsibility. Persons owe it to themselves to see to it that they realize, as best they can, whatever abilities, talents, and intelligence they have.

On the other side, we also recognize that an important part of individual responsibility is one's responsibility for others. Persons

1. Self-Responsibility and Other-Responsibility [5]

may owe it to themselves to develop themselves and realize their potential, but they also have certain duties and obligations to others. We teach our children to respect others, to be kind to them (or at least civil), to aid those in need or distress, and to help them (or at least not hinder them) in the pursuit of *their* considered interests—again, as best we can. The sense we have that we have some responsibility for others—that to some extent human lives and fates are shared[2]—may be the ground of our willingness, however reluctant about it some of us may become at times, to tolerate (at least some) welfare institutions in our social system. We are taught by venerated traditions of humanistic thought that there is a certain value that attaches to creatures who are persons and that this value should be reflected in our treatment of persons. The point has been expressed in different ways. It has been said that persons are "ends in themselves" (and thus are never to be treated as "means" only), or that persons have rights (sometimes called "natural" or "human" rights) just insofar as they are persons. Alternatively, it has been said that all persons are capable of happiness, or at least pleasure or well-being in some form, and that the happiness, pleasure, or well-being of any given person "counts" for as much as that of any other person. Alternatively again, persons have been said to possess equal worth, or intrinsic value, or innate dignity, and for this reason they are, *qua* persons, owed equal concern and respect.

So there are elements in our notion of individual responsibility that point in different directions. A person's individual responsibility incorporates a responsibility "toward" himself or herself, and it also incorporates a responsibility "toward" others. And clearly, this self-responsibility and other-responsibility may come into conflict in the course of life. We can imagine circumstances in which, if one were to follow the directives of self-responsibility in a reasonably full way, one would have little or no time or energy for responding (not to mention responding adequately) to policies of other-responsibility. (Think of a person whose natural gifts are very great and cry out for development.) Similarly, we can imagine circumstances in which following the demands of other-responsibility in a reasonably full way would entail neglect of oneself, that is, a severe failure to respond to policies of self-responsibility. (Think of a person who devotes himself or herself to the provision of relief to those suffering malnutrition, or aid to the handicapped, or care for a loved one with a lifelong illness.) Apart from the difficulties posed by conflicts between these sets of policies, we can recognize that each set by itself is enormously demanding. Meeting fully one's responsibility to oneself, and meeting adequately one's responsibility for others—each of these summary directives considered by itself is already a moral project for a lifetime. Either general policy might by itself be all-consuming of a person's time, energy, and native resources.

When viewed in this way the conflict between the elements of self-responsibility and other-responsibility has the appearance of a moral dilemma. The general policies in question may, in today's world, press us in incompatible directions. On the one side, the course of self-development and self-realization may simply not have much to do with what even we ourselves might consider to be a reasonable manner of meeting our responsibility for others. On the other side, the course of responsibility for others may indeed involve suspending or abandoning important projects of self-development and self-realization. If we proceed to follow one general policy at the expense of the other, then we fail to respond to the other policy, that is, we fail to do something that we ought to do. If we respond as best we can but (in the nature of the case) inadequately to both policies, then our inadequate response to both when we could at least have done better at one leaves us morally compromised: we only partially meet our responsibilities. Perhaps this is a conflict for which in the long run there is no fully satisfactory remedy. Perhaps the attempt to be a responsible individual cannot, in the circumstances of today's world, succeed.

2 / "Policies"

In the remarks above I spoke of self-responsibility and other-responsibility as if they were policies that might compete with each

2. "Policies"

other and even come into conflict in the course of life in a world like ours. Perhaps I should say something about my use of the term "policies" here. It may be that "policies" is not the best word to use in a discussion of individual responsibility. Policies, after all, are things that institutions have, committees try to formulate, politicians manipulate or twist, and ordinary people are suppose to obey but sometimes (for good or bad reasons) do not. Perhaps "policies" seems too political a term to associate with the moral idea of individual responsibility. But despite such connotations of the word it will be useful, I suggest, to approach the elements of individual responsibility in policy terms. In any case, I do not have anything very technical in mind by my use of the word "policy." Here are some general features of policies that lead me to want to discuss self-responsibility and other-responsibility as matters of policy.

In the first place, policies are *understandings* of what or how things are to be done in some area of life *that project into the future*. A policy decision may be occasioned by current difficulties, and the content of a policy may be informed by past practice; but the policy itself looks ahead and does not just terminate the current difficulties. Policies, as I shall understand them, have the forward-looking character of resolutions. This is not to say, of course, that our personal policies, any more than those of our community, organization, or society, cannot be changed, revised, abolished, or reinstated at a future time. But it is to say that a solution to a problem, or an answer to a question, that sets up no commitment for how future situations of a certain kind are to be dealt with, or responded to, is not a policy. The elements of self-responsibility and other-responsibility are themselves forward-looking in this way, I think, and to treat them in policy terms brings this out.

In the second place, policies are understandings that people *establish* rather than *discover*, and this too is a feature that seems worth emphasizing in a study of individual responsibility. Many points of philosophical interest are involved in the contrast between establishing and discovering something. Here I mention only two of them. First, our policies of responsibility, as things we establish rather than discover, are objects of human *decision*. In the cases we typically favor, they are objects of our decisions and hence are policies we choose to follow, policies we willingly commit ourselves to, policies we give our allegiance to. In other cases they may be the objects of others' decisions, and we may follow them reluctantly; we may emphatically criticize them and seek public opportunities to disavow and even disobey them. But in general, and unlike many things that we discover (such as certain facts), policies do not exist apart from human decision—even if the human decision that produces them is not in all or very many cases our own personal decision.

The second item of interest in the contrast between establishing and discovering is that establishing a policy involves *reasons*, and it does so at two crucial points. At the first point, a person or institution (such as an organization or a committee) has a reason (or reasons) *for making a policy*, that is, a reason for undertaking to resolve something regarding some new problem, or perhaps some recurring type of difficulty or opportunity. Persons or institutions ordinarily do not undertake to make policies when they do not need to do so—though indeed they sometimes attempt to anticipate needs well in advance, and they sometimes make policies they do not, as it turns out, really need. At the second point, a person or institution has a reason (or reasons) *for the policy itself* that he or she or it adopts. Here I refer to the considerations or factors on the basis of which the resolution responding to the problem, difficulty, or opportunity that the person or institution faces has the content it has. Policies do not fall out of the sky, and they are not mere fiats. They are vulnerable to criticism, and this itself shows that they are expected to have rational backing. Of course, this matter of rational backing or justification for one's policies can be very complicated. It can involve considerations or factors of very different kinds, such as those of self-interest, moral principle, personal or institutional circumstances, history, resources, and even the motivation available to support policies among relevant groups of people to whom they apply. Very often it is important to an adequate justification or "case" for a policy that the differences between these sorts of factors

2. "Policies"

be understood. To think about the idea of individual responsibility in policy terms is not to simplify that idea in any way, but rather to play up its complexity.

Finally, we may note that another main feature of policies is that they are open to *interpretation*. To call attention to this feature is also to emphasize complexity. For to say that policies are open to interpretation is to say that they raise questions about how the forward-looking resolutions they formulate are implicitly or explicitly *qualified* (thus affecting what limits they have), about the *scope* they have (thus affecting what exactly may be considered to fall under them), about the *weight* they have relative to other policies that persons or institutions may have or find in their histories, and so forth. It may be unnecessary to say that a great many of the conflicts and disagreements people experience in ordinary life are traceable to different, mistaken, or misunderstood interpretations of apparently shared policies. But my thought is that conflicts and disagreements of these sorts in fact arise in connection with the familiar elements in our idea of individual responsibility, and so, again, I propose to discuss these elements as matters of personal policies for conduct.

I will not elaborate further on the term "policy." My summary of these remarks about its use here is this. Our idea of what it is to be a responsible person, that is, our idea of individual responsibility, contains what I call the elements of self-responsibility and other-responsibility. I wish to construe these elements as if they were sets of broad, personal, long-term moral policies that are accepted by persons who take themselves and others seriously, but that might compete with each other and even come into conflict in the course of life. To treat the idea of individual responsibility in these policy terms is to construe it as a batch or group of more-or-less specific (*a*) forward-looking resolutions, which (*b*) we establish for ourselves rather than discover, that is, which we should have reasons for undertaking to make, and for whose content we should have justification, and which (*c*) are open to the problems and difficulties of interpretation, such as those of qualification, scope, and weight. And my thought is that within the idea of individual responsibility, the policy-elements of self-responsibility and other-responsibility may conflict.

3 / Questions

When we approach the idea of individual responsibility in the policy terms suggested above, the following questions seem natural.

There are, first, questions of *content* and *scope*. Thus, we may ask: what do, or should, our policies of self-responsibility and other-responsibility consist in and cover? That is, can we say—in a non-empty way—what these policies direct us to do? And when they involve us in the lives of other persons, can we say—again, in a non-empty way—how this involvement in the lives of others is to be understood, and indeed which "others" such policies should cover?

Second, there is an *ordering* problem. If our policies of self-responsibility and other-responsibility can come into conflict, as I have suggested they can, then we may ask how they are to be ordered, that is, which of them is to prevail over the other in the event of conflict. Can we say in general which of them (if either) is more important than the other, or which of them (if either) should weigh more heavily with us?

Finally, beyond questions about the content and scope of the policies of responsibility and questions about how they are to be ordered, there is a further question about *incentive*: what does, could, or should move us to act in line with a certain ordering of the policies of self-responsibility and other-responsibility? Given persons as they are in today's world as it is, what will motivate persons to be responsible individuals?

In this inquiry I offer discussions that touch on these several questions. Sometimes, in order to get at one of them, I must take up subquestions or special related problems. But the general aim of my inquiry is to throw light on these questions of content, scope, ordering, and incentive, and in that way to illuminate our idea of individual responsibility. I make no claim that I provide full and adequate answers to the questions I pose. I find the problems asso-

4. Troubling Facts

ciated with our idea of individual responsibility very difficult. There is little that is clear and much that is controversial about its component ideas of self-responsibility and other-responsibility and how they fit together. It will be enough if the studies I offer help sort out the difficulties a little and suggest a position that might be defensible.

Let me note too that I bring to this inquiry no very firm commitment to this or that general ideology or general moral theory. What I offer is not merely the application of some general theory lurking undiscussed in the background. Nor is what I offer (so far as I am aware) the result of positive or negative religious beliefs or commitments. My inquiry into individual responsibility is prompted in the first instance by certain troubling facts about human life in today's world.

4 / Troubling Facts

The second of the problems enumerated above—the question of how self-responsibility and other-responsibility are to be ordered—has, I think, a certain urgency for us in today's world. This is not to say that the other questions I indicated are unimportant. From a philosophical angle these questions come as a package, and a general account that said nothing about one of them would be radically incomplete. But, still, the seriousness of the ordering problem in today's world is worth noting. In my own case certain facts about human life in today's world raise the ordering problem and lead me to inquire into the idea of individual responsibility. My own puzzlement over how the ordering problem is to be answered motivates this study.

Let me characterize certain troubling facts about the human condition in today's world.[3]

1. DESTITUTION. In an address to the United Nations General Assembly in 1978, then U.S. Ambassador Andrew Young said that more than one billion persons in today's world "live in conditions of

abject poverty—starving, idle, and numbed by ignorance." And he added that the freedoms associated with cherished human rights, such as those of thought, speech, and press, "are hollow for any individual who starves to death."[4] Now, I will speak of the people thus referred to as *destitute* people. While it may seem grotesque to discuss the plight of destitute people in an analytic fashion, I will nevertheless make a few simple points concerning how destitution is to be understood. The reason for doing so here is that, for most of us, the plight of destitute people is disturbing and even offensive to our moral sense of what ought to be. The facts of destitution make us uncomfortable and uneasy: they affect our thinking about how self-responsibility and other-responsibility, construed as policies for conduct, ought to be ordered.

First, we may understand *destitution* to be a *a state of severe deprivation relative to basic human needs*. While it may be difficult in some cases to determine what are our own or others' needs, it will serve our purposes here to think of the idea of basic needs as covering those standing prerequisites of human existence that must be satisfied for persons to conduct the business of life, whatever that "business" may consist in for particular individuals. Examples of these prerequisites are "health and vigor, intelligence and imagination," and also "rights and liberties, powers and opportunities, income and wealth." Such prerequisites may be classified in different ways. It may be that those in the second group are more effectively within the power of societies to make available and control than those in the first group. But those in the first group are certainly things whose possession by individuals can be influenced by what other persons do. Thus, I can refuse to give you food, and thereby affect your health and vigor; and you can withhold education from me, and thereby affect the development of such intelligence, curiosity, and imagination as I naturally have. For purposes of this discussion, when I speak of destitution I will be referring to severe deprivation relative to the things in the first group, namely, health and vigor, intelligence and imagination.[5]

It is not necessary here to fuss over technicalities regarding how destitution is to be understood. Perhaps in some contexts the question

4. Troubling Facts [13]

of when health, vigor, intelligence, and imagination are adequate is extremely important. But in the present context it appears that this difficult question can be set aside. Destitution is *extreme* deprivation by *any* standards of when possession of the prerequisites for the conduct of life's business is adequate.[6]

Among the people of the world who are obviously destitute are those who are enervated to one degree or other by malnutrition. Beyond this extreme, there are people who actually live in such a way as to face death from starvation. It is, in fact, very difficult to die from starvation,[7] yet, according to one estimate, at least ten thousand people die of starvation every day; as many as two billion more are malnourished."[8]

Apart from those who suffer malnutrition or who face death from starvation, there are people whose destitution takes other forms. There are over fifteen million homeless people—refugees—in today's world, and hundreds of millions of children and adults lack education of the most elementary kind. Under the social, political, economic, and legal system of apartheid in the Republic of South Africa, there are approximately twenty million black people making up an underclass in a society involving, for them, vicious material deprivation and moral degradation; these people suffer destitution in the form of poverty enforced through oppression.[9]

Suppose we grant—as we must—that destitution in these several forms exists in today's world. Indeed, it is perhaps only relatively recently that destitution, or near-destitution, has ceased to be the condition of life for most of humankind.[10] I have mentioned only people who suffer destitution in the form of malnutrition, or who face death from starvation, or who are homeless, or who are nearly completely lacking in education, or who find themselves in a social system that imposes upon them poverty enforced by oppression. There are of course many other "cases" that could be mentioned— including the case of future people who live many generations after us but who risk destitution as a result of what we do, or do not do, now. Some of us may be personally aware of people in desperate poverty, and perhaps even destitution, within our own relatively affluent national community. One does not have to move one's attention to distant people to find the severe deprivation relative to basic human needs that is at the center of destitution.[11]

2. EXTREME DISPARITY IN LEVELS OF LIFE. The most cursory account of the facts of destitution draws attention not only to the extreme deprivation suffered by so many people in today's world relative to what are on anyone's theory their basic needs but also to the extreme disparity in levels of well-being (a large part of which involves material conditions) available to people in different parts of today's world. I assume that both of these features of the circumstances of humankind are morally problematic—which is to say that they disturb our sense of what ought to be. Together, they form a challenge to our understanding of the course of individual responsibility in today's world.

In connection with the second problematic feature, namely, the extreme disparity in levels of well-being available to people in different parts of today's community, I will touch on just two notions: the idea of an "affluent society" and the idea of "a reasonably well off individual enjoying liberty in an affluent society." To follow the earlier notes about destitution with reminders about what affluence is, what individual liberty is, and what it is to be reasonably well-off in a free, affluent society is to elucidate a second troubling fact about the contemporary human condition.

By "affluent society" I have in mind a national community (a nation state) in which the level of well-being available in principle to all its members is considerably beyond what might be commonly understood by such terms as "subsistence" and "relative comfort." It is not necessary to define "affluence" with great precision. Roughly, in an affluent society "the level of production far exceeds the requirements for a minimum standard of decency," so that "food, clothing, housing, education, medical facilities, and recreational facilities are available in great abundance and variety. In addition, large number of goods and services are available for newly discovered consumer wants."[12] Affluent societies, then, are societies of plenty. This is not to say that they are without problems. Some of those "newly discovered consumer wants" may be highly artificial (perhaps even

4. Troubling Facts [15]

spurious) "creations" of institutions (industries, businesses, advertising firms) that cater to persons' desires for material goods and services, and the extent to which this is controlled or uncontrolled may be a subject of controversy among members of affluent societies.[13] And, of course, such societies may differ in their means of giving their members access to the available goods and services, and these means too may be a subject of concern in their public discussion. Societies of plenty are not free from moral problems associated with the distribution of goods and services, the manipulation of human desires, and even the efficiency of production. But these problems attending affluence are not at stake in this discussion. The fact is: there *are* affluent societies in today's world community—the United States, Canada, the Scandinavian nations, and several countries in Western Europe are all probably examples—and the level of life available (in principle) to the members of such societies is remarkable when it is contrasted to the level of life available to destitute members of the world community. There are indeed very different "worlds" available to different members of the same "world community."

Just as there are affluent societies in the world community, so there are members of such societies who are "reasonably well off" in them. We may note at once that not all members of affluent societies are in fact reasonably well off in them. Even when a society has a capacity for affluence, such that a level of life well beyond that of subsistence or mere comfort is in principle available to all its members, there may be social and political obstacles in the way of the general distribution of goods, services, and opportunities. But even as we note this fact we may recognize at the same time that, in today's world, many of the obviously affluent societies have achieved a general distribution of goods, services, and opportunities that permits *most* of their people to be "reasonably well off."

The idea of a "reasonably well-off person enjoying liberty in an affluent society" is best understood as referring to a *social position* or *office* of sorts. I have in mind what (in Rawlsian terminology) might be called an individual who is *representative* of a certain part of the membership of (in this case) an affluent society.[14] Let me offer the following general remarks about the reasonably well-off representative individual, and then suppose that, for most readers, it will be clear enough in most cases when the idea applies and when it does not.

In general, the reasonably well-off representative individual is a person who is "average or better" relative to the opportunities and level of life available in the economic, political, and educational sectors of the affluent society.[15] This is a person who is economically far from "worst off" in his community, though he or she may or may not be among the few whose wealth is extraordinary. This is an individual who is typically relatively knowledgeable in a society whose educational opportunities are widely available and whose educational system is richly vertical, though this does not mean that all or even most persons who approximate the description of the representative reasonably well-off individual pass through the same educational regimen. This is a person too whose health is sufficient to support a productive life and who possesses a range of capacities, skills, and talents that allow him or her to contribute to the life of the community when its cooperative scheme calls for it. Finally, we may suppose that this representative individual is a person of some if not extreme moral sensitivity; in the vocabulary of the classical utilitarians this is a person who is influenced by the sentiments of both self-love and natural sympathy and is dominated exclusively by neither.[16]

It is important to add that *actual* persons in an affluent society may meet the standard-laden criteria of "average or better" economic position, knowledge, ability, health (etc.) involved in the characterization of the representative reasonably well-off individual to different degrees or extents. Some actual persons may barely meet some of these criteria and over-meet others. We must keep in mind, as we discuss the burdens of individual responsibility, that actual persons may have personal circumstances and difficulties that affect — perhaps even relieve or remove — those burdens to some extent.

Finally, we should emphasize the *liberty* available to the reasonably well-off individual in many affluent societies. The central position of liberty among the values cherished in certain of the world

4. Troubling Facts

community's affluent societies raises many questions of explanation and justification, among them (*a*) the question of what liberty is, (*b*) what its possession means in practice, and (*c*) why it should be central among cherished social values. I will not enter into current controversies over how these several questions are to be answered,[17] but simply outline the answers—perhaps themselves relatively uncontroversial—which are needed for this discussion. (I discuss liberty further in Chapter 7.)

First, we may understand that individual liberty is a set of rights that all members of society may be said to possess or hold; and the net result of their possession of these rights is to put them individually in a position in which they, on an equal footing with others, have what are generally thought to be opportunities to compete for or obtain such goods, services, and offices as the society makes available, and in which they, on an equal footing with others, are protected against arbitrary or gratuitous sacrifice of personal resources in the forms of time, energy, and personal goods. All that should appear on a list of these rights and how they should be categorized or classified (as, for example, "civil," "political," "personal," and so forth) are matters we need not settle here. When John Rawls speaks of these rights, or "basic liberties," he includes "political liberty (the right to vote and to be eligible for public office) together with freedom of speech and assembly; liberty of conscience and freedom of thought; freedom of the person along with the right to hold (personal) property; and freedom from arbitrary arrest and seizure as defined by the concept of the rule of law."[18] This enumeration of the contents of individual liberty will serve our purposes, with special emphasis, perhaps, upon *freedom of the person*, which I shall understand to include liberty in respect of *choice of work and style of life*.[19]

Second, it is important to understand that what liberty-possession in the form of rights *does* for persons in society is, among other things, to contribute toward making a number of important time- and energy-demanding aspects of human life, such as work, associations, and the pursuit of what is personally interesting, matters of individual choice. To possess individual liberty in a society is, regarding these demands, to be relatively free from "outside" controls of many sorts and to be relatively free to make one's own decisions about them according to one's own best judgment.[20] And the "affluence" of affluent societies of course affects the character of this liberty in many ways: in some ways it may help extend and deepen the areas of choice thus reserved to individuals; in other ways it may sidetrack and distort the deliberations required by choice, as, for example, in the creation of artificial needs mentioned earlier.

Finally, we may note that one plausible way of answering the question of why individual liberty should be central among the cherished values of social life is in terms of its bearing upon individual self-respect and integrity. Individual liberty may be abused by persons, of course, and persons may make choices that they or others regret. There may even be social and moral practices in a society that are meant to work against real or imagined abuses of individual liberty.[21] But the ultimate rationale for the centrality of individual liberty proceeds not in terms of the ends of particular activities, or even of "society" construed as itself an agent, but rather in terms of the positive impact upon individuals of the effective exercise of personal choice in the establishment of ends and the deployment of personal resources.[22]

The above remarks obviously yield only a sketch of the variety in the "human condition," and we might usefully investigate details at great length — though I will not do that here. It is enough for our purposes to emphasize that our world community contains millions of people in destitution, millions of people in affluence, and millions of people at the many many points between. For some human beings the human condition is simply and only a battle with extreme deprivation relative to the most basic needs of members of our species. For others the human condition is, or is potentially, a much richer affair. No human condition is struggle-free. But whatever its woes, the life of the reasonably well-off member of a free, affluent society, with its material base, its opportunities for self-realization, and perhaps its measure of luxury, is hardly a struggle with destitution.

3. EFFORTS TO HELP. I assume that for most of us it is a crude and moving fact that millions of people in today's world are desti-

5. Perspective

tute; I also assume that we are troubled by the gross disparity in levels of life available to different people in today's world. When the matter of destitution in the world community is thought about in the affluent societies of the world (within which such severe deprivation is rarely widespread and in which institutions are usually in place to deal with it when it is found), it is often conceived of as a problem to be addressed through programs of foreign aid responding to considerations of national self-interest and humanitarianism, and perhaps as well through individual contributions *via* private charitable institutions. But it would be difficult to conclude from the ongoing public discussion in the affluent nations that world destitution counts as much of a problem at all. For aid in the form of money, technology, and food directed from those nations to the world's destitute people is nothing relative to what could be made available, and some part of what little is made available is directed to political ends or lost through poor management and corruption.[23] The matter of the survival of millions of destitute people in the world, when it is not linked to national self- interest, is consigned to the secondary moral category of national or individual charity, or it is simply neglected.

5 / Perspective

It will be useful to equip ourselves with some general picture of the circumstances of humankind in today's world to help us put into perspective the extreme deprivation relative to basic needs and the gross disparity in levels of well-being that characterize our collective existence.

Suppose, all of a sudden, our current international collection of nation states were converted into a world state. That is, suppose the "grid" of national boundaries and all the apparatus of separate sovereign states were jettisoned and the people of Earth formed a single community—a world community. Notice that, upon the conversion, the affluent societies of the world are only pockets of prosperity amidst widespread poverty and human misery. On the whole, the new world community is not a society of affluence. It is not just America made a little poorer. It may not even be a society of subsistence. It may only be a society of scarcity, with enclaves here and there of subsistence and affluence.

Consider this general picture:

> If all the people in the world could be reduced proportionately into a theoretical town of 1,000 people, the picture would look something like this: In this town there would be 60 Americans, with the remainder of the world represented by 940 persons. This is the proportion of the population of the United States to the population of the world, 60 to 940. The 60 Americans would have half the income of the entire town with the other 940 dividing the other half. About 350 of these would be practicing Communists, and 370 others would be under Communistic domination. White people would total 303, with 697 being non-white. The 60 Americans would have 15 times as many possessions per person as all the rest of the world. The Americans would produce 16% of the town's food supply although they eat 72% above the maximum food requirements. They would either eat most of what they grow or store it for their own future use at an enormous cost. Since most of the 940 non-Americans in the town would be hungry most of the time, it would create ill feelings toward the 60 Americans, who would appear to be enormously rich and fed to the point of sheer disbelief by the great majority of the townspeople. The Americans would also have a disproportionate share of the electric power, fuel, steel, and general equipment. Of the 940 non-Americans, 200 would have malaria, cholera, typhus, and malnutrition. None of the 60 Americans would get these diseases or probably ever be worried about them.[24]

The perspective provided by such an account is striking. We may recognize, of course, that we suffer from poor information in this matter. One contemporary expert, focusing only on the problem of hunger in the world community, writes: "Perhaps most astonishing, we do not know the world's population within 400 million people.

6. Moral Reaction

In short, we do not know how much food there is, how much food people need, or even how many people there are."[25] And the same expert reminds us that every professional bureaucratic organization "exaggerates to its advantage the size of the problem it must tackle, and the hunger relief organizations are no exception."[26] But we can allow for the difficulties of lack of information and even bureaucratic manipulation of crucial notions (for example, "malnutrition")[27] and still see that there are millions of destitute human beings in the world by any sensible criterion for the satisfaction of any of the basic needs. We must remember that our concern here is with destitution in the world community construed as covering extreme deprivation of many kinds. Malnutrition is one kind; diet-related diseases, inadequate shelter and sanitation, even "severe" lack of education, are others.

6 / Moral Reaction

Our world contains both human destitution and extreme distance between levels of life available to different people, and efforts to change this situation through charity and nation-state programs of foreign aid are meager and inadequate. So what? What is our moral reaction to such facts? What are our moral emotions toward them? In fact, one's reaction may be complex and mixed, and its elements may be in tension. There may be different moral emotions, attitudes, and underlying beliefs running through it, and these may not all rest easy with one another.

The facts in question are offensive to one's moral sense of what ought to be. That much seems plain, as a feature of the moral psychology of interest in this discussion. Ignorance of these facts would be a blessing of sorts. (The greater blessing would be their absence from the world community.) Such facts are cruel and there is no sophistication about them. I have the impression that most experts agree that the destitution in the world community is a problem of distribution, and not a problem of lack of resources: "Little as we know about the food crisis, we know that it is a social, not a technical problem; the know-how, and even the food, to eliminate hunger are already here. . . . [L]iterally hundreds of millions of people today are living in poverty that is, technologically speaking, totally unnecessary."[28] I will assume that destitution in the world community is something that need not exist. Some part of it may indeed be due to natural causes, and some other part due to social causes; but however that may be it is ameliorable by human effort. Our *moral* sense of what ought to be—apart from certain religious convictions or fatalist ideologies—does not countenance a community in which (*a*) the human condition for many members is destitution, (*b*) there is wide disparity in levels of life, and (*c*) those who can respond to destitution do so, for the most part, in a way that fits neither their capacity to respond nor the magnitude of the suffering involved. The world community, as it stands today, is hardly "the moral community" of ordinary moral sensibility.

That the facts of destitution, grossly disparate levels of life, and meager response from affluent sectors of the world community violate our sense of what ought to be is reflected in the range of moral emotions we may experience. In the first place one may experience *sorrow* in reaction to the facts of extreme deprivation. These are, after all, matters of suffering, unmet basic need, and stifled lives, and they call up joy in no one. In some cases there is a question of the justification of the moral emotions we experience. Thus, a person may feel shame, say, but for no good reason, or suffer remorse but not really deserve to. But in the present case there is no controversy about the justification of the element of sorrow in one's moral-emotional reaction to the facts of destitution. No one will quarrel with the approriateness of this part of our reaction. But, of course, sorrow is sorrow, and not another thing. It is a form of passive, perhaps painful, sadness, and does not itself point to a positive course of action. It also does not by itself charge anyone with blame or portend punishment. A common prescription for relief from sorrow is a change of topic, a re-directing of attention.[29]

But sorrow is not the only element in our reaction to the facts in question. They also—especially the gross disparity in levels of life—may well call up in many of us something very like *guilt*. As someone who more or less fits the characterization of the reasonably well-off

6. Moral Reaction

individual in one of the world's affluent societies, the facts in question make me sharply self-conscious about my level of life. When I think of them, I become suspicious of the legitimacy of my efforts to secure *my* interests and my efforts to develop *my* talents as I see them. How can I be in life for myself (and those I care for, or otherwise acknowledge a responsibility for) when the situation in the world community is what it is? One is reminded of Rousseau's impatient pronouncement: "it is plainly contrary to the law of nature, however defined, that children should command old men, fools wise men, and that the privileged few should gorge themselves with superfluities, while the starving multitude are in want of the bare necessities of life."[30] Perhaps it is simply wrong for me to be-in-life-for-myself in such circumstances.

But—despite Rousseau's pronouncement—the element of guilt in our moral-emotional reaction to the facts in question may seem itself to generate in some of us a further element, namely, an anger of sorts. I have in mind the anger of *indignation*, and in particular the indignation of innocence unfairly accused. After all (let us assume), I did not cause anyone to be destitute. I more or less found the world the way it is, and I did not make it be the way I found it. Perhaps indeed the world is such that millions die every day of destitution in its various forms. But I am not responsible for that. I do not conduct my life (let us assume) in such a way as to damage the lives of others. And as long as this is so, I am of course entitled to pursue my interests and develop my talents as I see fit. There is nothing morally objectionable in my doing so. If others—or myself one day—wish to fly to the aid of those in severe need, then my admiration and best wishes go with them. But there is nothing wrong—and hence no justified guilt—in my not doing so. I am an innocent party to a world I did not create. And I have but one life to live.

Now, on this brief account the affront to the moral sense produced by the facts of destitution, disparate levels of life, and meager responses by affluent agents is internally complex. It may contain layers of such moral emotions as sorrow, guilt, and indignation. All these elements may figure in one person's reaction (as they do in mine), and there may be even more elements that would be revealed by further investigation (for example, an anger directed at the apparent cosmic unfairness of the human condition). But it is not my aim in what follows to exhibit further emotional complexity. My interest is directed chiefly to the evident tension between the second element (of guilt) and the third element (of indignation). I wish to explore the presuppositions of these different moral-emotional elements and attempt to understand the tension between them. The occurrence of moral emotions in us reflects the influence on us of moral conceptions, that is, moral views and principles. (This is what allows there to be a question of justification for a moral emotion, so that we can ask whether, for example, a person who feels guilt ought to feel guilt, or a person who feels indignation ought to feel indignation.) In the next chapter I sketch the moral conceptions that stand beneath or behind the elements of guilt and indignation clustered around the element of sorrow in the moral reaction I have described. The importance of understanding these background moral conceptions is that they control our approach to the questions of how far either of these moral emotions is justified.

7 / Fatalism and Pessimism

I should make plain that I assume that our moral-emotional reaction to the facts we are concerned with does involve some "mix" of guilt and indignation beyond the element of sorrow. Suppose this is not so. Suppose, for example, that one's response is only sorrow. Guilt and indignation are absent, or somehow negligible. Then what we might call *fatalism* or *pessimism* may be the main governing conception in one's response to the facts in question.

By *fatalism* I have in mind the view that holds that the facts of destitution and disparity in levels of life are metaphysically fixed parts of the general human condition. The situation we encounter in today's world community is, on this view, essentially the human condition as it has always been, and it is a kind of foolishness to think that the circumstances of human life can be changed—anyhow by human effort. Human beings are powerless to ameliorate such

7. Fatalism and Pessimism

facts of life. The situation that we react to with sorrow is what it is; and it will be what it has been. The sorrow we experience may indeed be real enough, but the prospect of amelioration is, at best, a vain hope. Alternatively, *pessimism* is the view that holds that, while the facts of destitution and disparate levels of life may not be metaphysically fixed parts of the human condition, the task of amelioration is nevertheless too much—too difficult—for human beings as we know them to carry out. The claim here is not that the prospect of change is in some deep metaphysical way impossible. It is rather that the prospect of change is in some deep practical way infeasible: the effort required is excessive relative to our capacities. At some point, so it is claimed by the pessimist, conditions that are not metaphysically grounded may nonetheless come to be, as a matter of practical fact, insurmountable relative to human effort. (Thus, in American society, for example, the mode of transportation involving the automobile, roads, and supporting technology appears to be so fixed in place that the prospect of eliminating it—as distinct from controlling or improving it—seems completely unrealistic.) On this account the human condition is only contingently tragic, yet the magnitude of the tragedy makes the situation irretrievable. In both cases—fatalism and pessimism—no program of amelioration is recommended; instead, some form of *resignation* to the troubling facts of the human condition is proposed.

Now, I mention these conceptions of fatalism and pessimism only to dismiss them. I will not argue against them in any systematic way, for to do so would only lead us (especially in the case of fatalism) into subjects that, while interesting, are too far away from the concerns of this discussion. In any case fatalism is ultimately, I think, a conception that denies that the facts of destitution and grossly disparate levels of life are morally problematic—and this seems to me very mistaken. And perhaps the best short thing to say about pessimism is that its emphasis on the impracticality of the task of amelioration is prematurely defeatist—or perhaps immorally escapist. Let us hope that neither of these conceptions is taken seriously by many members of the world community in a position to contribute to the relief of those caught, for whatever reason, in destitution.

2

CAREER CHOICE

1 / A Question of Individual Responsibility

What is the individual supposed to do about the troubling facts of destitution and gross disparity in levels of life available to different people in the world community? This is a moral question, and, as I understand it, it concerns what one takes, or should take, one's responsibilities to others and to oneself to be. We may treat it as a question of moral policy for a lifetime. What kind of person am I to be? Am I to be a person who lives solely or mainly for myself? Am I to be a person who lives solely or mainly for others? Am I somehow to hit between these two "extremes" (if that is what they seem), that is, somehow balance them off in a way that is best (for myself and others) on the whole? How far is my fate to be shared with that of others?

These large policy questions may arise in different contexts. But one of the most important contexts is that of career planning for oneself. "We must . . . fill out our span of life with activities," said Kant. "Work is useful occupation with a purpose."[1] What career shall I choose—one that allows me to serve others or one that allows me to serve myself, that is, pursue my interests and "realize" myself in the way mentioned earlier? I suppose one might object at once to the either/or cast of such a question. "Am I to live for myself?" "Am I to live for others?" Such questions seem simplistic. One might think that one can combine the projects of self-responsibility and

1. A Question of Individual Responsibility

other-responsibility. Surely one might choose a career in which one serves others *and* realizes oneself. But the problem is not that easily solved. In fact, the view that one can move readily into a career combining self-responsibility and other-responsibility in some significant way is itself simplistic. Even if there are some careers that combine these responsibilities in some apparently meaningful way, most careers—including the professions of teaching, law, and medicine—do not significantly do so in fact, if one keeps, for example, the destitution in today's world in mind. And, in any case, most of life's "careers," as they are termed in the marketplace of the affluent societies, serve neither form of responsibility in any serious way; if they serve anything, they serve the end of the aggrandizement of some product, person, social class, or luxury good. If one has the facts of destitution and gross disparity in levels of life in today's world in mind, the "world of work," as it is structured in the typical affluent society, is hardly a promising source of effective syntheses of self-responsibility and other-responsibility.

In what follows I discuss *career choice* as a moral problem for individuals. As I treat the problem it belongs to the theory of individual responsibility, though I recognize that a full treatment of it would require contributions from the theory of justice for the basic structure of society. My special interest here is in cases of individual decision-making about careers in which the values of *self-realization* and *service to others* are in competition with one another. I have in mind, for example, cases in which one's natural gifts are such that one might undertake, on the one hand, a self-realizationist career in which, say, artistic self-development or intellectual interests are pursued for their own sake, or, on the other hand, a service career in, say, the distribution of health care or the administration of an international human-rights organization. It is not necessary for me to specify in detail the "contents" of envisioned careers. The important feature of the cases I have in mind is that one's choice of a career appears prospectively to require one of these values (self-realization, service to others) to prevail over the other, or to be pursued pretty much at the expense of the other.[2]

2 / Common Opinion

Common opinion treats career choice as a paradigm of a matter for individual decision. No one is required to have a career, and our society certainly does not guarantee that those who seek careers will have opportunities to pursue them. Those who resolve to seek a career are supposed to negotiate the problem of choice involved on the basis of their own best estimates of their long-term interests, capacities, and circumstances. They may ask for information about lines of work and their own aptitudes, but no one is to set directions for them, or steer them into one field or another. Common opinion thus locates career choice in that area of Mill's "region of liberty" in which we are thought to have "liberty of tastes and pursuits, of framing the plan of life to suit our own character."[3] It is a thoroughly self-regarding matter. The good society does not assign careers, or even jobs—except perhaps in short-term fashion in an emergency, such as war. Even advising another person to take up this rather than that career—anyhow, outside one's own family—is to be avoided or kept to a minimum. All this perhaps evinces a certain respect for individuality: it seems natural to think that career choice is linked closely to the individual's own development and expression of the self, and thus to the self-realizationist component in our idea of the morally valuable human life.[4] Self-realization appears to be the main moral value that is supposed to guide the thinking of those who wish to select and pursue careers.

Of course, common opinion allows that service to others may be taken into account in one's thinking about a career. The life-long service career of, say, the American social reformer Jane Addams is a legitimate option. But, as I understand the common opinion, such a career is only an option, and even then only to be taken seriously when the projected service career is itself a self-realizationist career. Jane Addams once wrote that "the one test which the most authoritative and dramatic portrayal of the Day of Judgment offers, is the social test. The stern questions are not in regard to personal and family relations, but did ye visit the poor, the criminal, the sick, and did ye feed the hungry."[5] But this appears to go against our ordinary opinion if Addams' words are interpreted as proposing that career choice be guided by service to others *over* self-realization when the two conflict.[6]

The aim of my discussion is not to recommend a specific career or even a general line of work to any nameable individual. The aim is rather to consider how a reasonably competent individual should think about his or her choice of a career, and in particular how the values of self-realization and service to others should figure in his or her decision-making regarding careers. I will invoke the troubling facts about the human condition in today's world discussed above (1.4–5), for these seem to me relevant to career choice as a problem of morality for individuals. These facts place before those who are choosing careers in today's world some hard questions about the moral standing of individual lives. What degree of importance should I attach to the individual life that is, in fact, my life? What degree of importance should I attach to the individual lives that are not, in fact, my life? If the lives of many other people are frustrated and stifled, what difference should that make to my life? In this chapter I shall explore, and then make a first effort to support, a view that may seem extreme, namely, that in today's world morality requires that service to others be put before self-realization in the matter of career choice.

3 / Careers and Competent Individuals

What is a career? For the purposes of this discussion a career may be thought of as a long-term project for an individual life. One's career may be "in" business, law, teaching, entertainment, professional philanthropy, or something else; whatever it is in, it typically involves work and way of life such that the former has implications for the make-up of the latter. A person may or may not "make money" or "earn a living" from a career, but a person who has a career may very well seem internally related to the work and way of life so that they become a part of his or her personal identity for practical purposes. A large psychological investment may be involved. One's thoughts, hopes, aspirations, energy, and sense of worth may be wrapped up in and dominated by the materials and apparatus of one's career, that is, by its goals, techniques, and standards and by the conditions of its pursuit in one's social environment. In a way that is familiar from life (for those who have careers) but difficult to analyze philosophically, one may *be*, in important part, one's career. It may be a struggle at times not to reduce oneself to one's career, or, perhaps, to resist being thus reduced by others.

A career usually imposes certain terms upon its pursuit. For example, it may require a certain specific location or type of location, a certain kind of geography or climate, a certain mix of uses of body and mind, or certain kinds of education and training. Such terms generally force some elements into and others out of a person's way of life. Careers may not dictate all the elements of one's way of life so that a career choice is the *only* serious life decision one makes; but careers certainly restrict and focus options in the many sub-parts of human lives, and it would be difficult to exaggerate the importance of career choice among the major decisions persons can make. A large part of the practical answer to the Socratic question of "what kind of life one should live"[7] may be given in one's choice of a career.

We sometimes make a distinction between a *career* and a *job*, though we do so to make different points in different contexts. (*a*) The distinction may mark, for example, a difference in attitude toward work on the part of the career-pursuer and the job-holder. Perhaps the psychological investment—the making of the work a part of one's practical identity—is greater when one's work is one's career rather than (merely) one's job. For the job-holder, according to the distinction in this case, work is held at a distance. It does not define what one is, or even dominate one's identity. (*b*) In some cases the distinction may make a point about relative skill and difficulty. The work involved in a career is harder, less automatic or routine, more demanding. Here we may speak in a classificatory way of "the professions," "the trades," or "unskilled labor" and tend to associate the term "career" with the first and perhaps the second of these, and the term "job" with the last. (*c*) In some cases the distinction may

3. Careers and Competent Individuals [31]

mark a relative difference in work-required time and energy. A career may demand more preparation-time and energy in education or training, and then the pursuit of it may claim or anyhow dominate most of one's "waking moments." Some career-pursuers come to resist the time-and-energy demands of their careers and do not find the intrinsic interest of their work enough to compensate for a certain narrowing of their lives. (*d*) In some contexts the term "career," in contrast to the term "job," may be used in an honorific or laudatory way. "My son has a career now" may contextually imply the left-unsaid "And yours (merely) has a job," and we are thereby called upon to admire the son with the career. But the honorific aspect is not steady: one's son may pursue a "career in crime" and not be admirable at all. To be a career-pursuer is not necessarily to be in a superior moral position relative to a job-holder.

But this discussion does not require that the distinction between "career" and "job" be elaborated further. The central features of a career, for present purposes, are that it involves work that one anticipates doing and staying with over a significant period of time (many years, say), that one expects will regularly consume substantial portions of one's time and energy, that one anticipates will affect one's way of life in salient respects, and that one is prepared to be rather positively committed to (rather than, say, resentful of). As one takes up the question of what career one shall have, one thinks of it as calling for a decision about a multi-year project in one's lifetime.

Persons who are able to take up the problem of career choice I will call "competent individuals." These are persons who are *positioned* to self-realize and to contribute to the lives of others, and this implies many things about them. At a minimum they possess intelligence, knowledge, health, energy, talent, and imagination to a degree that is sufficient to support activities involving planning and following-through, plus some capacities, skills, and abilities that enable them to contribute to the lives of others. They are also persons for whom future time is in some significant amount "available," though this does not imply that only young people can be competent individuals. (More than one or even two careers may be possible in a lifetime.)

There is no intention on my part to restrict membership in the class of competent individuals. Even so we must recognize that many human beings are in fact not competent individuals: they are not positioned to realize themselves, or to contribute to the lives of others. In some cases their incompetence is temporary and their place among competent individuals is retrievable by medical, social, or political action. In other cases their incompetence may be permanent. Not all human beings are *able* to take up the problem of career choice. We should note too that some people do not aspire to a career. They do not want to have one. Sometimes this is a matter of the aspiration not occurring in them; perhaps there is no pressure toward a career in family background or social environment, and the idea, as it were, does not cross the mind. In other cases the not-wanting may itself be the result of thought about one's actual circumstances. The pursuit of a career may seem unrealistic, or not worth the apparent trouble of preparation. In still other cases a decision not to pursue a career may rest on a point of principle: for example, one might choose to avoid "channeling" oneself into any relatively fixed combination of work and way of life.[8]

Should one have a career? Or should one at least *aspire* to a career? "Career," as I use the term here, will not carry moral connotations that make the answers to such questions automatically "yes." It is imaginable that a person might meander through life without a career and have a richer, more diverse, and more exciting existence than a person with a career. It is also imaginable that a person might pursue a career—a career in crime, say—and be a force for evil. In general, it is as far-fetched to claim *a priori* that careers *per se* are evil as it is to claim *a priori* that careers *per se* have positive moral value. But even though the idea of career by itself is empty of moral content, it remains that careers *can* be vehicles through which moral values are realized. After all, the time, energy, and resources one puts into a career (if one pursues one) over a large part of a lifetime can touch many lives, including one's own, for good or ill. Careers are long-term projects through which, among other things, self-realization and service to others may be achieved.

Even for a competent individual, however, career choice can be a problem only in a society that is to some degree open in respect of opportunities. It need not be very open, but the choices available must be such as to require the weighting and ordering of the values of self-realization and service. Most (but not all) competent individuals in today's world probably find themselves with enough in the way of opportunity to satisfy this condition, even when they are members of societies with unjust institutions, and even in some cases when they are victims of such institutions. A society's degree of justice contributes to, though it does not by itself settle, the range of career opportunities available to individuals.[9] In this discussion I must set aside the many questions raised by the fact that a society's structural make-up can "affect" (block, encourage, thwart, promote) career options. The exclusion of these questions constitutes a large restriction of the topic. But for the moment I am concerned to approach career choice as a problem of individual morality. Its treatment as a problem in the theory of justice for the basic institutions of society may be taken up at another time.

4 / The Problem of Career Choice

There is, in fact, great personal risk for competent individuals in the matter of career choice. If the work at the center of one's career goes stale, or fails to sustain interest, or finally goes beyond one's energies or abilities, the result can be a life lost in a very real sense. If in the midst of a career the usefulness or general purpose of one's work comes to be in doubt, the result may be a demoralization that renders life "meaningless" or is threatening to self-respect. A career that goes wrong or becomes disappointing may cause regret, deaden energies, and shorten life.[10] If one is artificially kept out of a career to which one aspires, or pushed out of a career one has underway, one may be outraged. If one trains elaborately for a career involving work one relishes, only to find no opportunities to pursue it, one may be frustrated or feel cheated.

But there are not only self-regarding risks in how the career-choice problem is resolved. As I mentioned above, one may through one's career touch the lives of others for good or ill. Recall those troubling facts about the human condition in today's world that were discussed earlier: (*a*) there are millions of people in today's world who suffer destitution in some or many forms; (*b*) the levels of life affecting people's opportunities for self-realization are grossly disparate in today's world;[11] (*c*) efforts to ameliorate the destitution and gross disparity in levels of life through charitable institutions and nation-state programs of "foreign aid" are meager and inadequate. Now, it is neither strange nor implausible for an individual to consider such facts when deliberating about the choice of a career. Indeed, such facts may press themselves upon one[12] to the extent that one supposes that one *ought* to pursue what we may call a *service career*, that is, a career whose point is to contribute to the amelioration of such facts and thus to help others become positioned to develop their potential and, in general, realize themselves.

Given such facts about the circumstances of humankind in today's world, is a service career *morally required*? What of my own self-realizationist aspirations? Suppose I fit the description of the competent individual, but estimate that the career that best facilitates self-realization in my own case (relative to my own estimate of my real interests, talents, and capacities) would not, if pursued directly, speak significantly, if at all, to the amelioration of such facts as those listed above. Am I then called upon morally to set aside my own self-realization in order to contribute to others' being positioned to self-realize? If I were to sacrifice myself in this way and devote myself to service to others in whatever ways among the alternatives available to me seem to be the most effective, would I be meeting a moral requirement—or would I be going beyond what morality requires to do something that to some is admirable, but to others is simply extreme, foolish, or even in some sense wrong?

5 / The Moral Standing of Individual Lives: Three Perspectives

At this point the exploration of the problem of career choice directs our attention to the question of the moral standing of individual

5. The Moral Standing of Individual Lives

lives. This is a difficult subject, and a variety of views seems possible. I consider only three views, so my discussion is hardly comprehensive. Still, they are important views, and they come naturally to mind in cases in which career choice involves a clash between one's self-realizationist aspirations and one's recognition of the need for service to others.

First, a common feature: all the views I discuss are forms of individualism. This is to say that they all centrally value individual lives, and they give great moral weight to individually defined self-realizationist aspirations and projects.[13] These are views that speak in the vocabulary of the "inviolability," the "irreducible significance," and the "irreplaceable worth" of individual lives.[14] But the views I have in mind begin to come apart on the question of how and to what extent human lives fit together. Some of our most basic moral attitudes are involved in this question. (*a*) According to one of them, human beings are, morally, *in life together*, and the key to understanding our form of moral life is the proper interpretation or reading of this notion of being-in-life-together. My life is bound up with our lives; together—*ab initio*—we form a community in which, as it may be put, *fate is shared*.[15] (*b*) The force of a second basic attitude is given in the saying: "you have but one life to live." The theme here is that human beings are, morally, *separate persons* and that "there are *only* individual people, different individual people, with their own individual lives."[16] I may arrange with (some) others so that my life becomes bound up with their lives. We may make communities through agreements. But *ab initio* there is no community at all—only separate individual lives of "irreducible significance."[17]

Entire moral conceptions may be built upon such basic attitudes. Even though both attitudes seem to me similarly deep and equally fixed in ordinary thinking, moral conceptions may be developed that emphasize one of them at the expense of the other or that make an effort to accommodate both of them in some way. In what follows I call the moral conception that emphasizes the first of them *shared-fate individualism*, and the conception that emphasizes the second of them *separate-life individualism*. Insofar as different interpretations of each conception may be possible, the root attitudes seem like suggestive themes on which variations may be played. In any case these basic attitudes are very powerful in their hold on us, even in circumstances in which they come to clash. It is doubtful, I believe, that anyone raised in a form of life like ours, in which both attitudes are emphasized, could be brought to jettison either of them effectively. Accordingly, we may suppose that a moral conception might be developed that starts from one of these basic attitudes and then reaches out to incorporate the other in some way. A conception I call *liberal individualism* proposes to do this: it attempts to accommodate both convictions by arranging them in a certain way so that in certain circumstances the separate-life theme prevails but in other circumstances the shared-fate theme receives some emphasis as well.[18]

Now, my discussion does not include a comprehensive review of the many different implications of these three conceptions (shared-fate, separate-life, and liberal individualism) for individuals and the political order. I stay with the problem of career choice and illustrate how these conceptions differ in what they suggest for individuals (not for the state) regarding the situation in which the values of self-realization and service-to-others clash. The interest of doing so is that these forms of individualism yield contrasting accounts of the moral standing of one's own life, relative to the lives of others, in different circumstances. There are three main cases to characterize.

Consider the easiest case first. This is the case in which the human situation in general is such that all human beings are adequately positioned to undertake individually defined self-realizationist projects. This is not, of course, the actual situation in today's world, but were it to become so there would be no reason for the recommendations of the three forms of individualism not to coincide: one's deliberations about the selection of a career in such a situation need be guided only by the value of self-realization. In this case destitution and gross disparity in levels of life are not present (perhaps they have been overcome), and, in general, the factors that press us to take seriously the idea that a career of service to others should be chosen over a career of self-realization (when the two conflict) are absent. This is a fully intelligible situation, but it is (*ex hypothesi*) one in which there is no serious application for concepts that might figure

5. The Moral Standing of Individual Lives [37]

in appeals for the use of one's career time, energy, and resources in behalf of others, such as the concepts of destitution and gross disparity in levels of life.

The second case is that in which (*a*) not all persons are adequately positioned to realize themselves, but (*b*) there exists an institutional scheme[19] operating reasonably effectively toward the end of positioning all persons to do so. This is essentially the manner of operation aspired to (in principle) by liberal welfare states relative to their citizens. But if we think in larger terms and recognize *all* human beings (including non-citizens) as "equal moral persons," then this would be the situation in which a "world community" is equipped with reasonably effective services speaking to problems of unmet basic need for the entire human population of Earth.[20] There may of course be problems of poverty in such a community; a world community may be just as riddled with pockets of destitution and enclaves of affluence as is today's world. But the point is that (*ex hypothesi*) a set of institutions is in place to speak to these problems and amelioration is gradually taking place. In this community those with means of life above some level may be legally required to maintain the scheme of services—through income and inheritance taxes, say—but such a requirement need not extend to our careers. That is, the desired amelioration is occurring at a rate such that our work and ways of life need not be legally assigned to us.

In this second case the three moral conceptions we are considering show certain differences in what they recommend for individuals taking up the problem of career choice, and these differences begin to suggest different views of the moral standing of individual lives. For example, in the circumstances of the second case separate-life individualism imposes no moral requirement on individuals to choose careers with anything other than self-realization in mind. (It also objects to the world community's legally requiring support, through taxation, for the redistribution program.) It *allows* the individual to elect to pursue a service career (as it allows one to support private welfare schemes voluntarily). The point is not that separate-life individualism estimates that the amelioration scheme operating in the world community is adequate to the task of putting all members of the community in a position to realize themselves. It is rather that this form of individualism recognizes no community membership among persons prior to or independent of any bonds individuals create among themselves by agreement or consent. Morally, again, our lives are separate: my life is mine to lead; and as I deliberate about careers I am not already morally constrained by any responsibility for enabling others to realize themselves.[21]

The conceptions of shared-fate and liberal individualism make a different response to this second case. Under the pressure of the basic shared-fate attitude, these views accept the requirement of support (in the form of taxation, say) for the world-wide scheme of services. Such a scheme merely reflects what our common membership in a moral community implies when, for example, destitution and gross disparity in levels of life prevent many members of the community from being equipped to realize themselves. Indeed, the point of this scheme, under the shared-fate conviction, is precisely "to secure just background conditions against which the actions of individuals . . . take place,"[22] for it is only within such a structure that "individuals . . . are at liberty to advance their aims."[23] Without the background scheme, carefully "regulated and corrected," "the social process *will cease to be just*, however free and fair particular transactions may look when viewed by themselves."[24]

Accordingly, it is natural to suggest that these conceptions find the morally recommended course to be "self-realization *cum* service to others." That is, given that there exists an appropriate institutional scheme, individuals are free to put first the claims of self-realization in their own cases *provided* that they then pursue their careers in such a way as to help others less well-placed to realize themselves.

This way of thinking about career choice seems familiar. The common opinion mentioned above (2.2) probably admires this balance of the values of self-realization and service to others even if it does not require it. In any case the formula "self-realization *cum* service to others" is typically not onerous. Most of the aspirations toward self-realization that people pursue through careers (such as artistic self-development, the pursuit of knowledge for its own sake, the development of certain mental or physical powers) permit a ser-

5. The Moral Standing of Individual Lives

vice component of some sort. (One may be able at least to teach the thing, or about the thing, that one aspires to or is interested in to audiences whose lives will be "enriched" thereby.) Nevertheless, in contrast to separate-life individualism career choice *is* modestly constrained by service on these conceptions, even though the call for service is posterior to decisions based on self-realization.

In the third case I will touch on, the circumstances of the human condition are more familiar and more troubling. As before, (*a*) not all persons are in a position to realize themselves, but also (*b*) there exists no single general institutional scheme, or even collection of smaller schemes, operating toward the overcoming of that situation. This is an important case, and it is hardly unreal. It is in fact the characterization that best fits today's world, with its millions of destitute people, its gross disparity in levels of life, and its meager efforts at relief across national boundaries. It is also the case in which the three moral conceptions in question yield three different recommendations for individuals taking up the problem of career choice. This variety is philosophically interesting for its display of different views about the moral standing of individual lives.

Separate-life individualism stays with its same recommendation. My individual life is separate from that of others; it is mine to lead; and I am not—even in these circumstances—under any moral requirement to put service to others before self-realization in my choice of a career. I may elect (for whatever reasons) to pursue a service career or to combine a self-realizationist career with service to others, but I am not required to do either. Now, the moral teaching here appears to be that, as I make choices involving significant portions of my life, my life itself is to be thought of as having noncomparative worth. The teaching is not (necessarily) that of an egoism that claims that my life has standing "above" the lives of others or is somehow "worth more" than the lives of others. It is rather that my life is prized in a way that makes it immune to challenges based upon comparisons with existing lives that are frustrated or stifled (or, for that matter, with lives that are rich and exciting). The fact that others cannot realize themselves does not entail any sacrifice on my part of the pursuit of self-realization. And, of course, my life is not the only life that has this non-comparative worth. All individual lives have worth of this sort. But, again, individual lives are separate, and the standing of one is not affected by facts about the others.

At the other extreme, shared-fate individualism directly reflects, in the circumstances of this third case, the attitude that we are "in life together." The notion that all human beings are equal members of a moral community and that their lives are bound up together is reflected in this case in the recommendation that deliberations about careers are to be seriously constrained by the value of service-to-others. Morality requires, in these circumstances, a service career. If an individual can find some measure of fulfillment of self-realizationist aspirations in his or her service career, that is to be welcomed. But in these unfortunate circumstances service comes first—and stays first—until the conditions of self-realization are satisfied for all equal moral persons. Our common membership in the moral community requires whatever sacrifices of the competent individual's time, energy, and resources may be needed to put all members in a position to realize themselves.[25]

What does shared-fate individualism thus teach about the moral standing of individual lives? My thought is that it need not be interpreted as teaching either a simple altruistic reversal of egoism that finds others' lives "higher" or "worth more" than one's own life or a simple non-comparative valuing of "community" that places the collection of individual lives somehow "above" the individual lives themselves. What shared-fate individualism does is impose a *condition of legitimacy* upon the individual's pursuit of self-realization, namely, that such pursuit is acceptable only when all members of the moral community can realize themselves. This is no denial of the value of individual lives. It is rather the recognition that in certain circumstances those rankings or valuings of individual lives that give individuals moral *carte blanche* to realize themselves "no matter what" are moral luxuries of a sort. Even though I have but one life to lead, it does not follow that it is *mine* (in some private-ownership sense) to do with as I please. From the shared-fate perspective, all individual lives are so important that I cannot plead an entitlement to my life that exempts me from joining in the task of securing the conditions of self-realization for all. Perhaps there are some circumstances in which we can afford the luxury of "self-realization no matter what." But to follow that guide in the circumstances envisioned *would* be to deny the value of many—perhaps most—individual lives.

Liberal individualism stays with the same recommendation that it makes in the second case. The pressure of the shared-fate attitude is felt to the extent that self-realization is to be accompanied by service. But the pressure does not carry beyond this point. We are not morally required to sacrifice self-realization to the cause of service to others—though here too, as in the case of separate-life individualism, such a sacrifice is permitted.

What should we understand to be the teaching of liberal individualism about the moral standing of individual lives? The answer is not immediately clear to me. There is a look of uneasy compromise about liberal individualism. It certainly recognizes the hold on us of both the notion that human beings are "in life together" and the notion that "one has but one life to lead," and it accommodates these two convictions so that the latter prevails unqualified in the first case we considered and then becomes qualified by the former (so that self-realizationist careers must be accompanied by service to others) in the second and third cases. This suggests, I think, that for liberal individualism the notion that "one has but one life to lead" is ultimately the more important of the two basic convictions that concern us. But how such a claim is to be supported is not plain. In particular, why the liberal individualist stays with the recommendation "self-realization *cum* service to others" as we move from the second case to the third is unclear.

6 / The Selection Problem

If the circumstances of humankind in today's world are those of the third case characterized above, then the three broad moral perspectives or conceptions I distinguished yield different guidelines for the deliberations of individuals about career choice. (*a*) Separate-life individualism teaches a straightforward self-realizationist ethic in connection with career choice in these (or any) circumstances. One may, of course, pursue a service career if that appears to be the most efficient way of fulfilling one's aspirations for self-realization. Or one may pursue a service career rather than a self-realizing career for special reasons, such as the pressure of compassion or family tradition. But morality does not require a service career, even in today's world. (*b*) Shared-fate individualism teaches a straightforward service ethic, though it does not begrudge one the achievement of self-realization if one's service career should happen (in the fortunate case) to provide it. This perspective puts one in a community with others in which equal membership is taken so seriously that when it fails to obtain then all members who can contribute to its obtaining must do so. There is, on this view, a legitimacy condition imposed upon the pursuit of self-realization in my own case, namely, that all members of the moral community be in a position to realize themselves. (*c*) Liberal individualism attempts to occupy a middle ground of sorts: in the circumstances of today's world it "mixes" the ethics of self-realization and service so that individuals are to put their self-realizationist aspirations first in their thinking about careers, but then see to it that they implement their careers in ways that are of at least some service to others.

At this point the natural question is: which (if any) of these three conceptions is to be generally recommended, and why? Now, I am not completely certain how this question is to be answered. I am inclined to think—against what I take to be common opinion—that morality requires the shared-fate perspective in the matter of career choice in today's world. But there are difficulties in making such an assertion with confidence. In this section I make certain observations that are relevant to the problem of selecting among these perspectives, but which also indicate some of what makes the selection problem so difficult.

(*a*) In the first place, I believe that the serious alternatives in the problem of selection are those of liberal individualism and shared-fate individualism. When we keep the circumstances of today's world

6. The Selection Problem

in mind, separate-life individualism too easily permits callousness. Perhaps the account I have given is already enough to suggest how this is so. Separate-life individualism is of course not an unintelligible view, and it might have behind it certain claims about persons' rights that are theoretically interesting in themselves and for what they suggest for the assignment of powers to the state. But when the separate-life perspective is examined for what it recommends for individual responsibility (not for the powers of the state), its net effect is a claim of lack of connection among human lives that, in principle, allows the individual an extraordinary indifference toward others. This perspective is certainly not itself a view that *fosters* in persons the forms of moral thought and feeling in which the good of others is a serious matter.[26] My own thought is that no person raised in the form of moral life I am concerned with, in which both the basic attitudes I mentioned earlier are central, could in clear conscience maintain that, morally, relief for life's victims in today's world is at the whim of whatever "special reasons" (if any) competent individuals may have. We think, rather, that such relief is a moral burden that falls upon members of the moral community who are competent to discharge it. A view that glosses our situation in such a way that relief is not a moral burden at all will seem, at best, sophistical.

(b) But to reject separate-life individualism is hardly to settle the selection problem posed by the alternatives of liberal *versus* shared-fate individualism. Neither of these perspectives glosses away the moral burden for competent individuals raised by the facts of destitution and gross disparity in levels of life in today's world. But the choice between them involves a dilemma.

On the one side, if we suppose that morality requires that the shared-fate perspective guide career choice in today's world, and thus that we are to put service to others before self-realization in our own case, this makes us *risk* our lives in a way that may be too much for us, or many of us, to bear. That is, acceptance of the shared-fate perspective may make "excessive demands on human nature."[27] One can, after all, imagine the case in which the person who pursues the service career that is morally required incurs great costs in the form of the frustration of aspirations linked to self-realization. This may not happen, of course. One can also imagine the case in which one undertakes a service career involving the use of talents and capacities other than those one would have developed in a self-realizationist career, and, after a time, one experiences a certain interest and satisfaction in one's work, and no real regret over self-realization foregone. One may become "caught up" in one's service career. Or one may not.[28] In advance, it seems, one cannot calculate how these matters will turn out, and the *risk* of personal frustration of a most important kind is built into the acceptance of the shared-fate perspective for career choice.

On the other side, if one accepts liberal individualism, then an important risk of another kind arises. For in this case it is not at all clear that the job of making self-realization available to all members of the moral community could ever really get done. The magnitude of the problems of destitution and gross disparity in levels of life may very well require, as it were, a "crash program"—at least a concerted effort—by competent individuals over a generation or more.[29] It may well be that, in relation to the aim of achieving effective equal membership throughout the moral community, liberal individualism is not demanding enough. (Indeed, it hardly seems demanding at all.) Again, I do not see how, in advance, an individual can estimate with any confidence the impact of his or her career on this prospect. The acceptance of the liberal perspective for career choice thus risks leaving the problems of destitution and gross disparity in levels of life unaddressed or merely half-addressed.

(c) Consider further the choice between liberal individualism and shared-fate individualism. Suppose (as I believe) that morality requires the shared-fate perspective as a guide for individuals choosing and pursuing careers in today's world.[30] In that case we worry that morality imposes demands upon us that, if not impossible, may still be excessive. For it makes us risk the great unhappiness of frustrated self-realization. But this notion of "possibly excessive demands" is itself very problematic. A demand that is excessive for one person may not be for another; the standards of what is "excessive" may in some contexts be too lenient and in other contexts too stringent;

7. Replies to Two Objections [45]

something may be an excessive demand upon individuals in one set of circumstances, but still be *required by morality* in *another* set of circumstances. In the matter of career choice we may grant that the demand that service prevail over self-realization would be excessive when all members of society are more or less well positioned to realize themselves, or (perhaps) when an institutional scheme is in place and operating reasonably effectively toward that end. But it is not at all clear to me that that demand is excessive when relatively few are able to realize themselves, relatively many suffer destitution in some or many of its desperate forms, and no effective general ameliorating scheme is in place at all. It is not implausible to think that morality may, in extreme situations, make demands upon persons that would be excessive in non-extreme circumstances. If this is so, then in adopting the liberal-individualist perspective, and thus choosing a career under the guide "self-realize *cum* service to others," we may in effect be settling for a form of deliberating about career choice that is less stringent than the form we *ought* to adopt in the extreme circumstances of today's world. We end up resolving to self-realize (and hoping to serve) rather than resolving to serve (and hoping to self-realize). To do this is perhaps not flat-out immoral. But it may not be the moral thing to do either. It may be, in the end, a compromise with morality—a settling for what is, at best, "the easy way out."

7 / Replies to Two Objections

The discussion above is incomplete in many ways. Several objections come to mind. I close this chapter with a brief response to only the following two objections. First, it might be objected that I have not really *proved* that morality requires the shared-fate perspective and that insofar as this is so the claim that the familiar liberal-individualist perspective on career choice is a "compromise with morality" is premature. And second, it might be objected that the view I wish to recommend—namely, career choice under the shared-fate perspective, whereby we are to put service to others before self-realization—is simply outrageous. Surely morality does not require, or even urge, that we risk sacrificing our lives for others. It may require, or urge, the sacrifice of a part of one's income, occasional investments of time and energy, and so on. But the view I favor turns the "supererogatory" into "duty," and that is unacceptably extreme.[31] One would not, and should not, advise one's son, daughter, or close friend—someone one cares about—to put service *over* self-realization in deliberations about career. And if a view is such that one would not and should not put it into moral advice to one's child or close friend, then it cannot be right.

My response to the first of these objections is to grant its point, but then to suggest that the view I favor is anyhow not at a striking disadvantage in respect of "proof" relative to the other views I have sketched. I certainly have not "derived" the claim that the shared-fate perspective is morality's guide to career choice in today's world from prior propositions that "everyone agrees with" or from principles that are open to independent justification. But I do not see that a derivation of either of those sorts is available for separate-life or liberal individualism either. Somehow one must determine how one values individual lives, and this determination will be reflected in many of one's beliefs about the course of individual responsibility in different circumstances. The great interest of the career-choice problem is that it isolates the hard question, "Am I to be in life for myself primarily, or others primarily?" and then presses it upon us in a sharp fashion by directing our attention to the troubling facts of the human condition today.

There are of course different strategies for *expressing*, if not "proving," the shared-fate way of answering the hard question. For example, one might express the shared-fate answer by first recognizing a duty correlative to the rights of people generally to subsistence or to well-being,[32] and then construing those rights as so important that they prevail over the rights of individuals to pursue self-realization when the two sets of rights conflict. Alternatively, one might express this answer *via* a theoretical construction whereby,

7. Replies to Two Objections

say, hypothetical, specially credentialed rational agents in a morally privileged choosing position select the shared-fate perspective to govern career choice for (real) individuals.[33] But these strategies, again, do not prove the answer I favor; they only express it in ways of greater or less theoretical interest.

Regarding the second objection, I must say that I have no neat set of criteria indicating when a course of action goes "beyond the call of duty."[34] Nevertheless, in the form of moral life I am investigating, when it is considered apart from what it requires or permits in different sets of circumstances, there is *as much* pressure behind the shared-fate orientation as there is behind the separate-life orientation. When one asks the hard question formulated above with the circumstances of today's world in mind, I do not see that it could be clearly wrong, or especially "heroic," to answer "I must, in these circumstances, be in life for others primarily." A person who answers in this way of course reflects a moral sensibility that is significantly different from that of a person who answers in the separate-life or liberal manner. But if, under the pressure of attention to the crude facts about the human condition, the main elements in our form of moral life become so arranged that the shared-fate attitude dominates the person, I cannot see that this is a mistaken, extreme, sentimental, or otherwise weird result.[35] The elements within our form of moral life that support the shared-fate orientation are as familiar as those that support the other kinds of orientation, and the risks involved in not following the shared-fate view are obviously as serious as those involved in not following the other views.

These remarks perhaps already convey my response to the last part of the second objection I mentioned. Of course it would be difficult to advise one's son, daughter, or close friend that morality requires, in today's world, that one make the choice of a career under the shared-fate perspective. One does not propose lightly that one's child or friend incur the risk of frustrated self-realization. But today's world is nevertheless what it is: our circumstances are those in which the human condition is needlessly riddled with destitution, gross disparity in levels of life, and meager efforts at relief; and these circumstances could, through our efforts, be changed for the better. I do not see that our form of moral life teaches that we are to ignore these circumstances, or be indifferent to them, or pretend that they are other than what they are, in the context of career choice. And these circumstances *are* those in which the shared-fate advice is plausible and fitting. It is not the advice that is extreme, but rather our circumstances that are unfortunate. One might say that the other forms of advice seem to be for other circumstances.

3

MEMBERSHIP IN THE MORAL COMMUNITY

1 / A Problem of Definition

In the previous chapter I argued, in effect, that shared-fate individualism is not an implausible view. While initially it may strike one as extreme, I suggested that, when certain troubling facts about the human condition in today's world are given attention, shared-fate individualism loses its extreme character and begins to appear to be a serious view about what morality requires of "competent individuals." My general aim in this book is to defend and support shared-fate individualism. It is a moral conception that raises many problems, one of which may be sketched as follows.

Both liberal and shared-fate individualism are influenced by the element in our form of moral life that holds that persons are *in life together*: we are thought of as connected with each other such that *ab initio* we are members of a common "human" or "moral" community. Further, the discussion of the previous chapter suggests that both liberal and shared-fate individualism regard responsibility for others as *definitional* of the idea of membership in the moral community—even though they treat that responsibility differently in the third set of circumstances I sketched there, that is, the situation in which not all persons in the community are positioned to self-realize and there is no general amelioration scheme operating to remedy that fact.

It seems plain that neither liberal nor shared-fate individualism would be persuasive if it could be shown that other-responsibility is *not* definitional of the idea of membership in the moral community. In this chapter I wish to explore the basic claim that the idea of responsibility for others (under some interpretation) defines (in part) the notion of membership in the moral community. After setting out the problem in more detail (in section 2), I will introduce (in section 3) certain considerations that appear to dispute that claim. Then (in section 4) I will defend the claim against those considerations. Later (in section 5) I will sketch some "grounds" for the claim, that is, some conditions under which persons might be supposed to find it natural to build the element of other-responsibility into their idea of membership in the moral community. Finally (in section 6), I will briefly specify a practical condition of the existence and survival of the moral community thus defined.

Even if I succeed in showing that other-responsibility defines (in part) the idea of membership in the moral community, this will not be enough to show that we must accept shared-fate individualism as the appropriate moral perspective for competent individuals in today's world. The definitional point is shared by both liberal and shared-fate individualism, and to endorse it is not yet to select between these two forms of individualism. Still, the point is interesting in its own right, and if it is acceptable we may then be able to go on from it to provide further support for shared-fate individualism.

2 / Moral Agency as Membership in the Moral Community

We sometimes think of individual human beings in terms of the positions they occupy, the roles they play, or the offices they hold. So I may think of Jones *as* the city manager, or *as* a fellow jazz enthusiast, or just *as* a friend. Sometimes it is argued that to think of individuals in terms of their positions, roles, or offices is objectionable—that it is not only impersonal to do this, but somehow morally wrong. There may indeed be something to this point. It

2. Moral Agency as Membership in the Moral Community

would be not only impersonal but wrong to think of individuals as *only* their positions, roles, and offices—to reduce them, as it were, to concatenations of their social and conventional properties. On the other hand, it is not a practical possibility for us to junk altogether the forms of thought in which persons are construed in terms of their positions. Perhaps it is safe to think in such terms about human beings if one keeps in mind that they are not merely their positions.

Now, when liberal and shared-fate individualism view persons as members of the moral community, they treat them as occupants or holders of a kind of position, role, or office. At bottom, a certain way (among a variety of ways) of approaching the important and basic idea of "moral agency" is involved: the thought is that the task of understanding what it is for a human being to be a moral being is facilitated if we approach it as a problem of sketching the main defining features of a very basic and important role, position, or office a human being can occupy or hold. Attention shifts from, say, feelings, personal characteristics, or other facts about given individuals to properties of a position they may (or may not) hold.

An immediate consequence of approaching the idea of moral agency in this way is that it allows the intelligibility in particular cases of the question: how far is *this* individual human being a moral agent? For sometimes (as may be the case with most any position, role, or office) an individual human being may not be operating *as* a member of the moral community. We need not be simplistic about the cases in which persons do not operate as members of the moral community. They may be unable to operate that way, or fail to do so, or even refuse to do so. And in some cases there may even be reasons behind their inability, failure, or refusal to operate as members of the moral community.

In what follows my concern is to sketch some main features of membership in the moral community, and to consider how, so to speak, they should be arranged. The aim, as indicated above, is to explore (and endorse) the view of liberal and shared-fate individualism, namely, that other-responsibility is a defining feature of membership in the moral community.

3. Membership in the Moral Community

Let me formulate the problem in this way. First, recall our central ideas:

> Being a moral agent,
> Being responsible to oneself,
> Being responsible for others.

Then, to enable our discussion of the connections among these ideas to draw upon the contents of our intuitions, let us attach certain minimal interpretations (intended to be non-controversial) to these ideas. Thus, to allow ourselves whatever intuitive content attaches to the shift in attention from the personal characteristics of given individuals to the properties of the positions, offices, or roles they might hold or occupy, let the idea of moral agency involve, at least in part,

> (M) Being a member of the moral community.

And for the purposes of this discussion (recognizing that a fuller account will be offered later[1]), let the idea of self-responsibility be given a minimal "self-regarding" interpretation:

> (I) Having an interest in claims made on others.

Finally, let the idea of other-responsibility have a modest yet firm other-regarding edge to it:

> (A) Acknowledging (at least some) claims made on oneself in the interest of others independently of one's own interest.[2]

Now the problem is: how are (M), (I), and (A) related? The view I favor (with liberal and shared-fate individualism) is that (M) includes or "covers" both (I) and (A). That is, (M), (I), and (A) are connected so that the latter two notions are main defining elements of the first notion. On the view I favor (with liberal and shared-fate individualism) such claims as the following might be called "conceptual truths," for they would be considered definitional of the idea of membership in the moral community, and hence of the idea of moral agency:

> (MI) A member of the moral community (that is, a moral agent) has an interest in claims made on others.

3. On What Membership Includes

(MA) A member of the moral community (that is, a moral agent) acknowledges (at least some) claims made on himself or herself in the interest of others independently of his or her own interest.

3 / On What Membership Includes

It is plausible to maintain that (MI) may be construed as a conceptual truth relative to the idea of membership in the moral community for the reason that a member of the moral community is subject to moral demands and "a demand made on an individual is to be regarded as a moral demand only if it belongs to a system of demands which includes demands made on others in his interest."[3] That is, when (M) applies to Jones, (I) applies to him too, for the demands made on Jones so far as (M) applies to him are part of a system of demands that is such that being subject to it is (in one way or other) in Jones' interest. The point turns on what it is for a system of demands to be a system of moral demands: being subject to a system of moral demands is in one's interest just because some of the demands included in the system are claims made on others in one's interest.[4] It is not that the system is itself in one's interest independently of whether any of the demands that make it up are in one's interest. Since it may be arguable (perhaps along Rousseauian lines) that there is a possible reading of the distinction between my "general" or "long-range" interest and my "immediate" interest that makes sense of the claim that a system is in my (general) interest but contains no claims on others in my (immediate) interest, it would not follow directly that a system of demands that is in my interest, but that includes no demands that are claims on others in my interest, is impossible. But it does follow that such a system is not a system of *moral* demands. Hence, it is a necessary condition of a set of demands being a system of moral demands that a person subject to it have claims made on others in his or her interest. This allows us to see how (MI) is a conceptual truth.

P. F. Strawson grants that it would be "agreeable" to be able to argue that (MI) "carries with it the conclusion that mere self-conscious membership of a moral community implies at least in some degree extending one's sanction to its system of demands, to the extent of genuinely acknowledging as obligations at least some of the claims which others have on one." That is, it would be agreeable to derive, from the claim that (M) and (I) are connected definitionally, the further claim that (M) and (A) are connected definitionally. But, Strawson says, this cannot be done, for "to argue so would be to equivocate with the phrase 'membership of a moral community,'" that is, with the notion of (M).[5]

Why can't we construe (M) and (A) as connected definitionally? The reason is, according to Strawson, that "there would be nothing self-contradictory about the idea of one who recognized his interest in the system of moral demands and resolved merely to profit by it as much as he could, fulfilling its demands on himself only in so far as his interest calculably required it." Of course, a person's pursuing this policy successfully would require great skill at the practice of hypocrisy, and "it is an important fact that hypocrisy would be necessary."[6] But egoism of this sort is nevertheless conceivable, and, so far as it is, the claim that (M) and (A) are connected definitionally is defeated.

Strawson's line of thought does not end there. He goes on to draw attention to the important "fact of human nature" that "quite thoroughgoing" egoism of this kind is "rare" and to suggest that reflection upon this fact can lead us to see a different but nevertheless important conceptual truth involving (M) and (A). Although we cannot argue that *anyone* subject to moral demands must acknowledge some obligations under the system of moral demands, we can argue "that it is a tautology that the *generality* of those subject to moral demands must genuinely recognize some obligations under the system of demands." For "if this were not so, there would be no such thing as a system of moral demands and hence no such thing as being subject to a moral demand."[7]

In sum: in the case of (M) and (I) we can say definitionally that when Jones is a member of a moral community then Jones has an interest in morality; whereas in the case of (M) and (A), though we

4. Full Membership

cannot say definitionally that when Jones is a member of a moral community then Jones acknowledges some claims made on himself, we can say definitionally that the generality of members of a moral community acknowledge claims made on themselves. It appears to be the thrust of Strawson's view that we must reject (MA) as definitional of the idea of membership in the moral community in favor of a more modest definition, namely, that "members of a moral community in general" acknowledge some claims upon themselves.

4 / Full Membership

I suggest first that the claim that (MA) is a tautology relative to the idea of membership in the moral community can be maintained in the face of the conceivability of "quite thoroughgoing" egoism. On Strawson's account the egoist is characterized by (I) but not by (A) in that the egoist has an interest in the system of moral demands but resolves as a matter of personal policy not to acknowledge any claims on himself or herself that do not contribute to his or her interest. But Jones' being characterized by (I) but not by (A) need not provide a counterexample to the claim that (MA) is a conceptual truth. Jones' being characterized by (I) but not by (A) of course makes Jones a counterexample to the claim that

(IA) Those who have an interest in the system of moral demands acknowledge claims on themselves

is a conceptual truth. But Jones, when characterized by (I) but not by (A), only provides a counterexample to (MA)'s being such a truth on the supposition that Jones is also characterized by (M).

What this brings out is that the view that the conceivability of the egoist obliges us to say that (MA) is not a conceptual truth supposes that (MA) is the conclusion of an argument having as premises the two truths (MI) and (IA). When (MA) is so construed, then the conceivability of the egoist does indeed oblige us to give up (MA). But "giving up" (MA) in this context means rejecting (MA) as a conceptual truth *because* one of the premises from which it is supposed to follow is not such a truth. This, however, may not be to say that (MA) is either false or, more important, not definitional of the idea of membership in a moral community. For it may be that (MA) need not be construed as a conclusion from these two premises. And I think that it should not be construed as such a conclusion. What is at stake in this discussion is whether (MA), like (MI), can be asserted as one definition among others in a set of definitions that together elucidate the notion of membership in a moral community. But there is no rule here that one must approach a claim like (MA) *from* a claim like (MI), such that the former is a definition only on the condition that it be deducible from a definition like the latter plus other definitions. It remains open whether (MA) can be asserted as one among a set of conceptual truths elucidating the notion of membership in a moral community, even when it cannot be reached as a conclusion from some other such (alleged) truth in the set.

Of course, (MA) could not be so asserted if there were other definitional propositions in the set with which it would be inconsistent. But what the conceivability of egoism shows is not necessarily that (MA) cannot be asserted as such a proposition in the set, but perhaps only that (IA) is not such a proposition in the set. I see no reason yet to think that (MA) is not consistent with (MI). If (MA) is construed as a conceptual truth, then, even though it cannot be derived from (MI), the conceivability or fact of egoism is not denied. Perhaps there are persons who may be characterized by (I) but not by (A). Such persons could not then be regarded as having membership in the moral community in, as we might say, the strict sense. On this account, the view that the conceivability of egoism poses a threat to the status of (MA) as definitional of the idea of membership in the moral community is spoken to by construing (MA) as prior to egoism in such a way as to make the status of (MA) as thus definitional a threat to the title of the egoist to membership in the moral community.

It is worth noting too that reading (MA) as a conclusion from premises that are such that the conceivability or fact of egoism renders (MA) non-definitional has a consequence that may not fit with our ordinary conception of morality.[8] For reading (MA) in this way

4. Full Membership

leaves us without one of our usual, and strongest, reasons for *not* regarding the egoist as we would regard a member of the moral community. The fact that a person has an interest in a system of moral demands but acknowledges no claims on himself or herself other than those in his or her interest would, on this reading, provide no ground for thinking of or treating him or her any differently from the ways in which we think of and treat those who are members of the moral community. A person's being characterized by (I) but not by (A) would furnish in itself no reason to think that he or she cannot be characterized by (M), since on the account in question being characterized by (A) is not a necessary condition of being characterized by (M), while being (I) is. *Ceteris paribus* the egoist who is not characterized by (A) would be on a logical par with the non-egoist who is characterized by (A)—anyhow regarding having membership in the moral community.

But at the very least, knowing that a person does not or refuses to acknowledge claims of a certain kind upon himself or herself gives rise to a difference in what we expect of him or her as against what we expect of those who do acknowledge claims of that kind. Thus, we cannot expect that such a person will fulfill or satisfy claims of that kind when they are made (though he or she may respond to them in some other way). When the claims in question are not conducive to his or her interest but are conducive to the interests of others, then we cannot expect satisfaction from him or her of claims of this sort. But if we cannot expect the effort to satisfy these claims, then we are regarding him or her differently from those of whom we can expect this. Now, I do not find it strange or unfamiliar, as an observation about our form of moral life, to characterize the distinction between our ways of regarding a person of whom we can expect satisfaction of claims that are not in his or her interest and a person of whom we cannot expect this as the distinction between regarding a person as a moral agent and regarding him or her as not a moral agent. If this is not strange or unfamiliar, then the view that being characterized by (A) is not definitionally linked to being characterized by (M) is suspect, for on that view there is no reason in the fact that we cannot expect a person to satisfy claims that are not in his or her interest for characterizing the distinction between the way we regard him or her and the way we regard someone of whom we can expect satisfaction as the distinction between a regard for a moral agent and a regard for someone who is not a moral agent.

It may be objected, I suppose, that we all fail on occasion to satisfy legitimate claims on ourselves in the interests of others, and that we do so without threat to our title to full membership in the moral community. This is so, but its being so does not entitle us to infer that among members of the moral community there may be found some persons who do not or refuse to acknowledge claims that are not conducive to their own interests. A person may of course fail on occasion to acknowledge a legitimate claim that is not in his or her interest and retain his or her title to membership in the moral community; on such occasions we may ask him to justify his non-acknowledgment, or accuse her of moral weakness or of a lapse into selfishness, which question or charges are appropriate only on the condition that he or she does have this title. But one cannot fail on all occasions and retain this title, for when one *never* acknowledges legitimate claims that are not in one's interest, there is no room for justification of non-acknowledgment on a particular occasion (though there may be a question of justification of a general policy of non-acknowledgment), nor is there room for weakness or selfishness on that occasion (a person who never acknowledges claims neither is "weak" nor "lapses into selfishness" when, on a particular occasion, he or she does not acknowledge a claim). How many failures-to-acknowledge one may be charged with before one's title to membership is threatened I shall not attempt to decide here. (It seems like the question "How many insults can one deliver before one loses one's reputation for tact?") That matter is not relevant to the question of whether (MA) is a conceptual truth, for (MA) may be a conceptual truth whether the question "How many failures?" is answered "Many" or "Very few."

There may be other reasons for regarding a person as "outside" the moral community. On Strawson's account, a person's having no interest in the community's system of demands is such a reason. But my thought is that ordinarily one such reason is a person's acknowl-

4. Full Membership [59]

edging no claims on himself or herself other than those that are in some way conducive to his or her interest. Even when there are other grounds for treating persons as outside the moral community, on Strawson's account there would *have* to be other grounds, and this does not seem to me to reflect the character of our form of moral life.

Roughly, saying that a person's not being characterized by (A) is no reason not to regard him or her as a member of the moral community is like saying that a person's not acknowledging, or resolving not to acknowledge, the rules of chess as ever governing his or her behavior is no reason not to regard him or her as a chess player. But clearly, when someone is playing chess, the fact that he or she will not acknowledge the rules of chess as rules for his or her behavior is the best reason for denying him or her the title of player. The comparison between games and morality can be taken too far, but I do not think it is misleading in this respect: being a member of the moral community resembles being (for example) a chess player insofar as in both cases not acknowledging, or resolving not to acknowledge, certain constraints upon oneself independently of considerations of one's own interest counts as failing to hold the office in question. In the case of games we say of such persons that they are not really playing—if indeed we do not go further (when they are not, for example, children) and resent them.

Nothing hangs on the words "member of the moral community," and it does not follow from the fact that we regard some persons as outside the moral community that we think *badly* of them or that we consider ourselves to have a license to persecute them or ignore their interests. There are a number of ways in which persons are related to the system of demands of a moral community, and some of these ways can be short of "full" membership in the community without incurring the epithet "egoism." Small children and certain others may be "members" only in the sense in which some of us who are at some early stage or other in the process of learning a game are "players" of that game. Given the very general yet implicit character of the moral community, there are still others who are "members" in only the more rudimentary sense of being merely in contact with, or being unable to avoid being in contact with, the community's system of demands. It is a mistake to think that in general those who are in contact with a system but do not acknowledge claims on themselves do so *deliberately*, for example, out of some purposeful resentment of the system. There may be those who *simply* do not acknowledge claims on themselves, as well as those who do not do so from some special motive. This is to say that the general characterization "being (I) but not (A)" may cover more than egoism as it is ordinarily understood,[9] namely, as involving a *policy* of non-acknowledgment of claims upon oneself that are not conducive to one's interests; the general characterization, for example, may be blanketing a sense of "but not (A)" involving no deliberate policy. And the difference between these ways of falling outside the moral community may be of very great social and political importance.[10] But one may still insist that all this is compatible with the claim that full membership in the moral community entails acknowledgment of some claims upon oneself independently of what is conducive to one's own interest. The fact that persons may fall short of full membership in different ways and fall outside the moral community altogether in others does not require that we believe that there is no such thing as full membership in the community.

5 / Grounds

I have proposed that (MA) may be considered definitional of the idea of membership in the moral community even when egoism is conceivable or a fact, and that the view that being characterized by (A) is not tightly connected to being characterized by (M)—which follows from the view that (MA) is not so definitional—has a consequence that seems not to fit our form of moral life as we ordinarily understand it, namely, the consequence that a person's not being characterized by (A) would itself be no reason not to regard him or her as a member of the moral community. But the above remarks about how a tight connection between (M) and (A) may be preserved might seem somewhat defensive. Let us ask at this point: is

5. Grounds

there any positive ground for regarding (MA) as a tautology? What we are asking here is perhaps not plain. I take the question to be this: what could show that we consider ourselves members of a moral community such that (MA) is to be regarded as definitional of our idea of membership? Put another way: what must we suppose about ourselves and our circumstances to account for our needing, for purposes of moral deliberation and criticism, a notion of membership in the moral community that (in the Kantian metaphor) "contains" acknowledgment of claims in the interest of others independently of self-interest?

In what follows I sketch an answer to this question. I attempt to specify only some of what might figure in a full answer—which I think would be very complex—in an effort to make clear at least what kind of account would serve to answer the question.

(a) To begin, let us agree with Strawson that a system of moral demands (SMD) is (among other things) a system that includes demands made on those subject to it in the interests of all those subject to it, in the sense described above. This is to say that a system's including demands in the interests of all those subject to it is definitional of its being a system of moral demands. This characterization yields the claim that

> (SI) Those subject to a system of moral demands have an interest in claims made on others

is a conceptual truth, which in turns yields (trivially) the claim that (MI) is a conceptual truth, for members of the moral community are among those who are subject to the community's system of moral demands. It of course does not follow from (SI) that

> (SA) Those subject to a system of moral demands acknowledge claims upon themselves other than those in their own interest

is a conceptual truth. But the fact that (SA) does not follow from (SI) does not entail that the claim that (MA) is a conceptual truth is false, given my discussion above.

(b) Now, suppose that the practical circumstances in which persons are subject to (SMD) are such that it is a fact that

(F) Not all the demands of (SMD) made on any individual subject to (SMD) can be in his interest.

We may note that (F) is not a conceptual truth, for circumstances are conceivable in which an individual subject to (SMD) might never have demands made on him or her that are not in his or her interest. If this were the case for *all* individuals subject to (SMD), however, I think we would lose the use of the notion of something's being "in an individual's interest," though I shall not pursue this here. What is important for this discussion is that, when persons are subject to (SMD) and (F) is true, then there are demands on an individual subject to (SMD) that are in the interest of someone other than him or her. This is to say that one's being subject to (SMD) when (F) is true is a sufficient condition of having (some) demands made on one other than those in one's interest.

(c) This is important because we may now entertain the possibility that persons who have demands made on them other than those in their interest recognize it as a matter of policy either to acknowledge such demands or not. That is, we may suppose about them that they can see what policy options are open to them when they are subject to (SMD) and (F) is true. (See 1.2 for a brief discussion of "policies.") To say that they can recognize or see this as a policy decision requires that we suppose about them that they are "rational" in the sense of that term that goes with being able (for reasons) to establish forward-looking resolutions (subject, of course, to subsequent problems of interpretation) whose content should be justified.

(d) It follows that when persons are subject to (SMD) and (F) is true, and when they may be supposed to be rational such that they can recognize the question of acknowledgment or non-acknowledgment of claims independently of self-interest as a matter for policy decision, they at least have the idea of being subject to (SMD) in such a way as to acknowledge claims made on them other than those

5. Grounds

in their own interest. They must have this latter idea to be able to recognize the policy matter before them. It does not yet follow, of course, that they apply this idea they have to anyone, or even that they regard it as representing an option they should take seriously.

(*e*) But on the condition that they may be said to have the idea of being subject to (SMD) in such a way as to acknowledge claims independently of self-interest, we may entertain the further possibility that they might have reason to regard this idea as *important* such that they encourage themselves and others to live in such a way that the idea has wide application among them. All that would be involved in their having reason to regard the idea as thus important I will not attempt to specify at this point: the attempt to say something illuminating on this problem is the task of later parts of this book. But it is worth noting here that the explanation of their regard for this idea need not be narrow; for example, it need not proceed by appeal to social utility only. They might very well believe, and have reason for believing, that they are themselves individually important (they may believe that they are all "ends," that is, instances of value or possessors of rights) in a sense that entails that they are reciprocally deserving of acknowledgment by others. For the purposes of this sketch let us suppose that (in one way or other) they have or develop some such belief as this, and thus regard the idea of acknowledgment of claims independently of self-interest as important.

(*f*) On the condition that they regard the idea in question as important, we may then suppose further about them that their capacity for rationality extends to their developing criteria of the *legitimacy* of the interests by which proper objects of acknowledgment are identified. Making good this supposition would doubtless require, in part, certain assumptions about the relationship between their interests and what they may view as social utility, for example, the assumption that satisfaction of some interests is not as essential to securing utility as satisfaction of others. This can be compatible with their meaning in part by their belief in their individual importance that each person's interests are to be taken as seriously as any other person's; indeed, their notion of themselves as individually impor-

[64] 3. Membership in the Moral Community

tant may commit them to the view that each of them occupies a fundamental position in which their interests are valued and respected equally, albeit a position from which some interests may be sacrificed justifiably in terms of what is conducive to utility.[11]

(g) When these persons regard the idea in question as important and develop criteria of the legitimacy of interests, we may then say that they have the idea of being subject to (SMD) in such a way as to acknowledge legitimate claims in the interest of others independently of self-interest. And we may suppose that it is this latter idea that they regard as important, to the extent that they urge themselves and others to live in such a way that it has wide application among them. At this point we may suppose that they possess and endorse the idea of membership in the moral community that contains the idea of acknowledgment of claims independently of self-interest. That is, they consider themselves in relevant contexts as members of a moral community, such that (MA) is a conceptual truth.

I must repeat that the foregoing is merely a sketch of an answer to the question of "grounds" for regarding (MA) as a conceptual truth. It is not as it stands an argument in detail, though I hope it is suggestive of a kind of account that might provide an answer to the question of grounds. Roughly, the sketch suggests that a large number of conditions having to do with persons and their circumstances can, when satisfied, have as a consequence the fact that persons consider themselves to be members of a moral community such that they regard (MA) as definitional of their idea of membership.

What seems to me of interest in this manner of approach to the question of grounds is that an account of having the notion of membership in the moral community such that (MA) is a conceptual truth relies upon appeal to certain facts about persons and their circumstances rather than upon appeal to special forms of intuition, divine imperatives, or philosophically special principles of reason. The account has a certain plainness to it, despite the fact that it would be complex if fully laid out. For example, this way of accounting for the notion that membership in the moral community "contains" acknowledgment of claims independently of self-interest rests in part on (F), which I have said is not a conceptual truth. One may ask: is (F) true? The answer is surely "yes," but the interesting task is that of making clear why this is so. I suggest (without discussion here) that the ground of the truth of (F) is the fact about ourselves in society as we know it that our interests sometimes "collide." More elaborately: collision of interests among persons like ourselves is a sufficient condition of its being the case that, if we have a system of demands that operates in the interests of all those subject to it, it will be such that not all its demands on any one individual subject to it can be in his or her interest. But I doubt that it is a conceptual truth that we are beings whose interests collide (even if it is a conceptual truth that we are beings who have interests), and, if this is so, it may be doubted that it is a conceptual truth that we have need for the notion of membership in the moral community that contains acknowledgment of claims other than those in one's interest. But I am suggesting (*a*) that *if* collision of interests is a fact about us, then it follows that our having this notion is possible, and (*b*) that this is but one condition among many others that taken together form a sufficient condition of our regarding ourselves as members of a moral community such that (MA) is a conceptual truth.

6 / On the Existence of the Moral Community

I have been considering the view that we cannot claim definitionally that *any* members of a moral community must acknowledge some obligations under its system of demands, for this would be to "equivocate" with the notion of membership in a moral community; at best, according to this view, we can claim definitionally that the *generality* of members of the moral community acknowledge some obligations under its system. I have argued, in effect, that while it is true that not every last person subject to a moral community's system of demands acknowledges claims upon himself or herself independently of self-interest, nevertheless this fact does not provide reason for denying that membership in the moral community entails acknowledgment of such claims. It only does so upon enlargement of (or equivocation with) the notion of membership so as to include in it everyone "subject to" the community's system of demands. But there is no need to enlarge the notion of membership in this way, and to do so is surely to lose a useful distinction. Also, I have suggested in a programmatic way that we can describe a set of facts about persons and their circumstances from which it would follow that they regard themselves as members of a moral community who ("by definition") acknowledge claims independently of self-interest.

What, then, of the claim that the generality of members of the moral community must acknowledge some obligations under its system of demands? On the view I have been concerned to defend, according to which (MA) is a conceptual truth, this generality-claim follows trivially. But there is another way of reading the generality-claim that gives it great practical importance. Or perhaps better put: there is another generality-claim relevant to the situation of those who construe (MA) as a definition whose content and truth it would be of practical importance to ascertain. This is the claim that the generality of those *subject to* the system of moral demands of the moral community must acknowledge some obligations under its system of demands. When construed in this way the generality claim states what may be a practical condition of the existence and survival of a system of moral demands when (F) is true, and when (SI) as well as (MI) and (MA) are conceptual truths. It points to the fact that communities cannot survive when a certain number of those in direct contact with them do not maintain them. Such a claim has practical interest in the manner of an empirical hypothesis about the survival of (SMD) when (F) is true and (SI) and (MA) are conceptual truths; it would be important to find out whether and in what form such a moral community, in contrast with other sorts of community, survives when something less than the generality of those in contact with it acknowledge obligations under its system of demands, that is, when less than the generality of those in contact with it are members of it.[12]

6. On the Existence of the Moral Community

I suggest, however, that though this generality-claim may be of interest as an empirical hypothesis about the existence and survival of the moral community, it is less than what may be maintained to be definitional about membership in the moral community, namely, that members acknowledge some claims upon themselves independently of self-interest.

4

PARTICIPATION AND POLICY

1 / The Moral Acceptability of Policy

In the previous chapter I endorsed a view held by both liberal individualism and shared-fate individualism, namely, that moral agency, understood in terms of the metaphor "membership in the moral community," includes "by definition" acknowledgment of (legitimate) claims independently of self-interest. I defended this view against some considerations meant to dispute the claim that moral agency can be defined in this way, and then I suggested that there are conditions under which moral agency would be defined in this way.

I want to say that in certain conditions it would be the policy of persons to understand themselves in terms of an idea of membership in the moral community that includes (in part) the idea of acknowledgment of claims independently of self-interest. Later I will also want to say that in certain circumstances shared-fate individualism would be the policy considered applicable to "competent individuals" by the membership of the moral community. I mean by this, of course, not merely that these *would be* the policies of the members of the moral community, but also that they would be their policies *because* they are *morally acceptable*. But then a general background question arises: what is it for the policies of a community to be morally acceptable? In this chapter I explore one way of dealing with this question that seems to me relevant to our inquiry into the ideas of individual responsibility and moral community.

2 / A Dilemma

A direct and perhaps natural approach to our question is that of democratic theory. According to democratic theory, acceptable policies must reflect and respond to the interests of members of the community. But, of course, reflection immediately suggests that not any policy reflecting and responding to the members' interests is morally acceptable. Sometimes a policy is merely a bargain or compromise; it may be acceptable to those who are parties to it and affected by it but nevertheless be without moral credentials. The policy may, in the terms of a familiar distinction, reflect or respond to persons' *wants* or "perceived" interests, but not thereby reflect or respond to their *needs* or "real interests."

This distinction between perceived and real interests is, I think, a commonplace. Let us suppose that it has some point. But then an apparent dilemma arises.

On the one side, democratic decision-procedures (such as plurality voting and coalition politics) are designed to take in and articulate persons' wants, and these (ideally) are then serviced by the laws, agencies, and other governmental instruments of democratic society. On this account, political democracy is responsive to persons' perceived interests. But if the commonplace distinction just indicated has some point to it, then political democracy is not necessarily responsive to persons' real interests. And this we may view as a difficulty. For, as many critics charge, persons' wants are often "morally and prudentially defective"—and perhaps especially so in "advanced capitalist societies" equipped with powerful mass media, advertising industries, and other means of inculcating in people desires linked to profitable commodities and services. But in that case political democracy, as it operates in such societies, may serve something other than genuine needs; it may, in fact, be "an instrument of oppression; even of self-oppression."[1]

On the other side, however, if a society is to be responsive to persons' real interests, there must be some procedures, other than procedures that articulate persons' wants, whereby persons' genuine needs can be identified. But this too presents a difficulty, for in fact it is not clear what the relevant means of identification are. This is to say at least that we are uncertain, or that there is no general agreement, about how to determine real interests. This in turn brings to mind the situation in which "authorities," perhaps in the form of political elites, central planning bodies, or "technocrats," come to steer the course of life for members of a community—a situation that is unattractive to those who value autonomy. Thus, the "criticism of existing wants [is] quite naturally thought to be a precursor to tyrannical governmental interference."[2]

3 / Responses to the Dilemma

How shall we respond to the dilemma thus sketched? Is there some way of avoiding the twin risks of a community's catering through its policies to the known but possibly "defective" interests of persons or of its responding to their alleged real but perhaps speciously diagnosed and authoritatively imposed interests? Two views come to mind.

First, we might be inclined to agree that indeed there is no clear way, or no generally accepted way, of distinguishing wants and needs. We might view answers to the question "What are our real interests?" as essentially ideological, or anyhow intrinsically controversial; and we might view that consideration, together with the risk of imposition of answers to such a question by "authority," as a basis for *settling* for the satisfaction of expressed wants in the political arena. On this view there just is no real alternative, in societies actually attempting to be democratic, to gearing political instruments to respond to the interests persons perceive themselves to have. And, it might be added, the alleged risk of perceived interests' being "defective" can be exaggerated. After all, as the familiar saying has it, no one knows better where the shoe pinches than the wearer. This view, by which we are urged to settle for the satisfaction of perceived interests, has been described as the "classical liberal's preferred solution" to our dilemma.[3]

3. Responses to the Dilemma

But, alternatively, we might be enough tempted by the troubling thought that indeed perceived interests may be defective to resist the recommendation that we should simply settle, politically, for responding to wants. To do so, after all, may be to retain and reinforce a *status quo* involving related legal, educational, political, and economic institutions that, in effect, artificially limit freedom and the development of human potential. In brief, to settle for the satisfaction of perceived interests may itself be, from this angle, to diminish human autonomy.[4] And, so it may then be proposed, this danger *can* be avoided without incurring the risk of suspect authoritative imposition of conceptions of "our real interests." How? Well, by the proper understanding and skillful conduct of the political activity of *participation*. The thought here is that participation in decision-making by those affected by the resulting policies is not, or need not be, merely a matter of expression of wants leading to (mere) bargains or compromises. Rather, it is, or can be, a form of activity by which we may gain "a reasonably close convergence between expressed and actual interest"; also, participation (again, properly understood and conducted) is valuable in its own right, for it is "an essential means for the individual to discover his real needs through the intervening discovery of himself as a social human being."[5]

Now, the idea that we can secure a "convergence" between our wants and needs *via* widespread participation in policy decision-making is initially attractive, I think. But whether participation can be relied upon to bring about this result has been challenged. One critic has estimated, rather bluntly, that any such reliance upon participation is a "mere expression of . . . hope."[6] For "a moment's reflection discloses that participation in government is neither necessary nor sufficient for 'full moral development' "; nor is participation necessary for the "development of one's sense of self-esteem" or for "identifying one's interests"; and it is neither necessary nor sufficient "for being able to secure one's interests, although it is often a useful tool for so doing."[7] On this view participation has no value in its own right, and "so there is no intrinsic value in widespread participation in government which could balance off any instability or inefficiency which might result from it."[8] In short, there is no special magic in participation in decision-making such that, in principle, resulting policies favor real interests rather than possibly defective wants.

4 / Assumptions About the Participation View

So far I have sketched an apparent dilemma for proponents of political democracy and described two possible ways of responding to it: namely, the "settlement" view, that is, the classical liberal's preferred solution, and the "convergence" thesis, that is, the solution from participation. Neither response is problem-free. In what follows let us explore the solution from participation further—not so much to solve the problems of political practice addressed by democratic theory as to respond to the general question of when a policy is morally acceptable raised by the inquiry above. I begin by listing certain assumptions about the solution from participation that indicate some of its philosophical interest and thus provide reasons for giving further attention to it.

In the first place I take it that those who favor the convergence view have a loaded notion of what participation is. Thus, when critics argue that the view that participation will produce a convergence between perceived and real interests is a mere expression of hope, it is plain that any relevant reply will involve an account of what the intended concept of participation contains. What such an account should include is, I think, a philosophical question of some interest for our inquiry, insofar as it bears on "conditions of the acceptability" of policies for members of the moral community.

Second, I take it that when the theorist speaks of participation as promising a "convergence" of wants and needs he does not have in mind an activity in which one simply expresses interests already formed. Rather, he has in mind an activity in the conduct of which one determines real interests. It is in participating with others in decision-making concerning policies that it becomes clear what our

4. Assumptions About the Participation View

real interests are. And I interpret this to mean that to engage in this activity is to put oneself under constraints that operate so as to suspend or disallow considerations that are irrelevant to morally acceptable policies (considerations, for example, such as prior interests of a selfish or narrowly personal kind) and to reveal or push to the surface considerations that are relevant to such policies.

In line with the discussion of "policies" in 1.2 above, examples of policies are laws, institutions, and, in general, understandings of how things are to be done in some area of life among the members of groups or communities. Thus, for present purposes we might imagine the members of a community, or perhaps their agents or representatives—let us call them members of an *agreement group*—attempting to reach agreement on what their policy shall be (for example, what their laws shall be) concerning, say, abortion, or the availability of community funds to victims of disasters of certain types, or the degree of vulnerability of writers among them, such as journalists and scholars, to legal requests for disclosure of otherwise confidential sources of information. We might even imagine the members of a community attempting to reach agreement on what system of property they shall have; for example, we might imagine them deliberating between a system allowing exclusive rights of ownership to the things one has mixed one's labor with and a system that socializes the ownership of things so that decisions concerning possession are made democratically and not privately.

Third, I take it that, for the activity of participation really to promise morally acceptable policies, it must exemplify what has been called "pure procedural justice,"[9] or what I shall call "procedural moral acceptability." This is to say that the participation theorist is approaching the problem of determining morally acceptable policies from, as it were, the inside. His approach is *not* one in which we participate in decision-making, arrive at a result, and then test the result for "moral acceptability" by reference to independently known principles of right. Rather, we attempt to determine whether the persons involved in the effort to reach agreement on policy met certain standards, or fulfilled certain conditions, and we try to determine whether the routine (perhaps, for example, Robert's Rules of Order, or simply informal debate) used to structure their efforts to reach agreement was not itself closed to certain alternatives, and so forth. Then, if all such antecedent factors are in order, we are prepared to say that the agreement reached—whatever it is—is acceptable. Sometimes games of chance, such as five-card stud or blackjack, are held to be examples of processes the results of which—whatever they may be—are deemed fair just in case certain antecedent conditions are satisfied (the players know the rules, accept them, follow them, and do not cheat). Satisfaction of these conditions contributes fairness to the results. Now, I do not wish to discuss games here, but I will explore the participation-theorist's idea that there are conditions under which persons may participate in decision-making on matters of policy such that the satisfaction of those conditions confers moral acceptability upon the agreed-to policy, whatever it may be.

In connection with this theme of participation as an instance of procedural moral acceptability, notice that the participation theorist has a built-in and rather interesting conception of what "our real interests" are. When policies are the sorts of things that may (or may not) be in our interests, then to say that a policy is in our real interests is to say that it can be construed as the result of decision-making that satisfies the theorist's loaded notion of participation. On this account our real interests are neither the sum of our perceived interests, nor perceived interests we happen to share with each other, nor perceived interests that meet some independent (perhaps ideological) criteria of the good life. Rather, they simply are the interests that are responded to by the policies we arrive at *via* decision-making satisfying the conditions and constraints that elucidate the theorist's special concept of participation. And insofar as a notoriously slippery notion like "our real interests" (some call it the idea of "the public interest" or "the common interest") is open to interpretation, I see no objection to the participation-theorist's proposed understanding of the notion at this point in the inquiry.[10]

One further consideration in this area. It is in line with the assumptions I have been making that we may distinguish between a

4. Assumptions About the Participation View [75]

strong and a weak form of the participation theory. In its strong form the theory holds that when participation is properly conducted its result is morally acceptable, whatever it is. In its weak form the view holds that properly conducted participation *tends* to yield acceptable results; it may not always be successful, perhaps, but it often is. It should be clear that my interest is in the strong form of the participation view.[11] But perhaps it will already be asked: is the procedural-acceptability line even promising? That is, surely we always retain the option of questioning whether a policy agreed upon by persons is morally acceptable, regardless of the fact that it was *they* who agreed to it under *such-and-so* conditions.

We must be very careful how we respond to this point. To *insist* upon the option mentioned is, of course, to cut off the possibility of the (strong) participation theory at the outset and, in effect, to beg the question. I think we would be better advised to respond to the point in the following way. First, we may admit, as the inquiry begins, that we do not know whether there is a successful account of participation whereby participation guarantees the moral acceptability of resulting policies; though we may at the same time reserve the critic's right to inspect any proffered account of the relevant constraints on participation to determine whether we are persuaded that policies reached under them are thereby morally acceptable. It may be that conditions in addition to those proffered are needed; or it may be that we will discover as we go along that, for some reason, a successful account is not really possible. Second, we may recognize that the procedural-acceptability approach might in any case be a useful heuristic device. For that approach, even if it cannot culminate in a successful account, may nevertheless helpfully press us to formulate any moral intuitions we have about how the acceptability of policies depends upon how they are (or could, in principle, be) arrived at. I assume that we have some moral intuitions in this area. That is, I think we believe that the acceptability of policy has something to do with how it is (or could be) arrived at. Anyhow, some such belief seems a main part of our current "received" democratic ideology, to the extent that that ideology is evidenced in contemporary demands for community involvement in urban development and the control of schools, police, and even libraries and recreational programs, for student and faculty involvement in college and university governance, for workers' involvement in industry, and for recipients' involvement in the conduct of welfare programs.

In what follows, then, I will be chiefly concerned with this question: when, or under what conditions, does the participation of members of an agreement group in decision-making meant to lead to the formulation of policy confer moral acceptability upon any agreed-upon policy that results? In short form: when is participation an instance of procedural moral acceptability? This question asks for an account of the loaded notion of participation, that is, it asks for a listing of the conditions and constraints under which participation confers acceptability upon resulting policies. Beyond this question I will touch lightly upon the question of the practicality of participation thus understood. One of the standard objections to participation theory is that the model of decision-making it propounds is impractical for political systems in (large) states such as our own. Another objection is that some types of policy problems are not susceptible to solution by participatory processes. We may seek, then, for an account of the circumstances in which it is even reasonable to recommend the "practice" of participation in the loaded sense. But we must begin by developing an answer to the first question, for without some idea of what an account in its area contains we have no basis for moving to the question of practicality.

Finally, I should emphasize that in what follows I have in mind people who fit the description of the "competent individual" given above (2.3). I do not wish to invoke the concept of ideal observers, or of abstract individuals, or even the Rawlsian notion of contractors in an "original position." The job is to understand what conditions must be met by "regular" or "real" people, their agreement itself, and any means or routine they employ to reach it, such that we would be prepared to say that any policy they agree upon is morally acceptable.

5 / Conditions of (Strong) Participation

As I look ahead, of the several conditions I list all but four are conditions that the persons involved in (strong) participation must satisfy as they follow whatever routine they may have for attempting to reach agreement. Two of those four conditions are requirements on the policy to which they agree; the other two conditions are requirements on the means or routine they use to make their way toward agreement. I suspect that the list I offer is not complete, but perhaps it will provide some understanding of what is involved in participation in a relevantly "loaded," or strong, sense, and thus illuminate in one possible way, philosophically, what it is (in the abstract, as it were) for policies to be morally acceptable.

1. NON-COERCION. Procedural moral acceptability requires that persons participating in an effort to reach agreement on policy be *uncoerced*. They do not have special control over one another, and no one is able to force his or her conception of a preferred result upon others in the agreement group. The participants are uncoerced in at least three ways. (*a*) They are uncoerced by other *individuals*, that is, by other members of the agreement group, as regards the content or substance of the policy they are striving to reach. (Each citizen, as Rousseau required in the quest for the general will, must think for himself or herself.[12]) (*b*) Also, they do not allow *groups* to form that could put pressure upon individuals engaged in the effort. (Rousseau also required, we may recall, that factions be disallowed.[13]) (*c*) And, finally, they do not suffer coercion by the *circumstances* in which they find themselves.

As regards this last point, it may be that we can speak intelligibly about the moral acceptability of the policy agreements persons make, or have to make, when they are in forced, urgent, or desperate situations. (Think of shipwrecks, earthquakes, or enemy attack.) But the ideal situation, so far as procedural moral acceptability is concerned, is surely one in which persons are free from harassment by circumstances, whether in the form, for example, of shortness of time, imminent disaster, intimidating titles of policy alternatives to be considered, or even mild commotion. There is a point about degree to be made here. As the circumstances of persons become increasingly stressful, the moral acceptability of any policy agreement they make may be more and more in question.

2. RATIONALITY. Another condition is that the persons involved in participation be *rational*. For the historical social-contract theorists (but not for Rousseau) this meant not merely the negative point that the participants in the decision-making effort were not emotionally agitated, depressed, or otherwise distracted, but also the more positive point that they were in possession of the "laws of nature." On this account, rational beings are those who are aware of certain rules or principles and also of what it is to be constrained by them.

But we might properly be suspicious that the condition of rationality is here being worked too hard. We may think that the "ordinary" concept of rationality, as it applies to real people and not to (specially designed) beings in a (specially designed) state of nature, does not require that rational beings have in common such principles as those that appear on certain theorists' lists of natural laws. Rather, it requires simply that such beings can reason, and in fact do so in the effort in question; that is, it requires that they can (and do) argue from certain propositions to other propositions, as, for example, in the process of giving evidence or a defense for certain views they favor. It also requires that rational beings can (and do) estimate the consequences of what they project and that these estimates have a bearing on what they propose be done. And this ordinary concept of rationality admits of degrees.[14] Some rational beings are clearer or faster or less inept at reasoning than others. Procedural moral acceptability for real people requires (I think) that persons participating with others to reach agreement on policy be rational, but not that they be equally rational. If you are clearer or faster or less inept at reasoning than I am, it does not follow that our joint attempt to agree on a policy, under a procedure we both accept, does not yield a morally acceptable result.

5. Conditions of (Strong) Participation

3. ACCEPTANCE OF TERMS. A third condition, reminiscent, I think, of Hobbes' condition of "lawfulness" for valid covenants,[15] is that the persons attempting to reach a policy agreement must accept whatever operating rules their procedure imposes upon their thinking. The intuitive point is that persons must find acceptable the *terms* of the procedure by which they seek agreement. The acceptance-of-terms I have in mind also allows of degrees. It is intelligible to say that one person may find the terms of a procedure by which a policy agreement is sought to be more acceptable than another does. One may accept the terms of a procedure in the spirit of compromise; perhaps a certain procedure is the only one available that others will accept as a means of making the effort to secure an obviously needed settlement of a policy issue. But as the compromise is more and more severe, the idea that the policy arrived at is morally acceptable is increasingly controversial.

4. DISINTERESTEDNESS. A fourth condition on (strong) participation is that the members of the agreement group be *disinterested*. It is usually acknowledged that there is no special moral quality in the simple pleading of one's own special interests—though this is not to say that one's special interests are morally irrelevant, for they might coincide with, or be representative of, the interests of the members of a group or class that has been unjustly disadvantaged in, say, educational or economic opportunity. The simple pleading of one's own interests ("perceived interests" in the earlier language of this chapter), when accompanied by a tolerance of others' pursuit of their interests, might on occasion produce a bargain or a compromise. And such a bargain or compromise might be found to be acceptable by the parties to it. But we do not think that acceptable bargains are thereby morally acceptable policy agreements.

How disinterestedness is to be characterized is not clear. Rawlsian parties in the original position are disinterested in a technical sense. They are behind a "veil of ignorance"[16] in such a way as to be without knowledge of particular facts about themselves. It is not that they are setting aside such knowledge or suppressing it (that is, not letting it count) as best they can. Rather, they are literally devoid of it. But this is not, I think, a state to which *real* people can aspire. (We can suffer amnesia, of course, but we do not, normally, aspire to it.) I can try my best to set aside my knowledge of my relatively high or low position in the economic system, or I can try my best to look at an issue from the standpoint of someone who occupies an economic position that is different from my own. But I do not know what it is to be without my knowledge (it may be only my opinion) of my own position. Satisfaction of the disinterestedness condition for real people admits of degrees. One can be more or less disinterested than the next person. When Rawls discusses not the features of parties in the original position but rather how we (real people) may attempt to locate among our moral judgments those that are "considered," or those of which we are most "confident," he advises that we do this, in part, by *not* paying "excessive attention to our own interests."[17] This, I think, is much closer to the disinterestedness that can be aspired to by real people than is being behind the "veil of ignorance." It is, I suppose, negative in its thrust: it constrains us to push away or set aside special interests that seem linked to our economic status, social position, family background, and the like—those features of our personal situation that, in Rawls' apt phrase, seem "arbitrary from the moral point of view."[18]

5. JOINT AGREEMENT. But even though a morally acceptable policy agreement is something different from a (mere) bargain or compromise, it is, like the latter, a *joint* agreement. If R is the result of the efforts of real people to reach agreement on a policy under the conditions of (strong) participation, then R is not merely a coincidence among their choices. How to explain what it is for participation to be "joint" is difficult.[19] But perhaps the following is in the right direction: joint participation involves (*a*) that the decision-making by which the effort to reach agreement is made be conducted in such a way that each person has in mind that the achievement of a result requires the agreement of others, and (*b*) that the decision-making be conducted under the intention that the result R of the group's agreement is to stand as an object of commitment or of allegiance for all members of the agreement group. Again, how far

5. Conditions of (Strong) Participation [81]

the efforts of real people to reach agreement on policy meet the condition that their participation be joint (thus interpreted) is pretty clearly a matter of degree.

6. UNIVERSALITY. We may mention a further condition that is closely related, I think, to the condition of disinterestedness discussed above. It is that participants in the attempt to reach agreement must consider only possible *universal* solutions to their problem. The earlier condition of disinterestedness required negatively that participants push away or set aside special interests linked to their personal situations in life. The sixth condition is more positive and may also be associated with Rousseau. When Rousseau requires of citizens seeking the general will that they ask *the right question*,[20] he requires that each citizen consider only policies that affect himself or herself equally with everyone else, at least in the sense (as I interpret Rousseau for present purposes) that he or she be prepared to tolerate the agreed-to policy no matter what position he or she may occupy relative to its application.

7. COMMUNITY SELF-INTERESTEDNESS. And this leads to a further positive condition that also reflects the Rousseauian notion of asking the right question. It is that participants must attempt to select a policy that is *best* for themselves *qua* members of the group or community to which the policy is to apply. (How "best" is to be understood is a problem—one that I recognize but will not discuss here.[21]) This is to say that procedural moral acceptability allows self-interestedness, but only the self-interestedness of persons *qua* members of the group, community, population, or society on whom an agreed-to policy will have an impact.

Both the sixth and seventh conditions (universality and community self-interestedness) seem to be matters of degree in perhaps the way the fourth (disinterestedness) and the second (rationality) are. This is to say that one person can be "better at" perceiving "universal" solutions, or comprehending what it would be for a policy to be "best" for persons *qua* members of a community, than another person. It is also worth remarking that conditions 4, 6, and 7 fit together very closely. It may be that these three together provide an account of the moral notion of *impartiality*. That is, to be impartial—to think, deliberate, or reason impartially in participating with others in decision-making on a matter of policy—is (*a*) to think, deliberate, or reason without excessive attention to one's own special interests, (*b*) to consider only universal solutions, and (*c*) to choose in line with one's own self-interest *qua* member of the community to be affected by the policy. And perhaps this fits well with the Rousseauian notion of "asking the right question."[22]

8. EQUAL AND FULL INFORMATION. Finally, in this part of the list of conditions for (strong) participation, we must surely mention the necessity of *equal and full information*. That is, procedural moral acceptability requires both that participants be informed of such facts as may exist about the issue they face and also that they be equally informed of such facts. It does not allow some participants to be in possession of relevant information while other participants deliberate "blind." Yet, in practice, our ordinary real-life attempts to reach policy understandings are typically plagued by the failure to meet this condition. And insofar as participants are not fully informed, or not equally informed, the acceptability of their result is weakened.

All of the above eight conditions of (strong) participation I think of as requirements upon the *participants* in the attempt to reach agreement on policy. I will now quickly add four further conditions, two of which appear to be conditions on the policy itself, that is, on the *result* of the joint effort the participants make; the other two to be requirements on the procedure or routine itself, that is, the procedure construed narrowly as the *means* the participants adopt in making their attempt to reach agreement.[23]

9. NON-RISKINESS. The first of these further conditions is the Hobbesian requirement that the policy agreed to should be *non-risky* relative to the assurance of follow-through that the parties to it may have.[24] As such, this condition may be obvious or platitudinous. If the policy the participants agree to cannot be thought of by them

5. Conditions of (Strong) Participation [83]

as non-risky in terms of follow-through, then it is unclear what has become of their conception of themselves as participants in a joint effort to solve a problem by agreement. Even if non-riskiness is platitudinous it is important, for it emphasizes that agreement is an important value among participants: it helps to sustain their character as members of an agreement group whose policy understandings and changes are neither arbitrary nor forcibly imposed.

10. POSSIBILITY. The second of these further conditions may be similarly obvious. It is that the agreed-upon policy must prescribe something that is *possible*, rather than something that is contradictory or (more typically the question for practice) something known not to be feasible. This, too, reflects one of Hobbes' conditions of a valid covenant.[25]

The following and final two conditions are requirements on the procedure the participants adopt to structure their decision-making. I do not think procedural moral acceptability requires anything very specific by way of a proper means for persons participating with each other to reach agreement on a policy. For example, it does not select between Robert's Rules of Order and informal debate. But, in general, the procedure must allow for the satisfaction of all the conditions indicated above. I can think of at least two things that should be listed here (there may, of course, be more):

11. COUNT ALL VOTES. The first of these is the Rousseauian requirement that *all votes be counted*,[26] which means, put informally, that all participants must have the opportunity to register their "considered opinion" in the final step of the procedure, that is, the step that counts as bringing the joint effort to reach agreement *to* whatever the agreement is. (A last vote, for example.[27])

12. VOICE. The second condition on procedures is that they allow all participants a *voice*, and of course one that can be "heard" by all other participants in the agreement group in whatever steps the procedures prescribe prior to the final step. The intuitive point is that a procedure must allow all participants to "have their say." A pro-

cedure that makes certain participants mere *listeners*, or some analog of this, does not satisfy this condition of (strong) participation.

6 / Problems

I have now completed a small elaboration of the "loaded" notion of participation—an exploration conducted under the theme that participation may be thought of as an instance of procedural moral acceptability and may in that sense be supposed to yield morally acceptable policies. My account is indebted somewhat to certain views of Rousseau and Hobbes, though its historical sources are not of great importance to me here. The account has its basis chiefly in intuition and reflective hunch concerning what it is for policies to be morally acceptable in virtue of how they are arrived at, and is only loosely guided by the views of Rousseau and Hobbes.

Doubtless there are many problems in the account as it stands in this chapter. The elucidation and defense of propositions purporting to express the constraints of morality is a classical subject for large moral treatises. But if the account provides at least an understandable outline, the following may be among the main problems it generates.

In the first place, is the list of conditions complete? I suspect not. But what further conditions should be added and how the formulations of the listed conditions should be refined or developed are not clear to me. Detailed discussion of actual or imagined cases of policy-determination by participation might contribute refinement and additional content. My present discussion is short on the consideration of cases.

Second, the satisfaction of all the conditions is meant to provide a sufficient condition of morally acceptable policies; that much follows from the idea itself of construing participation as an instance of procedural moral acceptability. But does the satisfaction of the conditions also form a necessary condition of acceptability? Suppose a dictator lays down a certain policy for a community, and then, after revolution or assassination, the members of the community participate with each other under our conditions and eventually arrive at the

6. Problems

same policy. Shall we say that the dictator's policy was not morally acceptable, for it was not the result of (strong) participation? Or shall we say that the dictator's policy was acceptable because it would have been arrived at by (strong) participation? I am not certain what is to be said. But the issue at stake here, again, is whether satisfaction of the conditions is necessary as well as sufficient. It might be possible to argue "general proceduralism" for moral acceptability, whereby such conditions, under a suitable interpretation of "satisfaction," are necessary as well as sufficient.

The third problem concerns the legitimacy of what I have called the "agreement group." What is the morally correct make-up of an agreement group whose business is to determine policy? My discussion generally assumes uncritically that all those on whom a policy has an impact count as members of the agreement group, though there are places in it that suggest that we may think of the agreement group as made up of representatives of those affected. How to straighten this out is not plain. I recognize that we have a number of moral intuitions about the legitimacy of the make-up of groups claiming to have the responsibility for the formulation of policy, and also about the nature of representation. I think—but am not certain—that procedural moral acceptability tolerates representatives in the agreement group, but doubtless not on *any* interpretation of the nature of representation. It does not, for example, tolerate "representatives" who figure they have a mandate to determine policy in line with their own perceived interests or with their own conceptions of the perceived interests of others.

Finally (for present purposes), I am puzzled about whether procedural moral acceptability requires *unanimous* agreement to any policy resulting from (strong) participation. It seems clear that it does not require that individual members of the agreement group personally favor the result, that is, find it in line with their perceived interests. And, offhand, it is not clear to me that procedural moral acceptability does not tolerate plurality voting as a last step of (strong) participation.[28] It is a familiar point that simple majority rule, as a political procedure, does not by itself guarantee morally correct results. But we can imagine the case in which participants fully meet all the conditions listed and in which they employ simple majority rule as the concluding step in their procedure for decision-making; and in that case it is not so easy to suppose that the result might not be morally acceptable. On the other hand, it may be that, conceptually, *full* satisfaction of *all* the conditions somehow *necessarily* yields *unanimous* agreement on the policy result. This is the claim Rawls makes for the connection between his parties in the original position and the conception of justice as fairness.[29] But I am not, at this point, confident of how to argue for such a claim in connection with procedural moral acceptability for real people.

7 / Is (Strong) Participation Practicable?

Consider now the question: is (strong) participation practicable? This is a complicated subject, unfortunately, and I have just a few points of different sorts to make about it.

Recall that satisfaction of the conditions on participants in the account I have given is often a matter of degree or extent. This is to say that the moral acceptability of policy agreements among real people is not an all-or-nothing affair. Some attempts to determine policy by participatory processes may more closely approximate (strong) participation than others do, depending upon the extent to which the participants fulfill the conditions of being disinterested, non-coerced, equally in possession of full information, and so forth.

But this point about moral acceptability admitting of degrees brings to mind a difficulty that is reminiscent of an epistemological problem in Rousseau's doctrine of the general will. Just as Rousseau's distinction between the general will and any particular will, or even between the general will and the full set of particular wills (the "will of all"), may make us doubt whether there is any such thing as a practicable or workable decision-procedure that effectively guarantees that its result will not be contaminated by particular interests—just as we may doubt this, so we may doubt, I think, that the policy agreements to which real people are parties are ever such as to represent full satisfaction of conditions like those we have been considering.

7. Is (Strong) Participation Practicable?

I am not speaking here of real people who refuse, say, even to attempt to view an issue disinterestedly. Rather, I have in mind the difficulty of one's being confident—even just reasonably confident—that one's sincere attempt to be disinterested is not contaminated by elements of "perceived" interest or, perhaps more obviously, that the information one possesses is really "full" and equal to that of others. It may be that conditions of the sort I have enumerated are such that there is always, in principle, the possibility of skepticism regarding their full satisfaction by real people. If so, then there must always be an element of uncertainty about whether any policy agreement reached *via* the attempt to satisfy them is in fact an instance of procedural moral acceptability. It may yet be true, of course, that a morally justified policy—a policy that is in "our real interests"—is what would be agreed to by real people when they achieve full satisfaction of the conditions I have mentioned. The trouble is that we are not in a position in practice to figure out (that is, calculate) which policy would, under those conditions, be agreed to. For while we may understand that being disinterested or being uncoerced is a condition of (strong) participation, I do not think we understand how to determine when such conditions are partially, fully, incompletely, or sufficiently satisfied. In sum: it may be that in respect of the conditions of (strong) participation we are in the epistemological position that Kant thought we were in regarding the concept of duty; it may be, as Kant wrote about duty, that, so far as we can tell, full satisfaction of the conditions of (strong) participation is something "of which perhaps the world has never had an example."[30]

I think this is an important point, but I would add that there is no reason to exaggerate its importance. Its effect is to make of (strong) participation an *ideal* the approximation to which in practice is a matter of judgment but not of knowledge. So far as practice is concerned we may possess the theorist's formulations of what it is to be disinterested (and so on), and these may be meaningful guides for our conduct; but strictly we may nevertheless be in a limbo of uncertainty as to whether the guidelines have been fully met in particular cases. In the end our assessment of whether these conditions have been satisfied in practice becomes a matter of judgment rather than a matter of knowledge. But none of this is to say that the ideal of (strong) participation is something to which we cannot or should not aspire. In this matter, as in many others, we do the best we can.

But this "limbo of uncertainty" of which I speak has its impact on those who take part in decision-making under the conditions of (strong) participation, as well as upon third-party judges. Suppose you join with others in an attempt to reach agreement on a matter of policy. Let the problem be the large and important one of a choice of a system of property for the community. Suppose further that your attempt is successful, in the sense that a policy result is arrived at. Let us say that the property system agreed to is the one whereby property is "socialized" such that decisions concerning "things" are made not privately but democratically. And suppose finally that *all* the conditions I have listed are—as far as we can tell—*fully* satisfied. Then which of the following shall we say?

(1) That you (a member of the agreement group) find the socialized system acceptable, such that your rejecting it would be contradictory.

No, I think not. I have already suggested that unanimity in the sense that all parties to the agreement personally favor the result is not required by procedural moral acceptability. And your rejection of the result is in any case not contradictory, for you may finally decide to put your own interests, or those of your rich uncle, before "our real interests."

Perhaps, then, we should say:

(2) That you ought to accept the result, such that your rejection of it is morally wrong.

A partisan of procedural moral acceptability would probably say that this is correct. It seems right to say that you ought to accept the result, for *ex hypothesi* all the conditions were, as far as we can tell, fully satisfied. But someone might argue that, even so, the "ought" here is *prima facie* or presumptive at best, and may be overridable in some circumstances, such that the following is really all that we can say:

7. Is (Strong) Participation Practicable? [89]

(3) That you have reason to accept the result, but it is conceivable that your rejection of it might be rational and right.

My own inclination is toward the second of these three answers, under the proviso that it is true that as far as we can tell the conditions were fully satisfied. The move from the second to the more modest third answer becomes more tempting the less confident we are that the conditions were fully met. In real life, when many or all of such conditions are only more or less but probably not fully satisfied, the third may be the best practical general answer. And what I said above, namely, that we may always doubt whether such conditions are fully satisfied by real people, reinforces the view that the third answer is the best practical general answer for real life.[31]

But even if this is so, it does not suggest that the idea of (strong) participation cannot stand as a moral ideal for political practice—more precisely, an ideal of decision-making for those interested in the moral acceptability of their community's policies. It remains that to attempt to determine policy by (strong) participation is to attempt to meet certain conditions the satisfaction of which yields morally acceptable policies. However, we are not in a position to exhort (strong) participation as a panacea for determining policy in any and all circumstances. For we have not shown that it is practicable in any circumstances in which a community faces a policy issue. Under what circumstances is it reasonable to attempt to practice (strong) participation? I do not know that a complete before-the-fact answer can be given to a question of this sort, but at least two points that seem relevant to it emerge from my discussion.

The first point states an obvious necessary condition of the rationality of any attempt to practice (strong) participation. It is that the community's circumstances must allow the satisfaction of the various conditions listed above. That is, circumstances must at least *permit* persons to participate with each other rationally, disinterestedly, without coercion, and so forth. Perhaps it goes without saying that the circumstances of real life rarely permit all this.

The second point seems a matter of strategy. It is that the circumstances in which an attempt to practice (strong) participation may seem most attractive are those in which the community's policy problem cannot be solved by simple reference to accepted independent criteria of right,[32] and the members of the community do not overly distrust each other. There can be different kinds of cases here. For example, in one kind of case the policy problem might be "novel" so that an independent criterion of right is simply lacking; thus, a community's traditions and ideology may simply not provide normative resources relevant to a certain issue of policy; alternatively, a rupture or abrasive upset in the community's life may render tradition or ideology suspect or an object of discontent. Other kinds of cases are possible. Thus, plural criteria of right may exist and be accepted, but their relative weights may be unclear; or certain general criteria of right may be available and be accepted but not be policy-specific (they do not pick out *the* policy from a range of more or less tolerable alternatives).[33]

But no doubt many factors of different kinds enter into a judgment of whether or not the attempt to practice (strong) participation on some occasion is rational, attractive, strategic, or whatnot. My discussion may provide certain general considerations in this area, but nothing that eliminates the need for the balancing and weighing of factors present in particular cases.

8 / Two Further Problems

In section 6 above I indicated certain problems generated by a proceduralist approach to the idea of moral acceptability, and in section 7 I discussed briefly the question of the practicality — the "workability," so to speak — of the ideal of (strong) participation. But in addition to the problems discussed in those places, my account of procedural conditions for moral acceptability may seem to lack focus somehow. In real life "agreement groups" are not always very alike, and the account I have given, it might be thought, may risk smothering important differences. Among the many possibilities, let me speak briefly to just two further questions:[34] (*a*) What is the *context* in which the ideal of (strong) participation has its "natural" home?

8. Two Further Problems

That is, is there a "model" situation in which (strong) participation is appropriate? (b) What is the nature of the *deliberation* and *discussion* we are to imagine taking place among participants in the "agreement group" the proceduralist speaks of? And what is the connection of such deliberation and discussion to the moral acceptability that is the object of the proceduralist's attention?

Regarding the first of these questions, it might appear that a direct as well as convenient way of answering it would be by the designation of some type of decision-making circumstances as the model-type in which (strong) participation is appropriate. Thus (among the various types that come immediately to mind) one might suggest a pure-democratic model (for example, the Quaker meeting), or the model of the small committee responding to a "charge" from a larger or parent body (for example, a university educational-policy committee given a problem to solve by a faculty senate, or Dean, or Board of Trustees), or perhaps even the model of an elected representative assembly deliberating about the laws of a community (for example, a congress, parliament, or city council). But my trouble with this line of suggestion is that it responds to the question asked in too specific a way. In the course of designating some familiar type of decision-making context as preferred, it raises the problem of how it is to be argued that the type designated should be construed the as *model* context. And *this* problem seems to me to draw our attention away from what is important in the proceduralist approach I have sketched. In the sense of "context" in use here, there are many contexts, surely, in which it is plausible to think in terms of the satisfaction of the conditions I have listed. The degree to which participants have been, say, disinterested, uncoerced, equally in possession of full information, and so forth, is a legitimate topic of concern regardless whether their type of decision-making situation is that of pure democracy, the small committee, or the representative assembly.

I will add in this connection that a most helpful source for thought about (strong) participation seems to me to be the discussions of the idea of the state of nature in the historical social-contract theories. And this idea, of course, is notoriously a theorist's abstraction that does *not* clearly resemble any of the familiar types of decision-making situations mentioned above. I have in mind here not the perspective given by (for example) Hobbes or Locke when they are concerned to argue that the state of nature is a situation that should be moved out of, but rather the perspective given when they use the notion to characterize persons as in a *position* to make an *acceptable* policy decision. And as I interpret this part of the contractualist theories, it is not the type of context (for example, pure democracy, representative assembly) that figures in acceptability, but rather the satisfaction of precisely conditions of the sort I list above that does the work. This, of course, must remain a suggestion about interpretation in this discussion for I cannot now enter upon an investigation of the historical social-contract theories.[35]

The second question concerns the nature of the deliberation and discussion that the proceduralist account asks us to imagine taking place among participants in agreement groups, and the connection of these with moral acceptability. In practice it may be that discussion among participants in agreement groups is often contributory toward the end of acceptable agreement. In many philosophical traditions, perhaps especially in American pragmatism, there is an emphasis upon discussion as a means of clarifying problems, providing alternative views, and widening perspectives. But we can recognize that discussion *per se* is no guarantor of such benefits. We have all endured discussion, even among persons dedicated to being helpful, that meanders, obscures, sidetracks, and bores.

What I believe the proceduralist account suggests is the general view that discussion in real-life decision-making can be instrumental in the effort to secure satisfaction of conditions such as those I have listed. As is perhaps implicit in some of my remarks above, the effort of discussion can move participants closer to an understanding of the problem they face (what it is), and policy alternatives they have, and the information that is relevant to solutions they can entertain. I would speculate that discussion, if it does not go astray, can also facilitate the satisfaction of the conditions of (strong) participation, in particular those that I earlier associated with impartiality. But it remains, according to the proceduralist, that the satisfaction of the conditions is what renders the result of the effort to reach agreement morally acceptable. It is not that we must *add* "effective discussion," or something like it, to our list of conditions. Rather, the view is that discussion may promote satisfaction of the conditions, and if discussion goes wrong (for example, it sidetracks the participants) what is then jeopardized is the satisfaction of the conditions. How far this is in or out of line with our "ordinary" view of the role of discussion in policy decision-making, I find it difficult to say. If the ordinary view is that discussion is, or can be, a helpmate that aids in the effort to put us in a position to make a wise decision, then the proceduralist conception is quite compatible with the ordinary view. If, on the other hand, the ordinary view places discussion posterior to, or otherwise independent of, the satisfaction of the conditions in question, then the proceduralist view is counter to it.

9 / Observations

In this chapter I have discussed the idea of (strong) participation in an effort to illuminate what it is for policies to be morally acceptable, and I have suggested that to practice it would be complicated and demanding. It may be that in fact circumstances seldom permit the full satisfaction of the several conditions involved in (strong) participation in decision-making, as these are elicited under the idea of procedural moral acceptability. And in any event, so I have also suggested, there is an epistemological difficulty in the way of our ever being confident that these conditions are met in real life.

But even if the practice of (strong) participation is demanding and, when attempted, rarely fully achieved, our exploration has useful results. When we employ the idea of procedural moral acceptability as a means of eliciting the conditions of (strong) participation we provide ourselves with a philosophical account of what it is for policies to be morally acceptable. At the same time we provide ourselves with a catalog of sorts for the moral criticism of society and its policies. What the list provides is, from this latter angle, a set of criteria for assessing the moral health of a community as it is represented in its policies. Each item on the list, under a suitable interpretation, may be viewed as an entry in a catalog of ways in which communities may fail, morally, to be acceptable in their policies. Thus, even if the deliberative picture associated with the idea of procedural moral acceptability is logically coherent but unpromising as a program for political practice, the picture is useful as an imaginative means of eliciting the criteria of the moral adequacy of a society's policies. No pessimistic considerations concerning its practicality relative to actual decision-making impugn its capacity to stand as a radical ideal guiding moral criticism of actual society.

And from this angle it is striking to observe that the moral ideal of (strong) participation teaches something very different from the idea of participation involved in what I earlier called the "settlement" view. The latter idea calls for policy decision-making ensuing in bargains or compromises among persons on the basis of interests they perceive themselves to have. But this idea, while perhaps practicable, provides no *moral* ideal for practice, nor any criteria for the *moral* evaluation of a community's policies. It remains essentially a picture of the politics of accommodation. But "accommodation," in the form of bargains and compromises among the interests that persons perceive themselves to have, does not guarantee or even suggest moral solutions to the issues of policy a community may face.

5

FUTURE GENERATIONS,

PUBLIC POLICY, AND

THE MOTIVATION PROBLEM

1 / The Motivation Problem

In Chapter 3 I considered a definitional problem raised by reflection upon the other-regarding emphases (modest and strong, respectively) of liberal individualism and shared-fate individualism. I argued that the idea of moral agency can accommodate the notion of other-responsibility—and would contain it under certain conditions. In Chapter 4 I explored a problem of another kind raised by the terms of my discussion of shared-fate individualism, namely, what it is for policies to be morally acceptable; and I responded to this question in a way that is (as I see it) reminiscent of Rousseau's doctrine of the general will. At this point I turn to still another question that seems naturally raised by shared-fate individualism. I call it "the motivation problem." It arises as a problem insofar as shared-fate individualism teaches that serious sacrifice on the part of ordinary people may in certain circumstances be required by morality.

I believe it will be helpful to approach this problem by posing it in a different context from the one that opened my discussion. Accordingly, I now move attention from the problems of destitution, gross disparity in levels of life, and meager efforts to help that mar the human condition in today's world, and to certain troubling aspects of the legacy we seem to be leaving to members of distant future generations. To shift attenton in this way is not to abandon or diminish the importance of the problems in the human condition for current people. It is rather to place in sharper relief the terms of the motivation problem—a problem that is, after all, the same in both contexts.

I begin by asking us to make certain suppositions.

Suppose first that we are independent policy makers for a free society.[1] Our job is to formulate policies and put them before the larger community for approval. While we as individuals are members of the society we make policy for—we live in it and know it well—our appointments as independent policy makers give us enough security so that we may be disinterested and impartial in our work. We are free to consider what morality requires in the matters raised by the various policy questions we take up, and we in fact attempt to devise satisfactory policy solutions for our society's problems that are in line with what morality requires—so far, of course, as we can make out what morality requires in particular cases. But, given the context in which we work, we are also mindful of the fact that ours is a free society, and in such a society it is best for the implementation of public policy to flow from general *support* for it on the part of the people and not just from, say, legal coercion. Questions about the *availability* and *reliability* of such support recur in our work on policy questions.[2] Finally, our recommendations to the larger community are respected: they will be considered seriously. In the past our recommendations have often been accepted.

Our task at this point is to prepare morally principled policies concerning our society's legacy to "the world of the future."[3] These policies deal with many things, but (for convenience here) principally with the distribution and conservation of natural resources and the control and impact of our physical plant on the environment. Suppose it becomes clear that the policies we find emerging from our work—the policies we develop under the guidance of our conception of what morality requires of us in this matter of our legacy to the

1. The Motivation Problem

world of the future—will not be *easy* to implement. We see that they call for *serious* sacrifice on the part of ordinary people.

Now, since we are policy makers for a free society, and hence we seek to recommend policies whose implementation can command general support, the fact that the morally principled policies we have developed make heavy demands for sacrifice by ordinary people is something we cannot pass over lightly. We recognize that the people of our society—our fellow citizens—have deep interests in the ways of life they labor (hard and honestly, in most cases) to build and maintain. These ways of life reflect our fellow citizens' different interpretations of the value of self-realization, and in some cases their ways of life reflect aspirations they have for those close to them, such as their children, or even friends and associates. Such interests, values, and aspirations seem legitimate to us (though we may quarrel with their interpretations or contents in some cases). Indeed, as members of society we too have such interests, values, and aspirations. We may pause over the fact that the unbridled pursuit of self-realization can become corrupted into self-absorption.[4] But that is an extreme, and the possibility of its occurrence does not impugn our thought that there are things that the individual member of a free society owes to himself or herself. A person who takes seriously his or her personal development and the well-being of those close to him or her is not thereby morally unserious. We realize that a sacrifice can be perceived as being too great relative to one's legitimate interests in one's own realization, one's aspirations for others, and the ways of life related to these interests and aspirations. We recognize that to many of our fellow citizens these considerations may seem to be *defenses* against the demands for sacrifice involved in the policies we are entertaining.

Nevertheless, after further work, let us suppose that we see that the policies that demand this sacrifice are indeed *required* by morality and that these familiar defenses we have considered are *overridden*.[5] In that case we (independent policy makers for a free society) face this question: what (apart from legal or other forms of coercion) is available and reliable in the way of support for the morally principled policies we now see we must recommend to the larger community? Alternatively put: what in people can we draw upon to *motivate* them to follow the policies that morality requires regarding our legacy for the world of the future? I will refer to this as the *motivation problem* for public policy regarding the future.

2 / Notes

Here are some introductory points about how this motivation problem is to be understood.

In the first place, the problem at issue is not that of justifying morality to a thorough-going egoist, or what Hume called a "sensible knave."[6] The problem concerns the motivation of quite ordinary people, and they are not, in general (so I shall assume), egoists or knaves. Some may be, but not all or most.

Second, while it may be reasonably easy to generalize negatively that ordinary people are neither egoists nor knaves, it may be much more difficult to generalize positively about the motivation of ordinary people. What in fact moves people becomes at some point an empirical question, and this already suggests that there are limits to what philosophical work on this subject can achieve. A philosophical discussion of motivation available to support public policies guided by what morality requires for the world of the future will not, for example, yield statistical generalizations about the likelihood of the population of this or that nation state to be moved by a given motivational factor, such as a "sense of tradition" or the "love of mankind." But there are nevertheless certain aspects of the motivational problem that seem open to philosophical treatment. In what follows I restrict my attention to some of these.

Third, I assume that the availability and reliability of relevant motivation is a condition of the acceptability of proposals for social policy in a free society. Supporting motivational factors are of course only some among the many types of considerations bearing upon the acceptability of policies. (See Chapter 4, especially section 5.) But they may be of special importance in the context of the development of policies concerning our legacy for the future. I assume that policies are unacceptable when it is known that rational persons of integrity cannot follow them, or can follow them only with extraordinary difficulty such that they make demands nearly "exceeding the capacity of human nature."[7] Besides, as a purely practical matter, if we understand that our ways of life—our individual activities and collective projects, together with our means of conducting and implementing them—jeopardize or seriously risk damaging the interests and prospects of future people, and if we understand further that in these circumstances morality requires substantial—even radical—changes in our ways of life, then it would surely *help* in the choice of social policies developed with the requirements of morality in mind to determine what motivation in support of such policies is available and reliable among the people expected to follow them.

Finally, let me say again that the motivation problem I wish to explore is not unique to the policy context in which we deal with what morality requires for the world of the future. It may be that the problem typically arises when policy calls for sacrifice and the sacrifice is thought of as *for the sake of* people who are distant enough from us to be faceless and impersonal. Of course, the condition and plight (for example, the destitution) of *current* people who are distant from us can often be revealed to us through the gathering of particular facts. Individual current people, at any rate, can (in principle) become known to each other.[8] But the same opportunity to know future people in similar detail is not available to us. This, I think, affects our motivation to do (if not our understanding of) what morality requires for the world of the future. But it does not restrict the motivation problem to the context in which we are concerned with acceptable policy for the future.

3 / "Concern for Generations to Come"

Some theorists claim that people as we know them are not, and even cannot be expected to be, motivated by "a concern for generations to come" to act upon what morality requires for the world of the future. Robert L. Heilbroner, for example, offers the following overview of our situation.

> A crucial problem for the world of the future will be a concern for generations to come. . . . [H]umanity may react to the approach of environmental danger by indulging in a vast fling while it is still possible. . . . On what private, "rational" consideration, after all, should we make sacrifices now to ease the lot of generations whom we will never live to see?
> There is only one possible answer to this question. It lies in our capacity to form a collective bond of identity with those future generations. . . . *Indeed, it is the absence of just such a bond with the future that casts doubt on the ability of nation-states or socio-economic orders to take now the measures needed to mitigate the problems of the future.*[9]

Heilbroner here raises the motivation problem I have in mind. It may be useful to be aware of his own estimate of its seriousness:

> There seems no hope for rapid changes in the human character traits that would have to be modified to bring about a peaceful, organized reorientation of life styles. . . . [T]herefore the outlook is for what we may call "convulsive change"—change forced upon us by external events rather than by conscious choice, by catastrophe rather than by calculation. . . . [N]ature will provide the checks, if foresight and "morality" do not. Thus in all likelihood we must brace ourselves for the consequences of which we have spoken—the risk of "wars of redistribution" or of "preemptive seizure," the rise of social tensions in the industrialized nations over the division of an ever more slow-growing or even diminishing product, and the prospect of a far more coercive exercise of national power as the means by which we will attempt to bring these disruptive processes under control. From that period of harsh adjustment, I can see no realistic escape. Rationalize as we will, stretch the figures as favorably as honesty will permit, we cannot reconcile the re-

4. Stipulations

quirements for a lengthy continuation of the present rate of industrialization of the globe with the capacity of existing resources or the fragile biosphere to permit or to tolerate the effects of that industrialization. Nor is it easy to foresee a willing acquiescence of humankind, individually or through its existing social organizations, in the alterations of lifeways that foresight would dictate. If then, by the question "Is there hope for man?" we ask whether it is possible to meet the challenges of the future without the payment of a fearful price, the answer must be: No, there is no such hope.[10]

This is (to put it quietly) a troubling view. It rests directly upon a pessimistic claim about the motivation of ordinary people: namely, that they do not, and perhaps (given their social conditioning) cannot, feel responsible for future people deeply enough to move them to "acquiesce" in policies demanding substantial "alterations" in their "lifeways."[11] If my assumption is fair—that the availability and reliability of relevant motivation is a condition of the acceptability of public policies in a free society—then this pessimistic motivational claim presents a matter of great importance to the design and adequacy of any policies for natural resources and our physical plant that we propose seriously for adoption in a heavily industrialized "affluent" society such as our own.

Let me ask what this *concern for generations to come*—which is said to be absent or weak—consists in and amounts to. In what follows I explore a small number of ways in which such a motivational factor may be interpreted.

4 / Stipulations

Let us call people who live fifty generations after us "future people." Let us call ourselves "current people." In order to begin my exploration of the motivation problem, I must make four initial points. They are stipulations, and I will not attempt to argue for them.

The first point is that morality requires something of us regarding our legacy to the world of the future. Morality, as it were, speaks on this subject. *What* morality requires of us regarding future people is a full philosophical problem in its own right, and I do not take up that problem here. I only suggest some maxims that might stand as the "requirements of morality" regarding the world of the future.

We may begin by agreeing with Joel Feinberg's remark that "surely we owe it to future generations to pass on a world that is not a used up garbage heap."[12] Beyond this, let us suppose first that morality requires (among other things) an equal-opportunity maxim, according to which what we owe to future people is a world at least no worse off than the one we received. As Brian Barry puts it, "the overall range of opportunities open to successor generations should not be narrowed." Second, it may require (among other things) what we might call a custody maxim, according to which current people are to regard themselves as "custodians rather than owners of the planet, and ought to pass it on in at least no worse shape than they found it in." This is to say, I take it, that morality may require a change in our attitudes (and relevant practices) toward the things of the earth. We may have to give up the view of the world as a cluster of resources that we can come to possess or own, and to adopt a view of the world as a cluster of resources of which we are temporary custodians or stewards.[13]

I will not attempt to argue either for these maxims or against other candidates that may come to mind. Let us simply regard the maxims I have mentioned as plausible candidates to figure in an account of what morality requires of us in behalf of the world of the future.

The second point is that what morality requires of us is indeed what we (current people) would count as sacrifice. What exactly the sacrifice consists in I must leave indeterminate. Experts appear to make different estimates of what our natural-resources situation is and of what shape our physical plant is in. The fact that current humankind is organized into nation states is not helpful in this matter of information and estimates. Our approaches to the facts get cluttered, so to speak, with politics.

But however far away we are from accurate information about our

4. Stipulations [103]

physical plant and resources, I share with many people a growing uneasiness about our situation. As laypeople relative to the technical matters sometimes involved we have the impression that our resources are drying up or being squandered and that our physical plant is in disrepair or of the wrong kind to serve human needs in growing populations. All this portends sacrifice. The future has the bleak look of a burden about it. The vocabulary of the policies we are asked to consider is that of "pulling back," "seeking alternatives," "using less," "curbing," "lowering," and "restricting." Those who see something objectionable in ways of life supported by affluence and considerable energy consumption may welcome the prospect. But many of us do not.

The third point is a distinction that allows the motivation problem to arise: it is one thing to understand what morality requires, another thing to be moved to do it. If understanding what morality requires operated in us in such a way that, in Kant's words, the actions that we recognize to be "objectively necessary" were also "subjectively necessary," then the motivation problem I have in mind would not arise. But—so I assume here, following Kant—this is not so.[14] There is no *tight* connection between understanding what morality requires and being moved to do what morality requires. It does not follow, of course, that understanding what morality requires has no motivating power. But it does follow from this distinction that an account[15] that shows what morality requires in some category of cases does not *thereby* make clear (at least not directly) the motivation of people to do or act upon what morality requires in that category of cases.

The last point I offer here is a set of notes about the idea of motivation. I should say at once that I bring no antecedently worked-out theory of human motivation to this discussion. Yet I owe the reader some account of what I have in mind by "motivation." Of course, many factors of different kinds "move" people to do the things they do, and the things they thus do may include (on occasion) things that are required by morality. Love, Hate, Fear, Ambition, Respect for Others, Concern for Reputation, Power, Self-respect, Self-interest, Pity—all these would be on the list. And so would factors of the kind Hume enumerated so effectively: "Inward peace of mind, consciousness of integrity, a satisfactory review of our own conduct; these are . . . very requisite to happiness, and will be cherished and cultivated by every honest man, who feels the importance of them."[16] For this discussion let me offer the following skeletal characterization of motivation of the sort I am interested in and hope it will serve present purposes.

Consider the case in which it is true that a person, Jones, is moved by a motivational factor of the sort I have in mind to follow a certain policy. Let the policy be one that imposes sacrifice upon a group of people (to which Jones belongs) for the sake of certain other people. Then, among other things, the following several features obtain.

In the first place, when Jones is thus moved by a factor of the sort I have in mind, he makes the policy of sacrifice a *presumption for conduct*. That is, Jones, moved by this factor, resolves to act in line with the policy unless there is overriding reason not to. This is what it is for Jones to be motivated by this factor; the being-motivated shows up in Jones' making the policy of sacrifice a presumption for conduct.

In the second place, when Jones is moved by a factor of the sort I have in mind, that factor is viewed by Jones as *"internal" rather than "external."* Jones may indeed experience the motivational factor as a pressure or demand of sorts, but (in the cases I am interested in) it does not seem to Jones to "come from without," as, for example, in the manner of a threat of coercion.

Third, when Jones is moved by a motivational factor of the relevant sort, then Jones fits our general conception of what the standing *"positive" emotional nature* of a *decent* or *good person* is—even as we recognize that that nature may not infallibly move us to do what morality requires in particular cases.[17] Alternatively expressed, being "movable" by a factor of the sort I am interested in is part of the emotional nature we would cultivate in people were we able to "design" them for membership in a community in which benevolence prevailed, that is, a society in which persons naturally take the good of others into account.[18] Even though, for example, pity, like compassion, can be "mistaken" and "lead us astray," as Sidgwick ob-

4. Stipulations

served,[19] we still believe that the decent or good person can be moved by pity and compassion, and we desire to make the capacity to be moved by them a standing part of the emotional nature of, say, our children as well as ourselves.

In the fourth place, when Jones is moved by a motivational factor of the sort I have in mind, then that factor seems to Jones *not* to be the factor of "*self-interest*" as it is ordinarily and narrowly construed. That is, what moves Jones is not conscious attraction to something he understands to be his "personal benefit" in the form of social or material advantage—though, indeed, the end result of Jones' action in line with the policy of sacrifice may be (or turn out to be) something to his personal advantage.

Finally, when Jones is moved by a factor of the sort I am interested in, it has certain *feeling-tones* associated with it. There is an experiential side to the motivational factors I have in mind—enough so, at any rate, to make it seem plausible to suppose that one might be able to distinguish phenomenologically among such factors. There is a difference between, say, hate and pity, or pity and sympathy, that is beyond those differences in source, object, and rationality that may distinguish them; there are characteristic experiences or feelings associated with such motivational factors as they occur in human lives, and any account that leaves these out would appear to be incomplete.

I will not attempt to develop this general characterization further. Examples of familiar motivational factors that meet the characterization, I think, are a person's love for another person, or pity for that person, or respect for that person—and, of course, love, pity, and respect are factors that may motivate one to do what morality requires in certain circumstances. The "sentiment of natural sympathy" that receives attention in the tradition of utilitarianism may also fall under this characterization. Something that does *not* fit the characterization is external coercion, even when it is filtered through the mind *via*, say, the emotions of fear, anger, or distrust. Thus, "fear of punishment" is not an example of the type of motivation I have in mind—though, obviously, fear of punishment may be motivating, albeit not in the "positive" way I am interested in. When one is moved to do what morality requires by fear of punishment, one does not, I think, see either the punishment-in-prospect or the fear of it as "internal" to one. It seems, rather, pushed, intruded, or imposed upon one from outside. Nor does one see such a factor as a part of the positive emotional nature of a decent or good human being. Rather, in the case of fear one seems (to one degree or other) *driven* to make a certain policy one's presumption of conduct, and one's recognition of this may lead one to resist following through.

5 / Notes About Future People

Future people (those who live many generations after us) are faceless and impersonal to current people. The details that make people at least interesting to each other personally are missing. We do not know what their lifestyles are, what they stand for, whether they think much of us, or whether they are concerned about people who live many generations after them. Face-to-face encounters are out of the question.

We are not totally ignorant of what future people are like, of course. If (*ex hypothesi*) our descendants are still *people*, then we have now a body of "salient facts" about them.[20] They will almost certainly have wants and needs and hopes and fears; they will almost certainly love and hate, and perhaps even experience resentment and feel guilt. We may say, in overview fashion, that future people will have interests. And current people can do things now, so it seems, that affect those interests. We can do things now that hurt future people. We can damage the environment, for example, or use up finite resources (without researching and providing for alternatives), and thereby affect how many future people there are or make the circumstances in which future people live very difficult to bear.

These facts—that future people will be *people*, and will have *interests* that current people can affect—may make it *intelligible* to say that people of both sorts (future and current) have rights and, in an abstract sense, belong to one moral community. And if this can be said, perhaps it in turn helps show that indeed morality requires something of current people relative to future people.[21] But, of course,

6. Motivation and Particularity [107]

even if such claims are intelligible, it does not follow that we should adopt them or base social policies upon them.[22] Indeed, the whole idea that we and future people are members of a common moral community may seem strange. There is no mutual cooperation in such a community, and there are no exchanges "in kind"; as a consequence this community is not characterized by mutual benefit or joint participation in common activities in *any* familiar ways.[23] The one "exchange" I can think of is that, for the sacrifices we make in order to deliver an inhabitable globe to future people, they are grateful. They at least do not think little of us. But this "exchange" is hardly "in kind," and, in fact, it never reaches us.

In what follows I explore what these few notes about future people suggest concerning the motivation of current people to make the sacrifices required by morality in behalf of future people.

6 / Motivation and Particularity

It would be unrealistic for policy makers to rely on *love* or *concern* to motivate current people to do what morality requires for the world of the future.[24] Future people cannot arouse love or concern in current people—at least not in the way other (typically nearby) current people can. Whatever may be the full explanation of this fact, it involves, I think, the non-particularity—the facelessness and impersonality—of future people. As I remarked above, the details that make people at least interesting to each other are missing in the case of future people, and *the capacity to interest* is a precondition of, or perhaps a constituent part of, the capacity to arouse in us such "motivational factors" as love or concern. Somehow being moved by love or concern for a person, or group of people, involves having more of him, her, or them before one than one has in the case of future people.

But perhaps this might be replied to: we noted earlier that future people will have interests—call them "salient-fact interests"—that we can know about now and that we can affect now. Isn't that particularity enough to make it possible that love, concern, or some other strong feeling might be aroused? Perhaps we can love or have concern for future people insofar as they may be construed as interests we can affect now.[25]

But I do not think this response is helpful. I do not think one can love or have concern for interests *per se*, and so it does not help make motivation in the form of love or concern flourish or even exist to quasi-reduce future people to their interests. What is at stake here *is* motivation and, in particular, that motivation to do what morality requires that meets the terms of my earlier general characterization. The fact that future people have interests that we can affect now may indeed be relevant to the philosophical problem of determining whether or not we have responsibilities to future people, and beyond that to the philosophical problem of determining what, morally, is adequate provision for future people. But, again, what thus helps us see or understand what morality requires is not thereby what motivates us to do what morality requires. And in any case the non-particularity problem remains. The interests of future people, construed as derived from their wants, needs, hopes, and fears, are radically indeterminate. Insofar as this is so (and risking the air of paradox), the interests of future people do not have the capacity to interest us. Therefore, so I suggest, a condition of their having the capacity to arouse love or concern or other strong feelings in us is not satisfied.

I said above that it would be unrealistic for policy makers to rely on love or concern to motivate current people to do what morality requires for the world of the future. Perhaps the term "unrealistic" is after all too weak. The discussion I have offered suggests that policy makers *cannot* rely on motivation in the form of love or concern, because motivation in this form is not available in the context of policy for the future. More exactly, what is not available is love or concern that has as a condition of its possibility (*a*) the capacity of its object to interest us, (*b*) which capacity involves what I have called "particularity." (I have not said how this idea of "particularity" is to be analyzed, other than that it has to do with detail and determinateness.) If a person were to profess or claim to be moved by love or concern for future people, or even for future people *qua* interests,

I would have to say that something other than the love or concern I have indicated is being referred to, or perhaps that what I earlier called "feeling-tones," or characteristic feelings associated with the love or concern I have indicated, were aroused by something else, that is, something other than future people or future people *qua* interests, or the idea of either of these. (Perhaps they were aroused by a drug.)

In general, insofar as motivation to do what morality requires is tied down to particularity about persons, such motivation is not available to support widespread acquiescence in public policies meant to implement what morality requires for the world of the future.

7 / Community Bonding and Reciprocation

A second form of motivation that is sometimes available to prompt us to do what morality requires may be labeled (for purposes of this discussion) as *community bonding*. Even if this term is not ordinary, what I have in mind is familiar enough. We are commonly and often moved to act in ways that may be in line with principles (and hence, on occasion, with moral principles) by a regard for other persons that derives from their membership with us in a common community, association, enterprise, or project of some sort.[26] At a minimum motivation of this sort involves a *sense of belonging to some joint enterprise with others*. The motivational factor constituted by this sense of belonging may carry with it the feeling-tones of solidarity, comradeship, loyalty, mutual confidence and trust, or at least a sense of being-on-the-same-side. And the sense of belonging with others to a joint enterprise has a certain directionality to it. It is not indiscriminate in its objects. It selects *those* "others" who belong with one to that common enterprise. It picks out others who stand *with* one as co-members of some identifiable body, association, or community. In the event that one fails the association, or violates the community, or lets down the side, one may incur feelings of guilt, or be dismayed, or experience regret.[27]

My thought is that just as there is a condition of the occurrence of motivation in the form of love or concern, namely, what I called "particularity," so there is a condition (probably many conditions) of the occurrence of motivation in the form of community bonding. I will title this condition *reciprocation*. By reciprocation I have in mind the exchange of ideas and conceptions of purposes that must be available to persons before they can be considered to stand as joint participants in a common project. We should distinguish this condition of reciprocation from that of prospective mutual benefit. Joint participation in common enterprises often has mutual benefit as its aim. But reciprocation is at a deeper level than the cooperation appropriate to mutual-benefit associations. There are communities, associations, enterprises, and projects that we participate in or endure (perhaps reluctantly), but that we do not view as directed toward mutual benefit. But still, participation in or endurance of these different associations and enterprises may arouse motivation in the form of community bonding,[28] yet these various modes of joint participation cannot occur in the absence of the reciprocation I have in mind. People may find themselves in routines and regimens in which their behavior is controlled for them (for example, as unwitting victims of medical experimentation), and these routines and regimens may occur in the absence of reciprocation (and give rise to still different kinds of "motivational factors," such as resentment). But such modes of control or manipulation of behavior are not communities, enterprises, associations, or projects. The latter rest on a ground of exchange of ideas and interpretations of ends among participants in them—an exchange that is sometimes one-sided, no doubt, but nevertheless (to whatever minimal degree) present.

If we ask at this point whether motivation in the form of community bonding is available and reliable to support policies designed to implement what morality requires of us in behalf of the world of the future, I think the answer must be no. We (current people) and they (future people) are not positioned in such a way as to be able to reciprocate with each other concerning the constituent ideas and controlling aims of any associations or enterprises that we jointly participate in or endure.[29] In the absence of the possibility of such reciprocation, I do not see how motivation in the form of community bonding can arise. The feeling-tones of solidarity or loyalty, or even the sense of being-on-the-same-side, are foreign to our relationship (whatever it is) to future people. Accordingly, the experiences of guilt, dismay, or regret, as they are known to us from our acquaintance with what it is to damage or destroy the associations we have with persons with whom we exchange ideas and interpretations of ends—these experiences cannot arise from our relationship (whatever it is) to future people. If a person should claim to feel guilt as a result of faults in his or her conduct toward future people, I would have to say that the experience of guilt referred to is of a different kind from that which may be explained by reference to motivation in the form of community bonding.

In general, insofar as motivation to do what morality requires is tied down to reciprocation with other persons concerning the ideas and aims of shared enterprises, as is so in the case of community bonding, then it is not available to support policies implementing what morality requires for the world of the future.

8 / Extended Shared-Fate Motivation

Finally, let me take up—or, more exactly, speculate about—a form of motivation that seems very different from love or concern and community bonding. In those cases the motivation was construed as grounded either in the particularity of other persons or in reciprocation with them concerning the ideas and aims of joint enterprises. The motivation I wish to touch on now is more abstract in character. I will call it *extended* or *unbounded shared-fate motivation*. I have in mind the *sense of common humanity* we have (if we have it, and to whatever extent we have it) that involves at some level the notion that in a very general way human beings as such "belong together," or are "in life together," *irrespective* of differences in time and location among them.

Let me offer a series of thoughts, in no special order, about motivation of this kind.

First we need some account or picture of what extended shared-fate motivation consists in, or at least what it is like. The following passage from Rawls' *A Theory of Justice*[30] is suggestive, I think, regarding the possibility of the form of motivation I have in mind.

> Individuals in their role as citizens with a full understanding of the content of the principles of justice may be moved to act upon them largely because of their bonds to particular persons and an attachment to their own society. Once a morality of principles is accepted, however, moral attitudes are no longer connected solely with the well-being and approval of particular individuals and groups, but are shaped by a conception of right chosen irrespective of these contingencies. Our moral sentiments display an independence from the accidental circumstances of the world.

What attracts my attention in this passage is just its suggestion that motivation may be grounded in an *idea* in a way that is independent of what I have called particularity about persons or reciprocation between persons. Given my general approach in this chapter, let us ask what such an idea would have to be *of*, in order to serve as a ground for motivation supporting public policies operating in behalf of the world of the future.

So far as I can see, the most straightforward candidate for an idea that could serve this function—analogously to the role of particularity in the case of love or concern, and the role of reciprocation in the case of community bonding—is the idea of a community of persons who may be at any temporal or social location and who nevertheless construe themselves as "being in life together" or "sharing fate" according to the contents of an appropriate conception of what morality requires of the members of such a community.[31] And we must note at once that the idea of community thus brought before the mind (an idea very like, I believe, the Kantian conception of persons as members of "the realm of ends") is unusual in important ways. (*a*) It is an idea of a community not all or even very many of the members of which can reciprocate with each other, that is, engage in an exchange with each other over the ideas and purposes of their community. No real *joint* decision-making, no matter to what extent

8. Extended Shared-Fate Motivation

representation is employed, can take place in it.[32] (*b*) It is an idea of a community not all or even very many of the members of which have—in principle—*particularity* for each other. Most of its members are, and must remain, faceless and impersonal to each other. (*c*) It is an idea of a community the membership of which is *unbounded* in *all* the ordinary ways. Thus it has no national or even geographical limits, and its membership extends into the future indefinitely if not infinitely.

Once the idea that might ground extended shared-fate motivation is sketched in this way, we may ask: can an idea of this sort in fact be motivating among persons as we know them? That is, can we not only conceive of a community of this sort, and of ourselves as members of it, but also imagine ourselves developing *a sense of belonging to it*, such that *that sense* might be available and reliable in support of policies meant to implement what morality requires for the world of the future? It is one thing, we may suppose, for us to be able to form the conception of humankind as an unbounded (yet) shared-fate community, another thing for such a conception to arouse in us, say, affection for the community.

I will close with just three notes about the prospect of the idea of an unbounded community of mostly non-reciprocating persons who are non-particular for each other being motivating among people as we know them.

First, it is worth mentioning that reference to the idea in question is an occasional part of ordinary moral discourse—though this occasional use of the idea may not indicate serious appeal to the content I have suggested the idea might have. I have in mind, in the context of discussions of policy for the future, appeals to common humanity in the form of appeals to the fact that *persons*, after all, may be hurt by what we do now. As Feinberg remarks, "the vagueness of the human future does not weaken its claim on us in light of the nearly certain knowledge that it will, after all, be human."[33]

The second note is that, if we follow Rawls' lead, we may then think of the development of certain forms of motivation as describable by very general psychological laws linking their emergence to institutional structures and practices.[34] Thus: *given* a society or social setting of a certain sort, together with persons' natural sentiments, we may *expect* certain forms of motivation to be aroused in the human beings who live in that society or social setting. In this fashion, what Rawls calls "the sense of justice" is a form of motivation that is the *product* of life in what he thinks of as a "well-ordered society," that is, a society that is, and that is known to be, governed by the conception of justice as fairness. To think in this way about the development of motivation leads us in the present case to ask whether *our* society is such that we may reasonably expect the people who have their lives in it to develop extended shared-fate motivation.[35]

Finally, when we raise this latter question, my own estimate is that our society is not one that lends itself to the cultivation of extended shared-fate motivation. To show why this is so would be a large project, and I will not attempt it here. It would involve discussion of the structures, institutions, practices, and moral ideology characteristic of our society,[36] argument about how far this social entity as a whole meets the criteria of "well-orderedness," and then treatment of the still further questions of what sorts of social structures would lend themselves to the development in persons of a sense of belonging to an unbounded community of human beings that could be efficacious enough to be relevant to the motivational problem of making available reliable support for public policies implementing what morality requires for the world of the future. Without meaning to beg important questions, I suspect that this large project would find that certain elements in the make-up of our society—for example, the lack of good-samaritan rules in our legal system, the self-interested psychology of competitive appropriation fostered by our economic life, the emphasis on self-realization in our educational system, and the prizing of immediate sensibility so powerfully supported by everyday commerce and culture—all these elements operate *against* the development in us of what I have called extended shared-fate motivation.

In general, I think extended shared-fate motivation is intelligible —we can imagine its presence in persons—and I think it "fits" our thoughts concerning what motivation would have to be like to be serviceable in the context of policies implementing what morality requires for the world of the future. But there is nevertheless serious empirical doubt, I think, about its availability and reliability as support for public policies in a society such as ours. Given the influence on us of certain dominating institutional elements in the make-up of society, plus our current received moral ideology, it may be that motivation of the unbounded shared-fate sort is somehow beyond us, or too difficult for very many of us to develop, at this time. The discussion above of love or concern (grounded in particularity about persons) and of community bonding (grounded in reciprocation) brings to our attention features of our nature that are familiar to us. But extended shared-fate motivation is, while not unknown to us, nevertheless not similarly familiar to us.

9 / Summary

The discussion in this chapter is offered as an exploration of what I called the "motivation problem" in the context of the task of formulating morally principled social policies in behalf of the world of the future. I touched on motivation of three different kinds. (*a*) I suggested that motivation in the familiar form of *love* or *concern*, grounded in what I called "particularity" about persons, is not available to support policies for the world of the future. (*b*) I also suggested that motivation in the familiar form of *community bonding*, grounded in what I call "reciprocation" between persons, is similarly unavailable. (*c*) Finally, I offered a brief account of *extended shared-fate motivation* and speculated that while this may be intelligible to us as a possible form of motivation among human beings, it may not be widely available or reliable.

At the beginning I called attention to Robert L. Heilbroner's view that "a crucial problem for the world of the future will be a concern for generations to come." And I indicated that Heilbroner is very pessimistic about the availability of this concern as motivation that could support policies in behalf of the world of the future among current people. My discussion may deepen somewhat how this notion of "concern for generations to come" is to be understood, and, so far as it goes, the discussion supports Heilbroner's pessimism. If we imagine ourselves in the place of independent policy makers for a free society (as sketched at the beginning of the chapter), we may well be dismayed by the apparent fact that certain familiar sorts of motivation are not available to support policies demanding serious sacrifice for the sake of future generations, and we may well be discouraged by the further apparent fact that the cultivation of a form of motivation directly supportive of such policies might require something close to an overhaul of main elements in the make-up of our society that influence the moral psychology of citizens.[37] Whether these difficulties would or should be enough to make us recommend policies other than those required by morality (for example, less demanding policies) or, indeed, no policies for the world of future at all, I am uncertain. It might occur to us that we should stay with our recommendation of the policies required by morality, even at the cost of reliance upon coercion of some sorts for implementation. But in that case it appears that we face the problem of determining what kinds and levels of coercion would be tolerable—a problem whose difficulty is emphasized by the fact that ours is a free society.

6

PUBLIC POLICY AND

THE INTERPRETATION

OF PERSONS

1 / When Public Policy Is Weak

Destitution in today's world, gross disparity in the levels of life available to people, risk to the lives of members of future generations—all these are at once grave issues for society and challenges to individuals. In what follows I continue my discussions of public policy and individual responsibility by bringing these subjects together in a certain way: I consider certain difficulties that arise when there are differences in the levels of sacrifice each demands. We may sometimes think of public policy, in a society that aspires to respect for individual liberty, as making demands on its individual members that are something of a burden, if not always a great struggle, for many of them to meet. In some instances we may have reason to regard certain of the policies of an (imperfect) society aspiring to respect for liberty as morally objectionable, so that individual responsibility requires protest or even principled disobedience. But in what follows I have in mind cases of another sort, namely, those in which public policy is "weak" or "shallow" relative to what (arguably) morality requires. I wish to explore how we are to think of the course of individual responsibility in the latter circumstances.

6. Public Policy and the Interpretation of Persons

Let me begin with certain suppositions to provide context for the discussion.

Suppose first that *J* is a person who is capable of moral duties "pitched at what the ordinary person can bear."[1] *J* is neither a hero nor a slacker nor what Hume called a "sensible knave."[2] *J* is, let us imagine, reasonably competent and reasonably conscientious, in the manner of the "competent individual" in 2.3 above. But *J* is also busy and has many responsibilities. She has a family to support, perhaps a career to pursue, certain causes to further, some talents to develop, and networks of personal and professional relationships (some of them demanding) to maintain or cultivate.

Suppose, second, that *J* lives in *S*, which is a society that aspires to justice. In *S*, of course, persons have interests that sometimes conflict (otherwise *S* would not need to "aspire to justice"). (See 3.5.) But individuals and groups persist in efforts to further their interests, and so they make agreements, transactions, bargains, and compromises with each other, many of which involve varying degrees of give-and-take and some of which involve occasional adjustments in individual conceptions of interests. It is important to add that these pursuits of interests take place within a "framework" meant to deal with problems within *S* of artificial limits on opportunities and losses of well-being and meant also to facilitate certain special projects of wide interest to the people of *S*.[3] There may be quarrels about the means for remedying the difficulties about limits on opportunities and about the levels of provision against losses of well-being; and there may be occasional changes in or additions to these means and fluctuations from time to time in the levels of protection against losses of well-being. But let us imagine that *S* is, relative to other societies, rather affluent, and *J*'s lot in *S* includes a share of the good things made possible by *S*'s affluence. *J* may not be wealthy by the standards of a few members of *S*, and *J*'s life may not be free of problems, but *J*'s problems are not (*ex hypothesi*) those of extreme poverty or unjustified restrictions on opportunity.

Suppose, third, that *S* also has a set of policies—and an appropriate staff and "physical plant" for their implementation—for "ex-

1. When Public Policy Is Weak   [119]

ternal" problems, that is, problems concerning S's security, well-being, and standing in a world of societies. There may be, again, debates in S's public discussion about the extent to which this or that threat to S is real or imagined, or serious or unserious, and there may be fluctuations from time to time in levels of support for S's policies, staff, and powers of implementation in this area. We may imagine that J participates in these debates when her concern is aroused, and even that J's personal convictions do not preclude joining in, say, the defense of S when the need is plain.

At this point let us suppose that certain unusual problems begin to make an appearance in the public discussion in S and that J becomes aware of them.[4] For example: (*a*) attention is called to the fact that in the larger world of societies (the "world community," as some refer to it) there exist *major* problems of destitution, that is, problems of severe deprivation relative to the basic needs of millions of people ("fellow human beings," as some call them); (*b*) attention is also called to current estimates (plausible estimates, so far as J can tell) according to which the generations of the future (that is, the lives of future human beings) are *seriously* endangered by current practices of consumption and loss and abuse of natural resources.[5]

Now, we need not suppose that S and its citizens are unresponsive to these unusual problems. We may imagine that concern about them begins to surface and then deepens. A number of factual studies of these problems appear in the public discussion, along with expression of opinions ranging from "alarmist" through "moderate" to "debunking." Insofar as the view that these problems *are* serious comes to prevail, policy alternatives begin to be explored. These policy alternatives vary in the demands they make on the individual members of S. Some seem "light" in their demands; but others seem "heavy," and still others seem "extreme"—even though in both of these latter cases the policies proposed, intellectually and morally, seem neither incoherent nor even implausible relative to the seriousness of the problems they address.

For our purposes, let the following be an example of the theme of a "heavy" policy proposal:

(FG) It is proposed that the future-generations problem requires equal-opportunity and stewardship programs regulating our legacy for the world of the future that entail major "alterations of lifeways" of current people in affluent societies and, indeed, deep changes in their attitudes toward the things of the earth.[6]

For our purposes again, let the following be an example of the theme of an "extreme" policy proposal:

(D) It is proposed that the destitution problem cannot be effectively dealt with through private charitable organizations or national programs of aid, but requires the abolition of the world's "system" of independent societies in favor of a genuine "world community" with a general mode of governance, scheme of taxation, welfare institutions, and even affirmative-action programs applying to all the people of the earth.

As the last step in our story, let us make two further assumptions. First, let us "inflate" (FG) and (D) into moral requirements. That is, let us suppose—or stipulate, since I cannot argue for these points here—that (FG) and (D) *are* "what morality requires" in their respective problem areas.[7] Second, let us suppose that in the end S does *not* adopt (FG) and (D) as (among) its public policies in those problem areas. It instead "settles" (see 4.3 above) for something less. Perhaps it settles, in the case of the destitution problem, for increasing its foreign-aid budget a little, or relaxing political-interest constraints on its existing budget somewhat, and calling in striking and colorful ways for greater charitable efforts by individuals in a "War Against World Poverty." In the case of the future-generations problem, perhaps it settles for providing some incentives for conservation and putting modest funds into researching alternative sources of energy. But we need not specify the details of the policies that are finally accepted. The essential points are that S does have public policies in the problem areas of concern, but that they are something less than what morality requires.

2. Two Limits on Responsibility

Here are some questions that are raised by the story of *J* in *S*, together with the stipulation that (FG) and (D) are required by morality, plus the supposition that *S* settles for public policies that are something less than (FG) and (D), that is, for something less than what morality requires.

(*a*) Why is (FG) considered a "heavy" policy and (D) an "extreme" policy in the public discussion in *S*?
(*b*) Why does *S* adopt public policies that are something less than what morality requires?
(*c*) Are *S*'s public policies *wrong*?
(*d*) What, in the circumstances of *J* in *S*, is the course of individual responsibility? That is, what is *J* supposed to do, morally, when what morality requires is "heavy" or "extreme" relative to *S*'s public policies?

In what follows I attempt to speak to these questions, though not in anything like the tidy order of their presentation above. Clearly, any philosophical treatment of such questions requires some background discussion of what it is for candidate public policies to be *excessive* or *too demanding* for the people of a given society, or in some other way *beyond* them, and of the bearing of the demanding character of such candidate policies on our understanding of "what morality requires" of them in respect of the difficulties addressed by the candidate policies.

2 / Two Limits on Responsibility

To begin, let us return to the supposition that *J* is capable of moral duties "pitched at what the ordinary person can bear." There is much of importance to the development and formulation of public policy lurking in this notion that duties are geared to what the ordinary person can bear. Let us ask this question: what affects "what the ordinary person can bear"?

Now, there are of course many considerations that affect "what the ordinary person can bear" in the way of duties. The number of

6. Public Policy and the Interpretation of Persons

these considerations may even seem to multiply when one models "the ordinary person" on oneself, or one's son or daughter, or one's neighbor down the street. But the purposes of public policy require that one not particularize the idea of "the ordinary person" in any such familiar way, but operate (in most contexts) with a smoothed-out conception that is capable of significant generality. Differences in individuals and their circumstances can be allowed for, of course. Certain facts may affect the physical and mental competence of some people so as to provide justified *individual exemptions* from duties that, in general, "the ordinary person" *can* bear. There are individual-specific considerations of health and intelligence (including handicaps), blocked information, economic conditions, and even special dependency relationships that policies developed with "the ordinary person" in mind can recognize and allow for.

But even as we operate with as general a conception of "the ordinary person" as we can, there are some considerations that may in fact influence what some people believe they can bear in the way of duties that are *spurious*, that is, they ought not to be taken into account as possible grounds either for cancellations of duty or for individual claims of exemption. I have in mind, for example, those bits of ideology that tend to deflate the duties of aid, for example, the alleged profundities that "poverty is natural" or that "life is unfair," or those scope restrictions that make those duties weaken or run out when recipients are located at a distance, or in the "further future," or outside the familiar circumstances in which we think it natural to feel the pressure of responsibility for others.[8]

Now, suppose *J* cannot claim individual exemption from the duties of aid, and suppose *J* is free of the obfuscating duty-deflating and duty-limiting views I have just mentioned. Suppose, following the characterizations given earlier (1.4.2 and 2.3), that *J* is an "ordinary person" who meets both the description "reasonably well-off individual in an affluent society" and the description "competent individual." What can that "ordinary person" bear in the way of duties? What are some legitimate, that is, non-spurious, limits on the demands that the liberty-possessing reasonably well-off competent individual in an affluent society can be expected to endure? Given

2. Two Limits on Responsibility [123]

our interest in the "heavy" public-policy proposal (FG) and the "extreme" public-policy proposal (D), here are some notes on two very different kinds of limits on the duty to aid and how they might affect society's "settling" for less than demanding public policies.[9]

The first sort of limit might be called the limit of practical impossibility. In general outline, a practical-impossibility case is one in which the demand that we do a certain thing is coherent; the difficulty in the case is not one of unintelligibility or even one of overcoming logically contingent but nevertheless *fixed* facts. Rather, the task we are asked to perform or carry through is beyond what persons as we know them could carry through, where the emphasis is more on the phrase "persons as we know them" than it is on the word "could." Again, the problem is not that the prospect of change is in some deep metaphysical way impossible; it is rather that the prospect of change is in some deep practical way not feasible; the effort required of us is *beyond* our capacities rather than "excessive" relative to them. At some point, so it gets claimed in this sort of case, facts that are not metaphysically grounded or otherwise fixed may nonetheless come to be, as a matter of practical fact, insurmountable by human effort, that is, the effort of "the ordinary person." Thus, in American society, to repeat an earlier example (1.7), the mode of transportation involving the automobile, roads, supporting technology, and huge numbers of "dependent" individual lives appears to be so entrenched that the prospect of eliminating it (as distinct from controlling or improving it) seems completely "out of the question." So the public-policy proposal "Abolish the automobile!" (that is, the "system" of transportation involving the automobile) may simply be beyond our capacities, not (merely, as it were) excessive relative to them. We can think the abolition of the automobile, but we *cannot* carry it through. On this account, the magnitude and depth of a society's commitment to a given "way of doing things" may make that way of doing things irrevocable.

The second sort of limit I have in mind is more a matter of degree. The word "excessive" now becomes appropriate. In this case what is demanded of us is what (perhaps) we already do—but not enough. We must do *much* more. What we are asked to do is not *beyond* our capacities, but, rather, a great *strain* on them. Perhaps the general call for conservation is, or could become, an example. Here the sacrifice involves cutting back in levels of life, and this could be carried to a point at which the diminishment of life becomes too extreme. People are no doubt different in respect of what elements in their "way of life" they can sacrifice, but there comes a point for most of us at which the capacity to sacrifice runs out and the continuing demands become "too much."

Now, my thought is that candidate public policy (D) may seem "extreme" in the sense that it demands of us something that is, or is nearly, a practical impossibility, and that this is a consideration that could lead society S to settle for public policies in this problem area that are less demanding than (D) is. What policy (D) calls for, namely, the abolition of nation states (that is, the nation-state apparatus) in favor of a world state, is coherent enough. But it hardly makes practical sense at all to make the abolition of nation states the policy aim of a nation state and its citizens. It is not at all clear what S and its people would or could do to obey or implement policy (D). The other candidate public policy seems to me (potentially) "heavy" rather than "extreme." If we are to approach our legacy for the future in equal-opportunity terms, this may exact increasing sacrifice from us to a degree that at some point becomes excessive relative to our capacities. And this again is a consideration that could lead the people of S to settle for something less demanding, or possibly to abandon the idea of having public policies (of sacrifice) in this problem area altogether.

So far I have said that in some cases a candidate public policy might involve a practical impossibility, and thus be beyond our capacities, and that in other cases a candidate public policy might make demands on us that are excessive relative to our capacities. Perhaps (D) is an example of the former, and perhaps (FG) is an example of the latter. If (D) and (FG) are such examples, does it follow that (D) and (FG) are not, as I stipulated earlier, "what morality requires" in their respective problem areas after all?

I want to answer this question in the negative. That is, I want to

2. Two Limits on Responsibility

say that (D) and (FG) could still be required by morality even if the former is beyond our capacities and the latter is excessive relative to our capacities. The reason this is possible (I suggest) is that there is a distinction between what it is for someone to be "an ordinary person" in (for example) the sense of "a reasonably well-off individual in an affluent society" and what it is for someone to be "a member of the moral community." Now, a single individual can of course be both an "ordinary person" and a "member of the moral community." But the interest of the distinction is that the "capacities" associated with "the ordinary person," respecting which candidate public policies might "go beyond" or "be excessive," are not necessarily the "capacities" to be associated with "the member of the moral community." It might be, this is to say, that S cannot have (D) and (FG) as *public policies* for the reason that those policies go beyond or exceed our capacities *as* reasonably well-off, liberty-enjoying individuals in an affluent society, yet (D) and (FG) may still be *what morality requires* of us *as* individual members of the moral community.

It is not clear that what strains or goes beyond the capacities of the citizens of an affluent society, and thus leads the society to settle for policies that are not "extreme" or "heavy," is what should strain or go beyond the capacities of members of the moral community. In the context of the development of public policy in S, our conception of what the capacities of the "ordinary person" can bear may make it a practical impossibility for J *qua* citizen of S to respond to (D) and too demanding for J *qua* citizen of S to be expected to tolerate sacrifice at the level demanded by (FG) (at that level, perhaps, at which J must give up a self-realizationist, consumerist way of life that her possession of liberty helps make possible for a way of life of severe conservation and service to others). So in this case the people of S do not take (D) and (FG) seriously in their public discussion. They move instead to candidate policies that are more "practical," "realistic," and "reasonable." But — so I want to say — it may still be a duty of J *qua* member of the moral community to respond to (D) and to meet the demands of (FG).

3 / Two Notes and Two Questions

If the distinction between "the ordinary person" and "the member of the moral community" is sound, then one is helped to see that public policy, even in a society that aspires to respect for liberty, may settle for less than what morality requires. It may be that as individuals, that is, as members of the moral community, we must occasionally (or often) go beyond the demands of public policy to undertake something more strenuous. The course of individual responsibility might be more demanding than that set by public policies, even public policies in a society that aspires to respect for individual liberty. The person who pursues the more demanding course of individual responsibility may be public-policy supererogatory but *not* morally supererogatory.

But, still, the distinction that helps us formulate these points is puzzling. Perhaps our conceptions of the capacities of the ordinary person in our kind of society are in fact heavily influenced by considerations about the level of life our society can make available plus considerations about what people may expect, for better or worse, from life in our kind of society. But what exactly do we let ourselves in for conceptually when we lift the idea of the member of the moral community off the idea of the ordinary person? *Should* we make the two distinct?

In the sections that follow I explore the distinction between the ideas of "the ordinary person" and "the member of the moral community." The distinction seems to me philosophically interesting in its own right, and an understanding of it may also throw light on the cases I indicated above, namely, cases in which the "demands" of public policy seem weaker than the "demands" of individual responsibility. To introduce the exploration that follows, let me offer two notes about the distinction, and then ask two questions that we may hope the exploration will help to answer.

The first note is that the distinction itself has perhaps a natural home in views and theories that approach the problems of individual responsibility from a deliberately ahistorical and "impersonal" per-

3. Two Notes and Two Questions

spective. When I attempt to figure out what my responsibilities to others are, I must do so, according to such views and theories, *from a standpoint in which the social and historical particularity of people (including myself) is ignored or considered irrelevant*. The distinction in question fits with a theoretical inclination (which may nonetheless be reflected in "ordinary" moral thinking) to be rather abstract with the idea of the morally responsible individual. The standpoint at issue may be, as Brian Barry puts it, an "atemporal perspective." In connection with the equal-opportunity policy for future generations, Barry writes:

> The basic argument for an equal claim on natural resources is that none of the usual justifications for an unequal claim—special relationships arising in virtue of past services, promises, etc.—apply here. Taking an atemporal perspective, there is nothing to single out any generation as having better or worse claims to enjoy the earth's resources. There are the resources and there are the successive generations: in the absence of any powerful argument to the contrary, there would seem to be a strong presumption in favor of arranging things so that, as far as possible, each generation faces the same range of opportunities with respect to natural resources.[10]

Rawls' theory of justice for the basic structure of society is developed (much of the time) with the atemporal perspective in mind as the relevant "moral point of view." Rawls calls it the perspective "*sub specie aeternitatis*" and writes of it:

> The perspective of eternity is not a perspective from a certain place beyond the world, nor the point of view of a transcendent being; rather it is a certain form of thought and feeling that rational persons can adopt within the world. And having done so, they can, whatever their generation, bring together into one scheme all individual perspectives and arrive together at regulative principles that can be affirmed by everyone as he lives by

them, each from his own standpoint. Purity of heart, if one could attain it, would be to see clearly and to act with grace and self-command from this point of view.[11]

The second note is that the adoption of this perspective tends to lengthen the list of factors that are to be thought of as irrelevant to our responsibility for others. As I suggested earlier, we may consider certain "scope restrictions" on duties to be spurious, such as those restrictions that make obligations to others weaken or run out when the others are geographically distant, or a part of the "further future," or otherwise outside the ordinary circumstances of justice. My thought in the present context of inquiry is that we may add another item to the list of factors that are arbitrary or irrelevant from the moral point of view: the suggestion here is that the fact that a certain candidate public policy either goes beyond our capacities or strains them excessively, that is, our capacities as "ordinary persons" in our kind of society, does not necessarily make the candidate policy fail to reflect what morality requires. It may make the candidate policy fail to be "practical," "realistic," and "reasonable"; but, of course, the use of that vocabulary only reflects the expectations, ideologies, emphases, and special pleadings involved in life in our kind of society and not necessarily the principles and constraints of rationality characteristic of membership in the moral commumnity.

But, as I said above, the distinction between the idea of the ordinary person (in certain identifiable social and historical contexts) and the idea of a member of the moral community (in no particular social and historical context) is puzzling. Beyond the notes just offered, a natural first question is: what *are* the "capacities" of members of the moral community? It seems intelligible to me that something might be put forward as a policy for the moral community that the members thereof *would* find to go beyond their capacities or to be excessive relative to them. Even members of the moral community, we may suppose, have *some* limits. But I must say that I have little idea what the capacities of members of the moral community are, and my drawing a blank on this question is, to me, an interesting and important fact. I am uncertain too about how to go

3. Two Notes and Two Questions

about figuring out what the capacities of members of the moral community are. I suspect, but do not know how to argue, that figuring out what the capacities of members of the moral community are is not, or is not entirely or even mainly, an empirical task; it is in major part, I suspect, a problem of decision—a policy problem for moral theory, as it were, if not a public-policy problem for any particular S—rather than a matter of discovery of facts about our nature. What we must do is establish, by argument and decision, a conception of the capacities to be associated with membership in the moral community, where that conception reflects an awareness of the fact that persons as individuals "have but one life to live" but are also "in life together," yet is not cluttered up with the contingent emphases, ideologies, and special pleadings of a self-realizationist, consumerist way of life in this or that affluent society.

This leads me to a second question: is it "fair" to people to double their memberships in the way I have been discussing? Is it unreasonably onerous to make people think that what is too demanding of them or beyond them as ordinary citizens of this or that society may not be too demanding of them or beyond them as members of the moral community? The direction of my thoughts in this connection is that it is not unfair or unreasonable to people to double their memberships in the manner in question. Indeed, that we have, or hold, these double memberships is, I think, a part (metaphorically expressed) of our "human condition."[12] But in any event the view I have is that we risk not taking our responsibilities for others seriously enough and that we risk being much too parochial about whom we count as "others." We may, in short, allow ourselves to be too much creatures of the view that the cultivation and realization of the self are the legitimate projects for our lives. Insofar as I believe that we "share fate" with human beings generally, including those in future generations, I find the distinction in question to be useful. Whatever the capacities of members of the moral community turn out to be, they will almost certainly be tolerant of more in the way of response to the basic needs of others than are those of ordinary persons fortunately placed in societies emphasizing self-realization and consumerism.

4 / Ordinary Persons and Members of the Moral Community

So far I have indicated that I think there is some need to distinguish between the ideas of "ordinary persons" and "members of the moral community." I have also indicated that the distinction seems puzzling. One wants to understand it, and the need to make it, more fully. In this section I offer some further discussion of the distinction: I examine a recent attempt to *deny* the distinction, and I suggest that the attempt does not succeed. My discussion is confined to an assessment of this recent effort, so it does not show that no attempt to deny the distinction can succeed; but perhaps it is nevertheless enough to give the distinction a certain plausibility.

The recent effort to deny the distinction that I refer to is a part of Michael J. Sandel's important critique of liberalism in *Liberalism and the Limits of Justice*.[13] Sandel's angle of approach to liberalism, the depth his discussion reaches, and the fundamental mistake he argues that the Rawlsian version of liberalism contains all seem to me to give his critique special philosophical interest. There is little in it that is directed to the usual questions about the content of or relations between the two principles that make up Rawls' conception of justice as fairness. Instead, Sandel offers an extended, very penetrating critique of what he calls the "deep individualism"[14] embedded in the premises of the Rawlsian theory—and, more generally, in the foundations of liberal political theories influenced by Kantian moral philosophy. This critique of the "deep individualism" of liberalism is, in effect, a challenge to the distinction between "ordinary person" and "member of the moral community" that I wish to suggest should be retained.

The novel element in Sandel's challenge to the deep individualism of liberalism is the special use it makes of the idea of community. Of course, laments about liberalism from "the value of community" are not novel. In the recent literature Michael Walzer's *Spheres of Justice*[15] asserts a "relativistic" and "pluralistic" treatment of justice as an alternative to the Rawlsian view (which Walzer does not sys-

4. Ordinary Persons and the Moral Community [131]

tematically or dialectically argue against), and here the idea of community, in the form of a proffered ground for justice in "shared understandings," is exploited to give plausibility to the relativism and pluralism.[16] But Sandel's use of the idea of community is altogether deeper and more philosophically interesting (so it seems to me): he proposes to take issue with Rawlsian liberalism about, in effect, the logical make-up of the moral nature of human beings, and his development of the view that persons are *constituted* by "community" is made to yield not the claim that justice is "plural" but rather the view that justice has *limits*.[17]

Sandel's specific challenge is to the "deontological" form of liberalism that he finds to be "prominent in the moral and legal and political philosophy of the day."[18] This is the liberalism that makes justice "primary" among values and that emphasizes the "autonomy" and (especially) the "independence" of the "self." It is the liberal idea of the self as autonomous and independent with which I associate the idea of persons as "members of the moral community." Sandel thinks deontological liberalism rests on an *incorrect* view of the self: the mistake he has in mind is not merely one of "impracticality"; it is, more fundamentally, a conceptual mistake.

> The central thesis of deontological liberalism is that . . . society, being composed of a plurality of persons, each with his own aims, interests, and conceptions of the good, is best arranged when it is governed by principles that do not *themselves* presuppose any particular conception of the good; what justifies these regulative principles above all is not that they maximize the social welfare or otherwise promote the good, but rather than they conform to the concept of *right*, a moral category given prior to the good and independent of it.[19]

The fact that "right" is construed as prior to "the good" is what makes this liberalism deontological, for "this fundamental priority allows the right to stand aloof from prevailing values and conceptions of the good."[20] In connection with this point, deontological liberalism reflects our tendency to think that existing values are to be evaluated, that is, such values are possible objects of *criticism*, and thus the business of liberal theory is considered to be to propose standards for this evaluation and criticism. Finally, deontological liberalism opposes both "consequentialism" and "teleology," for it involves the specification of duties that "take unqualified precedence over other moral and practical concerns," and the principles that provide this specification "are derived in a way that does not presuppose any final human purposes or ends, nor any determinate conception of the human good."[21]

Sandel then brings to the surface the specific target of his critique: deontological liberalism is said to be

> grounded in the concept of a *subject given prior to its ends*, a concept held indispensable to our understanding ourselves as freely choosing, autonomous beings. Society is best arranged when it is governed by principles that do not presuppose any particular conception of the good, for any other arrangement would fail to respect persons as *beings capable of choice*; it would treat them as objects rather than subjects, as means rather than ends in themselves.[22]

Thus, Sandel's critique asks us to reflect on the idea of self that is central to deontological liberalism (including Rawls' version of it), and we are to see that this self is construed as a "subject" that *stands apart from its ends*. It is this self's *capacity for choice* (rather than any particular choices) that deontological liberalism would have justice protect above all else, and this is to give justice "primacy" among the values that may be reflected in the basic structure of society.

To fill out what, in particular, the Rawlsian deontological liberalism holds to be the nature of this subject that stands apart from its ends, that is, "the moral subject," Sandel proposes "to . . . take the principles of justice as provisionally given and argue back to the nature of the moral subject."[23] The result of this strategy is an account that characterizes the liberal's "moral subject" as having three main features. (*a*) In the first place the Rawlsian theory requires a *plurality* of persons. "For there to be justice, there must be the possibility of conflicting claims, and for there to be conflicting

4. Ordinary Persons and the Moral Community [133]

claims, there must be more than a single claimant."[24] The importance of this apparently innocuous point is that Rawls' view thereby places "unity" (for example, cooperation) *posterior* to plurality and, so to speak, at the whim of the interests of the logically prior separate individuals. "We are distinct individuals first, and then (circumstances permitting) we form relationships and engage in co-operative arrangements with others. . . . In any particular instance, we just have to see whether or not the basis for cooperation exists."[25] (*b*) The second main feature is that the self is related to its ends and interests *via* the notion of *possession*. This is to say that the self is not itself reducible to its ends and interests; in fact, conceptions that have the effect of reducing the self to its ends and interests yield a "radically situated self" (as Sandel calls it), and these Sandel considers to be mistaken conceptions. Rather, "in possession the self is distanced from its ends without being detached altogether."[26] (*c*) The third feature that Sandel finds to mark the nature of the Rawlsian moral subject is *free agency*. There are really two points here: (*i*) the self that is one in a "plurality" of subjects and that is related to its own ends and interests *via* "possession" is *voluntarist* in character, that is, it is fundamental to it that it has the capacity for choice, and (*ii*) at the same time, the identity and "bounds" of this moral subject are thought of as "fixed" independently of its experience. As Sandel puts the point, this self is "an antecedently, individuated subject": "To be a deontological self, I must be a subject whose identity is given independently . . . of my interests and ends and my relations with others. Combined with the idea of possession, this notion of [antecedent] individuation powerfully completes Rawls' theory of the person."[27]

We are now, I think, in a position to see what Sandel believes is centrally wrong with Rawlsian deontological liberalism. His claim is that despite its efforts to avoid loading down liberalism with a view of the self that ascribes particular desires and ends to persons (as, say, Hobbes' view does), there is nevertheless a "deep individualism"[28] in the Rawlsian view that *is* substantive. That is, Rawls' view takes a position (to the exclusion of other positions) on the nature of the subject (if not its objects of choice), and this position is at its most basic level *anti-communitarian*. Some introduction to what Sandel means by this is given in the following passage:

> [T]he Rawlsian self is not only a subject of possession, but an antecedently individuated subject, standing *always* at a certain distance from the interests it has. One consequence of this distance is to put the self beyond the reach of experience, to make it invulnerable, to fix its identity once and for all. *No commitment could grip me so deeply that I could not understand myself without it.* . . . But a self so thoroughly independent as this rules out any conception of the good (or of the bad) bound up with possession in the constitutive sense.[29]

Sandel's point essentially concerns how we *understand* ourselves, and not, say, how we *feel* toward our community's culture, traditions, institutions, and policies. The Rawlsian view "rules out the possibility that common purposes and ends could inspire more or less expansive self-understandings and so define a *community in the constitutive sense, a community describing the subject and not just the objects of shared aspirations.*" In particular, the Rawlsian view excludes what Sandel refers to as "intersubjective" or "intrasubjective" forms of self-understanding, which are ways of understanding oneself that do not require the bounds of the self to be those of "a single, individual human being."[30] And, of course, Sandel wants to argue not merely that the Rawlsian theory "rules out," that is, conflicts with, the community-constitutive "position" about the self, but also the two further points (*a*) that Rawls' theory in some of its most distinctive doctrines (the notion that "natural assets may be a common resource," the idea of "social union") dialectically *requires* something very like the community-constitutive conception of the self, and (*b*) that, indeed, the community-constitutive conception is *correct*.

I will not here explore the extensive argumentation that Sandel brings to these further points. In the rest of this section I restrict my attention to the basic question of how the community-constitutive conception of the self is to be understood, and how it conflicts with

4. Ordinary Persons and the Moral Community [135]

the Rawlsian conception. I assume that these are important questions for Sandel's view and that answers to them are necessary to the support for the further claims. I have difficulties with Sandel's answers to these questions, as will be clear from what follows.

Three elements in Sandel's view seem plain. He wants to hold (*a*) that the "constituting" being referred to is a matter of building "community" into the moral *subject*, and not merely into certain of its "attributes" (for example, feelings, sentiments, aspirations); (*b*) that the result of this community-constituting of the self is a "mode of self-understanding" on the part of the individual, and not only an array of feelings the individual has toward his or her community (though such feelings may also be present); and (*c*) that within this mode of self-understanding one finds community "in" the self by, as it were, "discovery" rather than "decision." For the individual members of society, Sandel explains, "community describes not just what they *have* as fellow citizens but also what they *are*, not a relationship they choose (as in a voluntary association) but an attachment they discover, not merely an attribute but a constituent of their identity."[31]

I find it tempting to interpret Sandel's critique as claiming that Rawlsian liberalism rests ultimately on a (mistaken) conception of the self as "in itself" both transcendent and radically separated from "experience." Sandel's vocabulary suggests this when, for example, he explains that Rawls' denial that persons deserve their "natural assets" rests finally on the notion of the self as "pure" and "unadulterated."[32] Indeed, the whole critique approaches philosophical treatments of the "moral subject" by locating them on a continuum described as ranging from the "radically situated self" (whereby the self is collapsed too much into its attributes) to the "radically disembodied self" (whereby it is separated too much from them); and the Rawlsian idea of self is criticized precisely for being located too far toward the latter pole. In the end, Sandel proposes to replace the self of deontological liberalism with a self that is suffused with content, that is, constituted by community, and it is the point at which this replacement takes place that marks the "limits" of justice—or, at any rate, the limits of the justice that fits the characterization provided by deontological liberalism. In short: justice is limited as a function of the extent to which the self *is* constituted by community.

Now, Sandel's critique is guided by an important theme: it is surely possible and desirable to assess liberalism from the angle of what it claims or assumes about human beings and their moral nature. At the same time, the discussion that Sandel offers is filled with metaphor, and in places it might be characterized as an inquiry into the "metaphysics" of liberalism. I am puzzled about the force of his critical claims once the various "models" and "pictures" are set aside. Here are certain problems I have with Sandel's treatment of Rawlsian liberalism.

First, it is not at all clear what follows from Sandel's critique for the substance of and the relations between the principles that are to guide people's thinking about the institutions and practices that form (what Rawls calls) the basic structure of their community. Sandel does not argue directly against Rawls' conception of justice as fairness; nor does he argue for any particular alternative conception(s), appropriate to community-constituted selves, to be put in its place. Perhaps the principles that people are to employ to guide their thinking about the basic structure of society must be, for Sandel, somehow "relative to" the contents of the particular forms of "community" that constitute their selves. But, strictly, I do not see that even this *follows* from the critique as it stands. It might be, so far as logical possibilities are concerned, that the conception of justice as fairness ought to guide the basic structure of society *even if* Sandel is right in his view that the self is constituted by community.[33]

The second problem is also a matter of puzzlement about where Sandel's critique leaves us. He is quite right to emphasize, I think, that the justice of deontological liberalism is meant to protect the *capacity to choose* of the individual members of the moral community, and is supposed to avoid endorsing or proscribing particular *choices*, that is, particular interests or ends or "ways of life."[34] Liberalism aims, after all, to cherish *individualism* in many senses. But, somewhat surprisingly, I do not see clearly where Sandel stands, as a result of the critique, on the matter of this individualism (in its

4. Ordinary Persons and the Moral Community

many senses) that liberalism aims to cherish. He says in one place that "a theory of community whose province extended to the subject as well as the object of motivations would be individualistic in neither the conventional sense nor in Rawls'."[35] But I do not see from this how the community-constitutive conception is individualistic or, more important, even that it can be so in a principled way at all. (Its being so would appear to "depend" on the contents of the particular forms of community that constitute our selves.) I judge that Sandel has this concern in mind when he writes that "the scope of community ties, however expansive, is not without limit.... The bounds between the self and (some) others are thus relaxed on the intersubjective account, but not so completely relaxed as to give way to the radically situated subject."[36] But this is all I find in the text on the fate of individualism, and it does not provide guidance on the subject.

But apart from these puzzles about the normative implications—or lack thereof—of Sandel's critique, my main difficulty remains one about what it is for persons to be "constituted" by community. As my discussion indicates, I understand Sandel to hold that the community-constitutive conception of self is in theoretical competition with the Rawlsian conception of the self as "pure" and "unadulterated."[37] This is why I said above that Sandel's critique has the effect of challenging the distinction between "ordinary person" and "member of the moral community"—or, more exactly, the interpretation of that distinction associated with Rawlsian liberalism. Thus, whereas the Rawlsian account allows us to "distance" ourselves from our community ties, the view Sandel proposes makes us "participants in a common identity, be it a family or community or class or people or nation,"[38] in such a way that ties of the latter sort specify one's "mode of self-understanding." But there is a question, I think, about whether, logically, the community-constitutive conception can really be *in competition with* the Rawlsian conception of a "distancing" self. Rawls can, after all, agree that people understand themselves in ways that incorporate community ties.[39] But the sheer fact that people understand themselves in these ways *allows* that, logically, people can distance themselves *enough* from such ties to develop attitudes toward them and, finally, to evaluate and (sometimes) criticize them. And this seems to be so whether the ties in question are thought of philosophically as built into the "subject" or the "attributes" of the self.

I may think of myself as an American, and as a husband and a father, and perhaps also as a member of what some count as a profession. All these are, for me, examples of what Sandel calls "modes of self-understanding." They are not merely feelings I have about myself. They are parts of my identity as an "ordinary person," that is, parts of my self as "constituted by community." But so far as I can see I *can* also "distance" myself from these modes of self-understanding—enough so, at any rate, to come to hold them at critical arm's length, worry about them, perhaps plan to change them, and so forth. So, despite my efforts to do so, I am unable to keep the community-constitutive model of self *in competition with* the Rawlsian model of self such that theoretically I must select between them. Each candidate "constituent" of my identity, each community tie, I find I *can* slip away from *enough* to place it before me as an object of evaluation and, perhaps, criticism. And that seems to me *all* the transcendence, independence, or "purity" the self must have for the deontological-liberal project to get underway and for the distinction between "ordinary persons" and "members of the moral community" to make sense. We may grant that it does not follow from the fact that I can distance myself from my community ties in this familiar way that those ties are not deeply important to me. But what is deeply important to me ("central to my identity," I might say) may still be evaluated by me, even though it might in some cases be strange, painful, funny, or frightening to conduct the evaluation.

Late in his book Sandel argues that the Rawlsian view does not make sense of ordinary "self-reflection." "For Rawls, reflection 'on the kind of beings we *are*' rather than on the kind of desires we *have* is not a possibility."[40] The reason this is so is that the self, on Sandel's interpretation of Rawls' theory, "is conceived as barren of constituent traits, possessed only of contingent attributes held always at a certain distance,and so there is nothing *in* the self for reflection to survey or

5. End Note [139]

apprehend."[41] And then Sandel adds, in behalf of his own view, that "on the constitutive conception, the good of community was seen to penetrate the person more profoundly so as to describe not just his *feeling* but a mode of self-understanding partly constitutive of his identity, partly definitive of who he was."[42] My response is that one's *recognition* that such-and-so is "partly definitive" of who one is, in the ordinary contexts in which it might occur, seems possible only on the condition that one *can* distance oneself from such-and-so enough to allow its character as "partly definitive" to come into view. And this, I suggest, is to say that the "independence of self" that Sandel faults the Rawlsian view for assuming is a presupposition of our recognition of our community ties as indeed (sometimes) the constituting features of our make-up that they are.

When one reflects on the fact that one is an American, or Jewish, or Irish, or a father, or a Christian, and finds that that means something to one in respect of "the kind of person one is," one is *just then* "distanced" from oneself in the familiar but important way that I think the liberal's deontological enterprise requires. If this is so, then the community-constitutive conception of self that Sandel labors to show is ruled out by the Rawlsian view does not finally conflict with it at all. The community-constituted self is simply logically posterior to the distancing self. Thus, there is a distinction between "ordinary persons" and "members of the moral community," and, accordingly, we may (indeed) proceed to evaluate our community ties to determine what they are worth.

5 / End Note

I must observe that the point that I attempted to support in the last section is a limited one, and it does not itself "answer" the questions I posed in section 3 above. The point I attempted to support is that the ideas of "ordinary person" and "member of the moral community" are separable. It is one thing to interpret persons as "ordinary persons" and to understand them, in Sandel's vocabulary, as "constituted by community." It is another thing to interpret persons as "members of the moral community" and thereby to "distance" them somewhat from their community ties—their social and historical particularity—and thereby, too, to cast the latter particularity as an object of evaluation and perhaps criticism. To note that we can interpret persons in these different ways does not tell us directly, for example, what the "capacities" of members of the moral community are, or what their "limits" are such that certain policies "go beyond" or "exceed" those capacities. Nor does it tell us that it is always "fair" to hold persons to a notion of "what morality requires" that is more onerous than what is demanded by "practical," "realistic," and "reasonable" public policy. But, still, the intelligibility of the distinction at stake allows for the possibility that in some cases the course of individual responsibility might be, as I put it above, public-policy supererogatory but not morally supererogatory. Some of the implications of this point for the understanding and justification of the view I earlier called "shared-fate individualism" will be explored in the discussion that follows.

7

THE WEIGHT OF

ESTABLISHED LIBERTY

1 / A Problem of Justification

In Chapter 2 I argued that "shared-fate individualism" is not implausible as an account of what morality requires in the matter of career choice in the circumstances of humankind today. It is not a foolish, extreme, or otherwise strange view of what morality demands if one gives attention to certain troubling facts about the human condition and then, with those facts in mind, lets certain of our most familiar moral convictions settle into an order that seems natural. In Chapter 3 I backed up, as it were, and argued that a certain minimal interpretation of responsibility for others—an interpretation that both liberal and shared-fate individualism may be understood to take seriously—can indeed be built into the idea of membership in the moral community, that is, the idea of moral agency, without conceptual incoherence. This is to say that there is no logical difficulty in the view that the idea of moral agency already "contains" the idea of the acknowledgment of claims independently of self-interest.

But, of course, even if the other-responsibility of this minimal interpretation defines (in part) the idea of membership in the moral community, this would not by itself show that shared-fate individualism is the correct, or even an appropriate, moral perspective for competent individuals in today's world. (See 3.1.) We must now begin to revisit what in 2.6 I called "the selection problem." In 3.5 I suggested the possibility that persons who "have" the minimal conception of other-responsibility might have reason to regard it as *important*—to "inflate" it, so to speak. The question arises: what would be involved in its being reasonable for people to regard individual responsibility as involving a conception of other-responsibility that incorporates the "condition of legitimacy" I ascribed to shared-fate individualism in 2.5, namely, the condition according to which the pursuit of self-realization by competent individuals is acceptable only when all members of the moral community can realize themselves?

Shared-fate individualism makes, or appears to make, of individual responsibility a heavy burden. The responsibility-for-others it emphasizes is not narrowly focused on particular acts or acts of certain kinds, nor is it necessarily restricted to certain contexts or situations, nor is it limited to particular "others." It seems broader and more wide-ranging than the more focused forms of other-responsibility that come to mind. (In this it reflects the element in our form of moral life whereby we view persons as "in life together" such that *ab initio* we are all members of a common "human" or "moral" community.) This broad form of responsibility may seem not only "heavy" but also puzzling: it is not the sort of responsibility that carries with its violations a liability to *legal* punishment (cf. 2.6, note 30), and even if its violations make one liable to "moral punishment," it is not clear what is countenanced by the latter term.

The responsibility-for-others involved in shared-fate individualism reflects a certain position about what earlier (2.5) I called "the moral standing of individual lives"—a position that may indeed, so I believe, be or become reflected in one's attitudes and behavior toward (in general) the people who make up the membership of the moral community. What happens as a (logical) consequence of adopting the shared-fate individualist perspective, in the circumstances of today's world, is (among other things) that the legitimacy of one's pursuit of one's own individually defined self-realizationist projects is not automatically in place. That legitimacy is not, of course, abandoned. It is, instead, thought of as conditional upon others' being

1. A Problem of Justification

positioned to self-realize. I should add that to adopt the perspective of shared-fate individualism is not *per se* to "love others," or "take pride in them," or even "like" them very much. So to be asked to adopt this perspective is not to be asked to have certain emotions, feelings, or sentiments (though certain emotions, feelings, or sentiments may be typical or characteristic of those who adopt this perspective). It is, rather, to be asked to understand the terms of one's life with others in a certain way.[1]

As a perspective on individual responsibility rather than a cluster of emotions, shared-fate individualism is open to arguments pro and con. Philosophically, it raises a "justification problem." Perhaps it is already plain (from 2.7) that I am wary of the demand for a justification of shared-fate individualism that takes the form of an independent, positive argument, that is, an argument that derives shared-fate individualism from principles open to independent justification, or from other propositions that "everyone agrees with." I doubt that deep conceptions of individual responsibility bearing upon how the moral standing of individual lives is to be understood have available to them justification of that sort any more than do deep conceptions of justice for the basic structure of society. What, then, is the "case" for shared-fate individualism that selects it over its main rival, liberal individualism? In words borrowed from Mill's approach to the "problem of proof" for utilitarianism:[2] what could make good the claim of shared-fate individualism to be believed?

Here are some notes about the "problem of justification" for shared-fate individualism, and how I will approach it.

First, I should remark again that my concern is for the theory of individual responsibility rather than for the theory of justice for the basic structure of society. In *A Theory of Justice* Rawls writes that "substantial sacrifices ... are not demanded as a matter of justice by the basic structure of society,"[3] but he adds in a later essay that there is "no reason why a well-ordered society should encourage primarily individualistic values."[4] I take it that there can be a distinction between the demands of "individual responsibility" and the demands of the "principles for institutions" governing the "well-ordered society" such that the former demands do not necessarily imitate the latter. This is to say that even if the principles that make a society "well-ordered" collect together the values of liberty, equality, and fraternity in such a way as to make liberty somehow prior to, or more basic or important than, equality or fraternity, it does not follow that our conception of individual responsibility does not require, in certain circumstances, the substantial sacrifice of liberty. Shared-fate individualism, as a conception of individual responsibility, may be consistent with, say, the Rawlsian conception of "justice as fairness" for the basic structure of society, even though the latter does not by itself imply the former.[5] (The latter does not, for example, require individuals to put service to others before self-realization when the two conflict.) My attention in what follows continues to be directed to what morality requires of competent individuals, not to what morality requires of the basic structure of society.

The second note concerns the bearing of moral theories on the selection problem. It might seem that if one were, say, a convinced utilitarian or libertarian, or perhaps a Kantian or Marxist, then one could employ one's general theory (interpreted as a theory of individual responsibility) as an independent argument favoring one of the perspectives I distinguished (separate-life, liberal, or shared-fate individualism) over the others. For my own part, however, I find that the theories just mentioned seem either indeterminate or question-begging regarding the selection problem. (*a*) Utilitarianism, for example, is indeterminate in the sense that if one cannot make plausible estimates about the general frustration or satisfaction likely to attend a service or self-realizationist career, or the likely service impact one's self-realizationist career would have, then it is not clear how the appeal to utility can help individuals select among the perspectives in question. (This is not to say, though, that the outcome-*risks* I mentioned in 2.6 and 2.7 can be ignored. Morality may require in one set of circumstances that a certain risk be taken, and in another set of circumstances that a certain risk not be taken, and it may do this for reasons (for example, reasons of human dignity, the value of individual lives, or the preservation of some intrinsic good) that are independent of the terms of a utilitarian measure of

1. A Problem of Justification

outcomes, and independent as well of the likelihood or unlikelihood of some utilitarian-objectionable outcome actually occurring.)[6] (b) The libertarian and Marxist general theories seem question-begging regarding the selection problem insofar as they (as commonly understood) assume the priority of one of the basic attitudes I mentioned (the shared-fate attitude for the Marxist, the separate-life attitude for the libertarian) over the other, and thus provide no *independent* argument for selecting among the perspectives. (c) The Kantian texts (as I understand them) appear to regard both self-realization and service to others as duties, but not to choose between them, or to show how to choose between them, when they conflict. The net result of these (no doubt controversial) thoughts is that no ready solution to the selection problem is provided by the general moral theories I have mentioned.[7]

A third note concerns what, more exactly, is the "object" of justification here. Clearly, while shared-fate individualism is a moral conception it is not itself a "general theory" in the way in which utilitarianism or Kantianism are, nor is it a conception for the "basic structure of society" in the way in which Rawls' (Kantian) liberalism or Nozick's libertarianism are, nor is it something that identifies for individuals what in particular should be their careers or "vocations."[8] I think of shared-fate individualism as a *policy for individuals*, where "policy" means what I suggested in 1.2 and "individuals" means the "competent individuals" characterized in 2.3. The range of "serious life decisions" (see 2.3) covered by shared-fate individualism is not yet plain, of course, and I must say that I do not at this point have a systematic way of specifying the limits of that range. Obviously, I think shared-fate individualism "covers" the matter of career choice. It may also cover, for example, the serious life decisions involved in parts of what might be called "parental role-modeling" for children —to the extent, at any rate, to which such a matter of choice (threatened as it is by contingencies of all kinds on all sides) can be thought of by parents as something that falls under policies at all. But there doubtless are some serious life decisions that shared-fate individualism does not cover or apply to: whether to marry might be an example, whether to cultivate certain friendships might be another, whether to pursue certain activities or programs that help "keep the self intact," in a sense to be discussed later (8.2), might be still another.[9] And even in respect of one's own conceptions or interpretations of either self-realization or service-to-others in one's own case, shared-fate individualism dictates neither particular interests or aspirations, nor any particular strategies or techniques for pursuing or developing them. It speaks only to the matter of what standing one's own self-realization is to have in a world that is such that many of those with whom one is "in life together" are in no position to pursue self-realization at all. In general, shared-fate individualism is a policy for individuals that guides decision-making concerning long-term projects involving their time, energy, and resources. It sets a general direction and leaves the matter of "implementation" in particular circumstances to the judgment of the individuals involved in those circumstances.[10]

My fourth note concerns the normative character of the justification problem posed by shared-fate individualism. I take it that what is at issue here is not (merely) whether certain propositions can be verified, or how certain ideas are to be interpreted—though indeed a full treatment of the issue involves both establishing facts and analyzing concepts. The aim of justification in this case is the making of a *substantive moral decision*.[11] We ask whether there are considerations that lead us to decide in favor of shared-fate individualism. It is important not to lose sight of the fact that we do not find it incoherent or even unserious for a person who knows that the world is filled with stifled and frustrated lives to think that he or she may nevertheless legitimately "be in life for oneself." The real issue here is whether our serious life decisions concerning our long-term projects and personal commitments within a certain range *ought* to be governed by shared-fate individualism, that is, by the perspective on the moral standing of individual lives that makes it a condition of the legitimacy of one's being in life for oneself that all those with whom one "shares fate" are in a position to be in life for themselves. It is also important not to lose sight of the fact that the normative character of our justification problem calls attention to the *circumstances* of humankind. Clearly, in the fortunate case in which every-

1. A Problem of Justification [147]

one is positioned to self-realize, the question "Ought we to adopt shared-fate individualism?" is silly. But when the circumstances of humankind are such that huge numbers of human beings are, for no good reason, not in a position to realize themselves at all, but could be helped into that position, then that question seems (to me) not silly at all. Our justification problem for shared-fate individualism concerns the make-up of individual responsibility in, as it were, a transition period—or, more precisely, a period *that we could make into* a transition period leading toward a more adequate "human condition" for the members of the moral community.

My final note concerns the pattern my discussion follows in responding to the justification problem I have outlined. Even though I doubt, as indicated above, that there is an independent positive justification for shared-fate individualism, I am inclined to think that shared-fate individualism is *defensible* in the sense that it can withstand certain critical arguments directed against it. In this chapter I consider a critical argument "from established liberty." In the next chapter I shall consider certain further critical arguments based upon what might be called "the claims of the self." Toward the end of that chapter (8.6) I shall suggest not an independent positive justification for shared-fate individualism, but a moral-psychological consideration that seems to me to favor shared-fate individualism as a policy for competent individuals in today's world, over and beyond the natural support for it afforded by attention to the troubling facts of the human condition emphasized at the beginning of this discussion (1.4).

In general, a "critical argument" here is one that proffers a consideration that is supposed to resist the "condition of legitimacy" that shared-fate individualism imposes on the competent individual's pursuit of self-realization. Such a critical argument says, in form: x is a consideration that *defends against* the imposition of that condition of legitimacy. The burden of my discussion, again, is to show that shared-fate individualism can withstand the critical arguments I entertain. I doubt that the arguments I entertain exhaust the possibilities, though I think the ones discussed are interesting and important. My thought is that *if* one "starts" with shared-fate individualism, and then asks why one should *not* maintain it, these important arguments are *not* sufficient to lead one to give up shared-fate individualism.

2 / The Claims of Established Liberty

Suppose we hold that shared-fate individualism is correct as a position about individual responsibility in our time. Offhand, it appears that shared-fate individualism is consistent with, but not required by, *liberalism* understood as (in major part) a conception of justice for the basic structure of society. This appears to be so because (as indicated in my first note in section 1 above) shared-fate individualism is "for," or applies to, the responsibility of individuals, while the liberal conception of justice is "for," or applies to, the basic structure of society. We might say: liberalism *allows* the individual to adopt shared-fate individualism as his or her ("personal") perspective on individual responsibility, but does not *require* its adoption.

But then there seems to be an element of paradox in the picture. For if shared-fate individualism *is* what morality requires for individual responsibility, and the liberal conception of justice *is* what morality requires for the basic structure of society, why are the two conceptions "uncoordinated" in what they teach individuals? After all, the practical effect of the teaching of the liberal conception of justice is that the competent individual in the position he or she has relative to the pursuit of self-realization afforded by the *established system of liberties* characteristic of an affluent liberal society *is* morally permitted to exercise that liberty in the pursuit of self-realization. (See 1.4.2.) For liberalism, the use of that "established liberty" is not constrained by the condition of legitimacy specified by shared-fate individualism.

The question then is: are the liberal conception of justice and the shared-fate conception of individual responsibility somehow at odds? Why does the one merely "allow" what the other "requires?" Why aren't the two congruent? Shall we say, relative to the justification problem raised by shared-fate individualism, that the "established

2. The Claims of Established Liberty [149]

liberty" of the competent individual in an affluent society is a *defense* against the imposition of the condition of legitimacy prescribed by shared-fate individualism? Or shall we say that the established liberty of the competent individual in that sort of society is not a defense against the imposition of that condition of legitimacy on his or her pursuit of self-realization?

The response to this problem that I develop below is that the appearance of a lack of congruence between shared-fate individualism and the liberal conception of justice, in respect of what they "teach" about the liberty possessed by the competent individuals in the affluent societies of today's world, is deceptive. Shared-fate individualism teaches that individual responsibility involves, as a condition of the legitmacy of the pursuit of self-realization, that others be positioned to self-realize—and, of course, "others" here refers to all "members of the moral community" (or, in the language of liberalism, "all equal moral persons"). The discussion that follows involves several points. (*a*) First, I offer an interpretation of liberalism—an interpretation, more precisely, of certain doctrines of the most highly developed theory of liberal justice that we possess[12] —that strongly suggests that the *subject* of the liberal conception of justice is the *moral community* (that is, the community of "all equal moral persons"). (*b*) I also suggest that the best practical "instantiation" of the idea of "moral community" or "community of all equal moral persons" in today's world is in fact the *world community*. (*c*) The discussion involves as well the view (discussed briefly in 1.4 and 1.5) that *our* "world community" (the world *we* live in) is not at a stage of development that permits the effective exercise for all its members of the individual liberty held by the liberal conception to be the most fundamental of the several values (liberty, equality, fraternity[13]) that are collected together and ordered by justice. (*d*) Finally, I observe that the stage of development of the world community is such that the liberal conception of justice not only maintains that the sacrifice of individual liberty "for the sake of liberty" is *acceptable*,[14] but also itself provides no reason not to *require* that sacrifice. The liberal conception of justice for the basic structure of society, in circumstances such as those that mark *our* "human condition," in fact "gives way," as it were, without objection or qualification, to the shared-fate conception of individual responsibility. Taking these points together, my thesis regarding the alleged lack of congruence between shared-fate individualism and liberalism, stated in its most provocative form, is that the individual liberty so prized and relatively well established in anyhow several of this world's affluent societies is something that those who enjoy it are not now (morally) entitled to have. The theme here is that it is morally imperative for competent individuals to sacrifice that liberty—at least for a time (perhaps as little as a generation or as much as a century). And, so I claim, what grounds this imperative and gives it force is not shared-fate individualism alone, somehow "going beyond" liberalism to supererogatory extremes, but, rather, in part the *deep appeal* of the idea of justice itself *as* interpreted by liberalism.

3 / The Subject of Justice

My leading thought in the interpretation of liberalism is that certain main doctrines in the Rawlsian theory of justice make its resulting liberal conception of justice "universalist" in its scope. I recognize that, logically, it might be possible to devise a form of liberalism—even a form of liberalism that rests on recognizably contractualist foundations (as Rawls' does)—that was not universalist in its scope. Indeed, regarding one historical instance of contractualist liberalism, the late Alexander M. Bickel wrote that "Lockean contractarian doctrine, proceeding as it does from natural rights, is not, as might appear, universalist; it is intended to support and justify the national, constitutional state. The notion of contract presupposes parties, and the parties are citizens."[15] The question here concerns, in effect, what the liberal conception of justice is to apply to. Rawls has answered this question in part, for he has argued[16] that the liberal conception is to apply to *the basic structure of society*, where "basic structure" refers to the "major social institutions" such as "the political constitution and the principal economic and social arrangements" that "distribute fundamental rights and duties and determine the division

3. The Subject of Justice

of advantages from social cooperation."[17] But what is not argued in Rawls' work, as I read it, is whether there is any very definite, or any preferred, "instantiation" for the idea of society in the characterization of the subject of the liberal conception of justice. It is true that Rawls' careful development of his attractive theory is conducted under the *assumption* that the natural home of the basic structure he has in mind is what we think of today as a nation among other nations. Thus, Rawls notes that "the relevant systems here, of course, are the basic structures of the well-ordered societies corresponding to the different conceptions of justice," and then he adds: "Now I assume that the boundaries of these schemes are given by the notion of a self-contained national community."[18]

But despite the logical conceivability of *a* form of liberalism whose subject is the nation state, my thought is that the Rawlsian form of liberalism, given *its* background doctrines, is universalist in scope. I suggest, then, that Rawls' assumption that the natural home of justice is the "self-contained national community" is unexamined. I believe that in fact a case can be made, from the resources of the Rawlsian theory, that strongly suggests that *the subject of justice*, that is, what the liberal conception of justice applies to, is the basic structure of the *moral community*, the most plausible instantiation of which, in today's world, is the *world community*.

What shows, or tends to show, this? The combination of the following four considerations (each one a Rawlsian doctrine) suggests to me the view that the only legitimate home of the justice-governed basic structure is, in today's world, the world community.

(*a*) One consideration is the role of the idea of the "original position" in the Rawlsian development of the liberal conception of justice as fairness. My point is that this *way* of developing (explaining, justifying, testing) a conception of justice, relying as it does upon our thinking our way into the perspective of rational, mutually self-interested persons deliberating about the principles of justice behind a "veil of ignorance" concerning particular facts about themselves, suggests that the scope of justice is the total community of human beings any of whom the parties to the original position "might turn out to be." At a minimum, this manner of development of the liberal conception does not itself suggest that the basic structure of a *nation state* is to be the subject of justice. Indeed, as Rawls adds, "it is important that the original position be interpreted so that one can at any time adopt its perspective. *It must make no difference when one takes up this viewpoint, or who does so*: the restrictions must be such that the same principles are always chosen. The veil of ignorance is a key condition in meeting this requirement. It insures not only that the information available is relevant, but that it is at all times the same."[19]

In one place in *A Theory of Justice*, Rawls experiments with an "extension" of his theoretical approach to the problem of international relations. He writes:

> Let us assume that . . . the persons in the original position have agreed to the principles of right as these apply to their own society and to themselves as members of it. Now at this point one may extend the interpretation of the original position and think of the parties as representatives of different nations who must choose together the fundamental principles to adjudicate conflicting claims among states. Following out the conception of the initial situation, I assume that . . . while they know that they represent different nations each living under the normal circumstances of human life, they know nothing about the particular circumstances of their own society. . . . [They] are allowed only enough knowledge to make a rational choice to protect their interests but not so much that the more fortunate among them can take advantage of their special situation. This original position is fair between nations; it nullifies the contingencies and biases of historical fate. Justice between states is determined by the principles that would be chosen in the original position so interpreted.[20]

But, of course, one wants to respond that while one *can* think of an "original position" populated by nation-state representatives, the apparent direction for reflection set by the basic idea itself of developing a conception of justice *via* the standpoint of an "original position" does not suggest the two-step construction (justice for the

3. The Subject of Justice [153]

state, justice between states) that Rawls here follows. Indeed, it may be that the direction set by that basic idea yields an interpretation of the "original position" that in fact *criticizes* the nation-state organization of the world community. In this connection I find the following remarks by Brian Barry helpful:

> Rawls does not and cannot defend the assumption that principles will be chosen in the original position by men as members of pre-existing societies rather than by men as men who may wish to form sovereign states *or may wish to set up an overriding international state.* . . . [E]ven on Rawls' own account of the way in which principles governing the relations between states would be chosen in the original position, his minimal liberal principles of non-interference and non-aggression are no more than a fraction of what would be agreed upon, if indeed they would not be superceded altogether by agreement on an effective system of collective security.[21]

(b) Another consideration that suggests that Rawlsian liberalism should treat the subject of justice as the moral community (the most plausible instantiation of which, in today's world, is the world community) is its Kantian interpretation of the idea of "equal moral persons." This is to say that insofar as Rawls aspires to a Kantian interpretation of the beings whom the justice-governed basic structure is "for," then the natural move is to suppose that that structure applies to those beings that can be members of the Kantian "kingdom of ends." And this suggests that the preferred application of the conception of justice as fairness (the conception chosen in the original position) is *not* to the basic structure of this or that nation state (or some other particular community among other communities) to which some persons belong as members, but rather to the basic structure of the moral community to which, according to Kant, all "rational beings" belong and which is structured by *the* moral laws.

And, indeed, what Rawls says often suggests this interpretation:

> It seems reasonable to suppose that the parties in the original position are equal. That is, all have the same rights in the pro-

cedure for choosing principles; each can make proposals, submit reasons for their acceptance, and so on. Obviously the purpose of these conditions is to represent *equality between human beings as moral persons*, as creatures having a conception of their good and capable of a sense of justice.[22]

[T]he principles of justice manifest in the basic structure of society men's desire to treat one another not as means only but as ends in themselves. . . . On the contract interpretation treating men as ends in themselves implies at the very least treating them in accordance with the principles to which they would consent in an original position of equality. For in this situation men have equal representation as moral persons who regard themselves as ends and the principles they accept will be rationally designed to protect the claims of their person.[23]

[W]e think of moral principles as legislation for a kingdom of ends.[24]

(c) Rawls' discussion of *natural duties* provides still further support for the thought that the subject of justice must be the basic structure of the community of "all equal moral persons," or, for short, the total membership of the moral community construed as something much more fundamental than the nation state. He writes:

Now in contrast with obligations, it is characteristic of natural duties that they apply to us without regard to our voluntary acts. Moreover, they have no necessary connection with institutions or social practices. . . . Thus we have a natural duty not to be cruel, and a duty to help another, whether or not we have committed ourselves to these actions. . . . A further feature of natural duties is that they hold between persons irrespective of their institutional relationships; *they obtain between all as equal moral persons*. In this sense *the natural duties are owed not only to definite individuals, say to those cooperating together in a particular social arrangement, but to persons generally*.[25]

3. The Subject of Justice

We should observe that Rawls recognizes a *natural duty of justice*: "From the standpoint of justice as fairness, a fundamental natural duty is the duty of justice. This duty requires us to support and to comply with just institutions that exist and apply to us. It also constrains us to further just arrangements not yet established, at least when this can be done without too much cost to ourselves."[26]

(*d*) As a final entry on this list of considerations that show, or tend to show, that the subject of justice must be the basic structure of the community of "all equal moral persons"—where "all" really means *all* and not merely "those in this national community"—let me mention Rawls' account of justice across generations. First, Rawls make a "motivational assumption" about the parties to the original position:

> The parties are thought of as representing continuing lines of claims, and being so to speak deputies for a kind of everlasting moral agent or institution.... What is essential is that each person in the original position should care about the well-being of some of those in the next generation, it being presumed that their concern is for different individuals in each case. Moreover for *anyone* in the next generation, there is someone who cares about him in the *present* generation. Thus the interests of *all* are looked after and, given the veil of ignorance, the whole strand is tied together.[27]

Then, once the motivational assumption is in place, "no one is able to formulate principles especially designed to advance his own cause. Whatever his temporal position, each is forced to choose for everyone."[28] The point again, of course, is that the kind of reasoning that Rawls puts into ensuring that justice covers coming generations is the kind of reasoning that ensures that justice covers the community of all moral persons, and not some portion of it.

Perhaps I do not need to add further items to this list of considerations suggesting that the subject of justice is the structure of the moral community (of all equal moral persons). Let me conclude this section with the following point. Someone might urge, in the face of all the above, that it would still be logically possible to say that the parties to the original position might conduct their deliberations under the view that in the real world they are members of nation states and that, accordingly, they would think of the subject of justice as the basic structure of a national community. It might be added that the parties to the original position could of course find it reasonable to talk about a larger "world community" and that the principles for this larger community (the "law of nations") might be a suitable subject for *later* deliberations. This notion—that the parties to the original position may be understood to think in terms of membership in a nation state, that is, in terms of one society among other societies—is reflected in Rawls' writings:

> [T]he parties in the original position suppose that their membership in the society is given. This presumption reflects the fact that we are born into our society and within its framework realize but one of many possible forms of our person; the question of entering another society does not arise.[29]

My response to this point is that while this limitation on the thinking of the parties to the original position may be logically possible, it does not seem required, either by the logic of the notion of the original position itself or by the logic of Rawls' use of that notion relative to the conception of justice as fairness. *Ab initio* the parties to the original position may think of themselves as (in the real world) members of nation states or members of a world community. If so, then such considerations as those listed above may enter the picture, and make it plausible for them (us) to think of themselves (ourselves) in the latter manner. When they think of themselves in the latter manner, they then choose a conception of justice that applies to the basic structure of the total community of equal moral persons. If they then, in real life, find themselves in nation states, they must, insofar as the idea of justice is a serious ideal amongst them, take steps to bring into existence *the relevant community*, namely, the moral community whose membership is "all equal moral persons"— which is to say, in today's world, a world community with a basic structure operating in line with their conception of justice.

4 / World Community and Established Liberty

Suppose, as I suggested, that the subject of justice is the basic structure of the moral community, understood, in practical terms, as the basic structure of the world community. So what? To begin a response, consider this passage from *A Theory of Justice*:

> [I]f the persons in the original position assume that their basic liberties can be effectively exercised, they will not exchange a lesser liberty for an improvement in their economic well-being, at least not once a certain level of wealth has been attained. It is only when social conditions do not allow the effective establishment of these rights that one can acknowledge their restriction. The denial of equal liberty can be accepted only if it is necessary to enhance the quality of civilization so that in due course the equal freedoms can be enjoyed by all.[30]

In addition, suppose that, in fact, the situation in the *world community* is this: (*a*) there are some areas—some "pockets of prosperity"—in which the conditions that allow the effective exercise of individual liberty are satisfied; and (*b*) there are (many) other areas in which this is not so, that is, the conditions that allow the effective exercise of the basic liberties are not there satisfied. This is a situation, I take it, in which, in Rawls' words, "the denial of equal liberty can be accepted" as "necessary to enhance the quality of civilization so that in due course the equal freedoms can be enjoyed by all." It is a situation, that is to say, in which the sacrifice of liberty "can be accepted." Of course, since we have no world community (in the sense of a global organization forming a common "basic structure" for Earth), and hence little in the way of relevant experience as background for such a question, what forms such sacrifice might take may be unclear. Still, it is not implausible to understand such sacrifice as involving, for example, (*a*) individuals setting aside certain projects of self-realization (including certain first-choices concerning occupations) in favor of service projects of different types, (*b*) perhaps radical changes in ways and styles of life and patterns of consumption, and (c) even the surrender of certain political rights so that government could be "carried on in some authoritarian form if there were good reasons for believing that this would bring a great advance in material prosperity."[31]

But now a special problem arises. If we suppose the world community contains "pockets of prosperity" in which individual liberty flourishes, we may also recognize that the conditions of affluence and the general respect for individual liberty that characterize those parts of the world community *have been honestly hard-won*. And we may wonder: is this fact a defense against the demand for anyhow a severe sacrifice of individual liberty in the affluent parts of the world community? Is it in any case *enough* of a defense to make the matter of response to destitution in the world community be as if it were not something required by morality but merely permitted by it? This is to ask: what are the claims of established liberty—especially when this liberty is thought of as itself a moral achievement, hard-won in particular cases (perhaps requiring revolution, parental sacrifice, and so forth)? Do the claims of established liberty defend our (merely) "doing what we can" for destitute people in other parts of the world community, short of coercing our choice of work and radically reducing our styles of life?

I think that there are at least two possible "arguments from established liberty" here that may seem to resist the "condition of legitimacy" that shared-fate individualism imposes on the competent individual's pursuit of self-realization. (a) In one of these the defense in question is *from* the liberty prescribed by the liberal conception of justice itself, that is, the "long-range tendency" of ideal justice that is to establish a *system of liberties* whereby the individual pursuit of self-realization can be facilitated. But, of course, an "argument from established liberty" in this form would provide no defense in the context of our question since the establishment of this system of liberties is precisely what *justifies* the *sacrifice* of liberty in circumstances in which the conditions of its effective exercise are not satisfied for all. (b) In that case we may suppose that the defense in question is *from* the *character* of the liberty that flourishes in the affluent societies as a moral achievement, hard-won through collec-

4. World Community and Established Liberty

tive effort and personal sacrifice. But in connection with this second form of argument, I think we must distinguish two cases. (i) Suppose the liberty-in-affluence were hard-won *at the expense* somehow of destitute people in other parts of the world community. If that were so, then (so I assume) the sacrifice of liberty that is called for is in fact *owed as compensation* (or, more exactly, what it produces is owed as compensation), and the claim that the sacrifice is not called for is not defended. (ii) But we can imagine the case in which the liberty-in-affluence is not won at the expense of destitute people in the world community. It is, we may suppose, "honestly" hard-won in a way that is not parasitic on the fortunes of others. What then are the claims of "established liberty" against the claims of distant destitute people in the world community?

One must be careful to speak to this question from a defensible perspective, if one is concerned to respond to it in such a way as to understand "what morality requires." The Rawlsian approach to justice generally asks that we consider important questions from the perspective of those in the original position or, in some cases, from the perspective of the worst-off representative member of the society. (How the latter perspective is to be interpreted in the present case is not clear to me. Who or what provides the perspective of the worst-off representative member of the world community? The living destitute? The parties to the original position as they imagine being the living destitute?) But my thought is that, in the present context, the answer must surely be the same from *any* of the perspectives that would seem even possibly defensible to serious reflection, regardless of the various problems associated with defining such perspectives with precision. For it seems clear that when placed beside the claims of liberty-in-affluence, the claims of destitute people have a deep urgency to them that continues to press upon one even when one indeed cherishes individual liberty. One might ask at this point, of course: is having one's individual liberty sacrificed in the effort to respond to the latter claims a "worst possible outcome," such that even to relieve destitution we must not sacrifice liberty—or anyhow not very much? I want to say that it seems obvious that the condition of those who endure that sacrifice is not *worse than* the condition of the destitute people. If that is so, then the result of these few reflections is that the policy of immediate relief, requiring (perhaps radical) sacrifice of individual liberty, may stand as morally necessary, even in the face of liberty-in-affluence that has been honestly hard-won. This is not to say that the claims of established liberty "pale in comparison" with the claims of destitute people or that the issue between them is not serious. It is to say only that the claims of established liberty provide no clear defense against the imposition of the condition of legitimacy prescribed by shared-fate individualism. As I suggested above (section 1), *if* one "starts" with shared-fate individualism and then asks whether the claims of established liberty suffice to show that one should *not* maintain it, my thought is that the latter claims do not suffice to show this.

5 / Problems and Obscurities

Although it may be plain enough (even without elaborate philosophical discussion) that the claims of established liberty do not defend against the imposition of shared-fate individualism's condition of legitimacy, there are many puzzles (problems and obscurities) in the content and apparent direction of the line of thought sketched above. Let me outline and discuss briefly some of these difficulties in the following notes.

(*a*) Someone might object immediately that the idea of a world community is problematic (to say the least), such that the line of thought I offered is at best a piece of futile speculation. After all, there *is* no world community, and there *is* no "basic structure" for a world community. In fact, our situation *is* that of nations-among-nations, and it is perhaps most aptly characterized as more a Hobbesian "state of nature" than anything else.[32]

In response, I want to say: yes, the social facts are what they are—but they can be changed. The liberal conception of justice is an interpretation of an ideal, and I have argued that those who aspire to it (as I have construed it) are committed to justice for all equal moral persons. There is nothing incoherent in the liberal conception *qua*

5. Problems and Obscurities

ideal, and nothing in the current social facts that prevents that conception from standing as an ideal for us. (We may note in passing that if justice is indeed for *all* moral persons, then in fact even my interpretation of the idea of moral community such that the world community is the most plausible instantiation of that community at this time might be, as it were, theoretically "narrow"; for my interpretation may artificially *limit* the idea of moral community to "current people," whereas that idea might plausibly include members of future generations. (Cf. 5.8.)

(*b*) A second puzzle might be expressed in this way: someone might say that my account mislocates what needs to be sacrificed. One does not have to require the sacrifice of *liberty* in response to the facts of destitution in the world community; rather, what needs sacrificing is simply *affluence*.

But my thought, in response, is that I do not see that liberty and affluence can be neatly separated in the way the objection appears to suggest. They go together in our thinking in fact, and may even be internally related. Individual liberty, or that part of it that is designated "freedom of the person," is after all a set of opportunities and rights *connected to* what "affluence" provides or makes possible in a society. The sacrifice of liberty that is of special interest in this discussion is of course that projected by constraint on choice of work and style of life, and both of these are matters whose "content" is relative to the level of life provided by the degree of affluence achieved by a society. What is called for in my line of thought *is* a sacrifice of the liberty (those opportunities and rights) whose "meaning" is given, in part, by reference to the "way of life" made possible by a given degree of affluence. Insofar as this is so, the notions of liberty and affluence are fused in a way the objection fails to recognize. (Of course, if "affluence" in the objection only means "extra cash," then of course one could sacrifice affluence without sacrificing liberty—but to do so would not be much of a response to the troubling facts about the human condition. It would not, for example, be to ameliorate those facts any more than current charitable efforts do.)

(*c*) Someone might attempt to object to the direction of my account in this way: the line of thought suggests that the claims of established liberty do not defend against the imposition of shared-fate individualism's condition of legitimacy when one has in mind the plight of current destitute people in the world community, but that does not show directly that relief for destitute people is more important than, say, certain moral challenges "internal" to any given affluent society—in our (American) case, for example, the problems of overcoming racism and sexism where these exist in our collective life.

This objection seems to me, in its use of the notion of "more important," to direct attention again to the question of the "perspective" to be used in judging what might be called the seriousness of moral causes. I mentioned above certain perspectives recommended by the Rawlsian theory. But, from either of those perspectives, or from others that occur to me, I want to say that surely being-alive-but-destitute is at least *among* the most desperate situations human beings can be in. Perhaps that is already enough for the modest purposes of this discussion (namely, to show that "established liberty" does not defend against the condition of legitimacy prescribed by shared-fate individualism). Doubtless there are other situations in the general category of "desperate situation" (for example, being alive in a society that makes no provision for your handicaps in its distribution of opportunities, or being "victimized" in a society without humane penal institutions). How such situations are to be ranked is a problem for the theory of the original position or, more generally, for the theory of "moral perspective," but not a problem that must be solved for the purposes of this discussion. That destitution is *terrible* is not challenged by any serious interpretation of the "moral point of view" that I am aware of.

(*d*) Someone, with (*c*) still in mind, might be troubled by my account in the following way. It may seem that my view tends to construe the problem of ameliorating the plight of destitute people as importantly different in kind from problems like those of overcoming racism or sexism. The former is made to seem a *needs* problem, while the latter are *rights* problems. But this, the critic may

5. Problems and Obscurities

suggest, is wrong. The destitution problem is also an issue of rights. After all, my account calls for the sacrifice of liberty, and it calls for this *for the sake of liberty*, that is, for the sake of the satisfaction of the conditions of the effective exercise of the *rights* of all people.

In response, I think it may be granted that the destitution problem is also a rights problem. We call in all these cases (destitution, racism, sexism) for satisfaction of the conditions of the effective exercise of rights. But there is nevertheless an important difference in the *ground* for the call for satisfaction of these conditions. The non-satisfaction of the conditions of the effective exercise of rights involved in the case of severe deprivation in respect of basic needs is different from the non-satisfaction of conditions involved in suffering the indignities of racism or sexism. Those suffering the latter indignities may not be severely deprived respecting basic needs—though in fact those who suffer from racism (not so much those who suffer from sexism) have often *also* been poor relative to the level of life available in affluent societies.[33] But this latter poverty, albeit hardly "desirable," is typically not the destitution I have had in mind when speaking of the plight of destitute people in the world community—though that poverty may in cases dip down to the level of destitution, even in affluent societies, for affluent societies can, and do, have within them "pockets of destitution" (see 1.4, note 11).

(*e*) Finally, someone might object that my account wins its case (so far as it does) by *definition*. For in the end, the objection might claim, my call for a sacrifice of liberty (as required by justice) follows trivially from the account of what justice is.

My thought in response to this objection is that I have tried to avoid making the line of thought go through trivially *via* a loaded definition of justice that itself contains a demand for the sacrifice of liberty in the world community. There are two "synthetic" links involved in the line of thought: namely, (*i*) the link between justice (the liberal conception of it) and the world community, such that the latter is the "society" the "basic structure" of which is the *subject* of the former; and (*ii*) the link between, as it were, justice-in-the-world-community and the moral demand for the sacrifice of liberty. In neither case have I made the connections by stipulation. Regarding (*i*), I made the connection by interpreting certain doctrines of the (Rawlsian) liberal conception, and then designating the world community as a plausible instantiation for the idea of "society" given today's world. Regarding (*ii*), I argued that the liberty-sacrifice is required, even against the presumptive claims of established liberty, that is, the claims of an honestly hard-won system of liberties that enables the pursuit of self-realization to flourish.

6 / On What to Do

Let me finish this discussion by considering the question of where the line of thought sketched above leads. Two large questions arise that are at once philosophical and practical. (*a*) Is what justice requires in the world community required of *us now*, as we pursue our lives in the framework of an affluent national community and in the *absence* of a functioning world community with a basic structure in line with justice? (*b*) In the absence of a functioning world community with an appropriate basic structure, what burden falls on nations and individuals in the present nation-state framework?

Regarding the first of these questions, I want to say at this point that we have not yet found any real reason why the answer is not "yes." What justice projects is a situation in which the conditions of the effective exercise of rights are satisfied for all. We saw that the Rawlsian theory maintains that the liberal conception of justice as fairness finds that the sacrifice of liberty for the sake of liberty is *acceptable*. My claim is that the liberal conception of justice, as a set of principles governing the basic structure of the moral community, leaves room for shared-fate individualism, as a set of policies for the lives of responsible individuals, and that it does this in such a way as to provide no objection to the imposition of the condition of legitimacy prescribed by shared-fate individualism. Insofar as all this is so, then we are left with the view that there is no reason (so far) not to suppose that the sacrifice of liberty for the sake of liberty called

6. On What to Do

for by shared-fate individualism is not merely "acceptable" but *required*. This is required of us insofar as we are "moral persons" or "responsible individuals." And we may be such individuals even as we are also Americans, or Canadians, or whatever. All this is, of course, easy to say. But what does it mean for "practice"? What is the answer to the second large question?

Perhaps courses of action such as the following are plausible: (*i*) the cultivation of our view of ourselves as equal moral persons in a "community of ends" that is larger and more fundamental than a national community; (*ii*) the cultivation of the view that the most plausible instantiation of the idea of a community of all equal moral persons at this time is the world community; (*iii*) the development of a set of institutions providing content for the basic structure of the world community (even though the immediate task for these institutions, upon their creation, will be to organize and control the "sacrifice of liberty for the sake of liberty"). These several courses of action seem buttressed by what Rawls calls our natural duty to further justice (see section 3 above), and it is convenient in any case to view the institutions of the world community—its "basic structure" —as an elaborate *means* to the relief of the destitution of so many members of our larger moral community. The natural duty to further justice together with the natural duty to help others in need or jeopardy would appear to suggest as well: (*iv*) individual "foreign aid," plus the encouragement of national-community foreign aid, plus the support of any relevant private programs of food, education, population control, technology, and so forth that speak to the plight of destitute people.[34]

All this may seem *impractical*, I suppose. It may be that the problem of world destitution is a central overwhelming challenge to persons *qua* responsible individuals who are citizens of the world community, so far as their moral agenda is dictated by the liberal conception of justice and the shared-fate conception of individual responsibility. But this challenge appears to be placed out of the reach of effective solution by the nation-state system of organization. The nation-state system does not itself prevent "foreign aid," of course. But it might be argued that that system operates so as to put national self-interest in a central position among values, and thus to make our conception of justice guide the development of our own immediate national community, and thus to force aid to "outsiders" into a secondary moral category of benevolence or charity. And, curiously, what holds this pattern in place may be, in part, the achievement of respect for individual liberty within the affluent national communities. The pressure to maintain sometimes hard-won civil, political, and personal liberties as matters of right, and not just temporary affordables, in the world's pockets of prosperity contingently organized in the terms of nation-statism is precisely what makes foreign aid risk being a kind of tokenism at best and what makes the move to a world community seem almost so out of the question to practical people as to seem silly. The prospect of a world community in which justice guides political and economic life is, at this time, not the prospect of a moral community in which liberty can flourish in a position of centrality in a mutually acknowledged system of values. It is instead the uninviting immediate prospect (uninviting to the current possessors of individual liberty) of *suspension*[35] of the very value that justice itself may teach is of greatest importance to individual self-respect.[36]

So my conclusion is gloomy. There is no obvious course of action that seems relevant and realistic.[37] The parties to the Rawlsian original position, we might imagine, would secretly hope to avoid turning out to be *either* destitute in our world of nation states at different levels of development *or* possessors of liberty in its pockets of prosperity. For in the former case one's material situation cripples one's life severely, and in the latter case one's possession of liberty is morally defective and the general correcting of the situation is effectively beyond the ken of individual effort. The remedy does not require Communist Revolution or Liberal Reform, or even the Abolition of Private Property. The major part of what is required is the conversion of nation-statism into a world community operating according to the liberal conception of justice as a long-range goal— together with the willingness of currently free, affluent people to

6. On What to Do

suspend for a time the central moral achievement of their civilization. This latter requirement, unfortunately, may be either a "practical impossibility" or simply "excessive" relative to the capacities of ordinary members of affluent societies, even if it is not so for the capacities of competent individuals who are members of the moral community.

8

ON THE IMPORTANCE

OF ONE'S LIFE

1 / The Claims of One's Own Life

Perhaps it is plain enough that there is no logical difficulty in imposing the condition of legitimacy prescribed by shared-fate individualism on the pursuit of self-realization. I have suggested that there is no moral difficulty in doing so either. There is, of course, no way that I can be comprehensive in defending the latter claim. In Chapter 7 I argued that even when "established liberty" (a system of liberties) in certain of the world's affluent societies is honest and hard-won, it is no defense against the shared-fate conception of individual responsibility. But there are many more candidate "considerations" that might be thought to show that there is a moral difficulty in the imposition of the condition of legitimacy in question. In these last remarks I address what may seem to be the most natural of these candidate considerations. I address the objection that shared-fate individualism ignores *the claims of the self*. The idea here is that the policy for individuals recommended by shared-fate individualism overwhelms my life (by directing my time, energy, and resources into service to others) and leaves the morally relevant fact that this life is *my* life out of account.

If we make use of some of the distinctions and characterizations worked out in previous chapters of this study, we may say that

2. The Proper Care of Oneself

shared-fate individualism is a perspective on the moral standing of individual lives that sponsors the following proposition:

> The greater the mismatch between the world community and the moral community, relative to how far all persons capable of membership in the moral community are positioned to self-realize, and relative to the mismatch being contingent and ameliorable (for example, political) rather than natural and irremediable (for example, a matter of incurable congenital disease), the *less* weight the value of self-realization should have, and the *greater* weight the value of service to others should have, in the serious life decisions of competent individuals.

In response to this proposition, the objection in question makes certain claims in behalf of "one's own life" that are meant to defend against any pressure to reduce the weight carried by the value of self-realization in our deliberations connected with serious life decisions. There are a number of ways in which such an objection might be developed. In the sections that follow, I offer first a small discussion of the idea of *responsibility to oneself*. I consider some of what self-responsibility might plausibly be thought to consist in, and then I ask whether "the claims of the self," in the form of certain maxims of self-responsibility, can be supported in such a way as to defend against shared-fate individualism.

2 / The Proper Care of Oneself

Surely individual responsibility extends to or "covers" oneself. "The proper care of oneself"[1] is a part of individual responsibility. And this responsibility toward oneself can be violated: "man's inhumanity towards man is only equalled by his inhumanity towards himself."[2] When we think about responsibility, perhaps we are typically occupied with our responsibilities toward others. But that does not argue that we have no responsibilities toward ourselves.

Consider these remarks by W. D. Falk:

> It could be sound advice to say to a woman in strife with herself and tied to a demanding parent, "You ought to consider yourself, and so break away now, hard as it may be on the parent." One is then saying more than simply "If you wanted to you would have the right to." One is saying, "I know you are shrinking away from it, but this is what you ought to do, and above all else." In form this is an ought through and through, and an overriding one at that, but its ground is not other-regarding. . . . One cannot love one's neighbor as oneself if one has not also learned to accept one's own wishes as a proper object of respect and care, as one's own wishes are the paradigm of all wishes. There is a profound sense in which charity begins at home. For some this acceptance of themselves is hard, and it may confront them with a personal commitment as categorical and as onerous as any.[3]

We may agree that individual responsibility extends to oneself, even though we may sometimes find ourselves rightly chastised for excessive self-attention, "materialism," or just plain selfishness. We may be aware that concern with oneself may turn into an objectionable sort of self-absorption.[4] But while such "abuses" certainly exist, it does not follow that there is no legitimate moral object in the area of concern for oneself. It only follows that the content of the policy-element of self-responsibility must be described with some care.

What *is* one's responsibility toward oneself? Alternatively put, what is the content of self-responsibility? If we can be clear about what one's self-responsibility is, perhaps we may then be better able to assess the competition between self-responsibility and other-responsibility, as it may be pressed upon us by, for example, consideration of the facts of destitution in today's world or consideration of jeopardy to our legacy to the world of the future.

Certain familiar maxims come immediately to mind as serious candidates for inclusion among the policies of self-responsibility in some form. Some of the most familiar of these are not controversial for a proponent of shared-fate individualism. For example, Falk

2. The Proper Care of Oneself

points to an injunction "to preserve [oneself] intact as a living and functioning self,"[5] and this must surely be acceptable to any serious theory of individual responsibility. Perhaps persons who do *not* maintain themselves intact—persons who "let themselves go" or who "waste" themselves—somehow *degrade* themselves or (as a Kantian might say) diminishes their nature as rational beings. It may be that the injunction to "preserve oneself intact," when it is relevant to moral theory, involves a maxim of self-respect. In the *Lectures on Ethics* Kant wrote:

> [W]e must reverence humanity in our own person, because apart from this man becomes an object of contempt, worthless in the eyes of his fellows and worthless in himself. . . . Only if our worth as human beings is intact can we perform our other duties. A man who has destroyed and cast away his personality, has no intrinsic worth, and can no longer perform any manner of duty.[6]

Similarly, self-responsibility uncontroversially requires that persons conduct themselves in such a way as to be able personally to tolerate what they do. Falk, again, speaks of the moral agent, or conscientious individual, as a person who has a "stake in the kind of self-preservation which requires that one should be able to bear before oneself the survey of one's own actions." He adds that "responsibly reason-guided and ought-abiding living exists, in the first place, for the sake of sane and ordered individual being, and not for the regulation of the social order."[7] Falk's view here is reminiscent of Hume's remarks in the Conclusion of *An Enquiry Concerning the Principles of Morals*: "Inward peace of mind, consciousness of integrity, a satisfactory review of our own conduct—these are circumstances very requisite to happiness, and will be cherished and cultivated by every honest man who feels the importance of them."[8] Essentially, preserving one's integrity involves taking oneself, others, and the relationships between oneself and others seriously. One cares about oneself, others, and these relationships in a way that involves one in being prepared to answer for what one does. And being prepared to answer for what one does involves one in being both *principled* in what one does and *accountable* for what one does. What it is to be a person of integrity, that is, to be principled in and accountable for what one does, is a large subject that goes well beyond the bounds of my discussion here. My thought is that the possession of integrity involves one's having what I will call "personal moral absolutes," and I will limit my remarks on this (again, uncontroversial) element of self-responsibility to the following note about what it is to have personal moral absolutes.

Persons who are principled and accountable in the way I have in mind are persons for whom *there are certain things one aspires never to do*. Lists of such things may differ from person to person in this world. I do not see that we can guarantee *a priori* identical lists of personal moral absolutes among real people—though the situation may be different when we abstract from our "real" selves and consider ourselves as "members of the moral community." (If this is so, it would be an important fact for moral theory.) But even among real people there is probably great overlap among lists of personal moral absolutes. Perhaps the extent of the overlap is influenced by social circumstances and culture. But that persons who are "persons of integrity" have certain things they aspire never to do may still be a conceptual point about the idea of possession of integrity.

I suspect that *our* lists (yours and mine) would contain proscriptions on torture, and even cruelty. We would aspire never to let our children be degraded. We would prohibit rudeness to people caught in the helplessness of old age. And we would disallow the across-the-board placing of one's own interests before the interests of those (perhaps few, perhaps many) we care about, or are simply responsible for, for whatever reasons. The point, again, is that persons of integrity have things they aspire never to do, and these things they aspire never to do are *not* merely things they won't do "unless" there is good reason to do them. (The absolute says "I will not torture," not "I will not torture unless I have to.") Having a list of moral absolutes is a part of being a person of integrity as opposed to being (merely) a reasonable person. It is part of what it is to be principled and accountable relative to what one does. We may get tricked sometimes. We may realize after the fact, and with a shock, that we were cruel to someone. Or we see now—and it makes us angry at ourselves—that our children were humiliated, and we did not see it coming soon enough to protect them against it. Or we were gullible, or weak, or afraid, and knowingly sacrificed or violated our moral absolute. But, apart from getting tricked or in some way failing to understand certain situations for what they are, being concerned to guard against threats to integrity and being concerned to understand, refine, and correct one's list of moral absolutes are parts of the "being principled in and accountable for what one does" that I am attempting to characterize here, that is, they are parts of the self-responsibility element in our general idea of individual responsibility.

What is it about certain courses of action that makes us put them on our list of absolute proscriptions, rather than on our list of negative presumptions that we will allow to be overridden by "considerations"? I am not very clear about this. It is not always because those courses of action lead to physical pain. It is sometimes (I think) because they involve degrading people and reducing them to "objects" or "things." To be parties to such courses of action is to diminish or threaten our own self-respect and integrity. Here is one way of expressing the point: to violate these absolutes is to do damage to, corrupt, or cancel (perhaps only temporarily, depending on the case) our membership in the moral community.

3 / Self-Realization

So far I have mentioned certain maxims that might provide content for the idea of self-responsibility, but that seem uncontroversial relative to shared-fate individualism. "Maintain oneself intact" might be one such maxim, and violating it might appear in some cases to be something we would characterize as "degrading" or "wasting" oneself. "Preserve one's integrity" might be another such maxim; I suggested that at least a part of integrity is being principled in and accountable for what one does, and I elaborated this in terms of one's possessing "personal moral absolutes." As far as I can tell, maxims such as these (doubtless there are others) are not in tension with shared-fate individualism. Let us next consider a general maxim that is plausible as a part of the "content" of the idea of self-responsibility, but that seems controversial relative to the perspective on individual responsibility that I call shared-fate individualism.

The maxim I have in mind enjoins one to *realize oneself* or *develop one's potential*. It is a familiar view that persons "owe it to themselves" to cultivate their native endowments as these exist in the form of talents, skills, capacities, and abilities. As I mentioned much earlier (2.3, note 8), Marx held that one of the cruelest features of capitalist society is that it channels its members into fixed, repetitive modes of activity, and in that way it blocks the realization of the many talents and capacities that are to be found in any individual human being. Perhaps this talent-realization extends to the cultivation of one's rationality, though we may not ordinarily emphasize this part of one's natural endowment except as it may be manifested as a special skill (for example, strategy reasoning, or the ability to manipulate symbols) in a relevant context. But despite the familiarity of the maxim of self-realization, there are a number of ways in which it is unclear and problematic.

In the first place, it seems plain that how far one succeeds at the task of developing one's potential will depend on many contingent factors—factors more or less beyond one's control—such as what one's native endowments are in fact, what one has available to one in the way of resources for their development (energy, health, imagination, time, teachers), and what one's opportunities are for actually doing the different (and often difficult) things involved in self-realizing.[9] Nature is hardly egalitarian in its allotment of resources and opportunities. Some people appear to be less gifted "natively" than others; other people, of course, seem to be extraordinarily gifted "natively." It appears that there is no uniformity of natural endowments among human beings. It is clear in any event that there is great disparity in the quantity and quality of resources and opportunities available to individuals in today's world.

I am inclined to suggest that, in these circumstances, no uniformity in levels of achievement can reasonably be expected of individuals who make the effort to follow the maxim of self-realization.

3. Self-Realization [175]

We might say that the moral community—as distinct from this or that actual political or educational system—allows differential achievement among its members. One person's self-realizationist results may not be as technically proficient or artistically significant as another person's (there may be, after all, limited initial gifts, or resource and opportunity failures) but these results may still *be*, from the moral perspective, self-realizationist results. If self-realizationist projects are open to judgments of "success," "failure," or "adequacy," those who make such judgments may have to tie them closely to understandings of circumstances in individual lives, and their judgments may have to make room for consideration of an individual's intentions, sincerity, and strength of resolve. No very precise generalizations about level of success that are fair to the differential factors of individuals' circumstances seem possible.

Further, we should note that the notion of "native endowments" that is spoken of in connection with the maxim of self-realization is of indeterminate range. When we think of "native endowments" or "potential" as something to be "realized" or "developed," we obviously do not have in mind just the individual human being's genetic heritage or physiological equipment. What *I* consider to be *my* native endowments *now* are features of mine that have already been infused (to some extent) with training, education, opportunities seized (others lost), interests pursued (others forgotten), and so forth. It is most difficult to be precise in one's inventory and estimate of one's gifts-to-be-realized. Each of us may indeed *have* some such gifts (some talents and skills, say), but each of these is itself rather a *mix* of "basic" capacities (for example, intelligence, physical dexterity, mathematical insight) and what has been done *to* and *for* these capacities by oneself, by others (for example, parents and teachers), and by certain institutions and practices (such as schools, of course, but also the economic system, class structure, and "streets" of the society one lives in).

Typically, one is somewhere in mid-stream in respect of the development of one's native endowments. A talent—for singing, say, or abstract reasoning, or some form of dancing—is something one usually views as further perfectible. It may atrophy if one does not take steps (through practice, in the first cases that come to mind) to maintain it. A skill can be lost, then regained or retrieved, then improved (and perhaps lost again). Common opinion suggests that some skills or abilities (for example, bicycle-riding), once gained, are never lost. I am not certain that this is so—though the present discussion does not require that we settle this matter.

Finally, any responsibility we have to develop our potential, in this sense of cultivating and realizing natural gifts, does not cover any or all abilities. If I am skilled at cracking my knuckles, or belching at will, or insulting my colleagues, there is surely no *moral* injunction upon me to cultivate *these* items in my stock of prowesses. It may be, then, that the familiar maxim of self-realization has buried in it some teleological premises that make it seem attractive to us. Some conception of appropriate ends, aims, goals, or targets seems necessary.[10] But when we begin to think about *appropriate ends* associated with different items in our inventory of gifts, we may note how the realization of such gifts is relative to the *ways of life* available to us. Such ways of life are structured by material circumstances, modern agriculture, recent technological innovation, ideologies about the state of natural resources, easy or difficult communications systems, efficient or inefficient bureaucracies, modes of transportation, and the like—and the ways of life thus available to some people in today's world are just not available (in today's world) to other people. We might put the point in this way: the development of one's potential is something one implements under an *interpretation* referring to aims and ways-of-life available at certain times and places but not at others—though indeed there may be rough similarities in ways-of-life available at many different "times and places." In this way "realizing oneself" is, in terms of its content, relative to differential aims grounded in changeable historical and social factors. There is no fixed content for the general maxim of self-realization—though it does not follow from this fact that it is not a legitimate part of the policy-element of self-responsibility within our general idea of individual responsibility.

The discussion above suggests that the self-realizationist maxim, as a candidate policy of self-responsibility, is not something that can

3. Self-Realization [177]

be expressed in terms of fixed content. How it is implemented or followed will be expressed in terms of an interpretation referring to differential aims and ways of life, as well as to the different initial gifts, resources, and opportunities present in individual cases.

Apart from this "openness" of the idea of self-realization, we may notice another problematic aspect of it. It seems controversial whether one is *entitled* to the native endowments the maxim enjoins one to develop, and this may render it unclear whether self-realization has a special place, or any place at all, in our idea of individual responsibility. John Rawls has claimed that one's possession of such-and-so natural gifts, like one's race or personal handicaps, is "arbitrary from a moral point of view."[11] Robert Nozick, on the other hand, disputes this, holding that persons *are* entitled (in some sense) to their natural gifts, and, in fact, to what flows from them.[12] While this issue needs much unraveling, I am inclined to comment, for the purposes of this discussion, that no one, surely, is *owed* a certain talent or gift—a talent for music, say, or quickness at mathematics, or a skill at leathercrafting. On the other hand, a person may work hard to develop the talents he or she happens to have (but not as a result of being owed them), and for this (the hard work of development) he or she might be owed something—presuming, of course, that the ends served by the development of those talents are legitimate or otherwise "valuable." (No one is owed anything for working hard to develop the ability to crack his or her knuckles, belch at will, or insult his or her colleagues.)

Suppose it is true that no one is owed his or her natural gifts. What, then, grounds the maxim of self-realization? What is it that makes us think that it is, despite the openness of the notion of self-realization, plus the intelligibilty of the question about whether we are even entitled to our native endowments, a serious candidate for being a leading part of our moral idea of individual responsibility? Is it just that we—or most of us—*want* to "self-realize"? Or is there some other, perhaps somehow deeper, reason for thinking that individually defined self-realization is a moral imperative for human beings? It does not seem quite right to say that human beings *need* to self-realize if "need" here is to refer to "basic needs," such as (survival) needs for air, shelter, food, and so forth. A person may, after all, survive as a human being without "developing his or her potential" in the sense discussed above. Is there something in or about the individual human being in virtue of which regarding its self-realization as a centrally important moral imperative makes sense? Is there some *importance to one's life* (insofar as one is capable of self-realization under some interpretation) that can be characterized philosophically and then shown to provide a ground for the maxim of self-realization?

4 / Individuality

Certain appeals to *the importance of one's life* that seem relevant to our question about the ground of the maxim of self-realization come to mind. An especially strong assertion of such importance is provided by Henry Sidgwick in *The Methods of Ethics*[13]:

> [T]he distinction between any one individual and any other is real and fundamental, and . . . consequently "I" am concerned with the quality of my existence as an individual in a sense, fundamentally important, in which I am not concerned with the existence of other individuals. . . . I do not see how it can be proved that this distinction is not to be taken as fundamental in determining the ultimate end of rational action for an individual . . . even if a man admits the self-evidence of the principle of Rational Benevolence, he may still hold that his own happiness is an end which it is irrational for him to sacrifice to any other.

Now, given the sketch of shared-fate individualism that is provided by my discussion as a whole, this striking passage from Sidgwick appears to say that it is *irrational* for one to accept the construal of the moral standing of individual lives that is recommended by shared-fate individualism. But, so it seems to me, the passage from Sidgwick does not itself provide a reason for thinking this. Indeed, how it is to be *argued* that one should regard one's own happiness as

4. Individuality

"an end which it is irrational for [one] to sacrifice to any other" is, in general, unclear to me. The sheer fact that "the distinction between any one individual and any other is real and fundamental" does not by itself yield that claim.

Some recent work of Bernard Williams picks up (not explicitly) Sidgwick's notion that "the distinction between any one individual and any other is real and fundamental" and offers a philosophical picture of what that distinction amounts to and of how it is "real and fundamental." Let me offer a short account of what Williams' view is in an effort to test whether its characterization of the importance of one's life provides a ground for the maxim of self-realization, and hence a defense against shared-fate individualism.

It is necessary first to understand that the view of the importance of one's life that Williams offers is developed against the backdrop of a claim to the effect that the "conception of the individual" associated with certain major traditions of moral theory—utilitarianism and Kantianism—is inadequate. The utilitarian account is worse than the Kantian, according to Williams, but both are "misrepresentations" of what persons are, for both leave out the *substance* of life (the meaning of life) for individuals by systematically ignoring "the importance of individual character and personal relations in moral experience."[14] The utilitarian view is worse in the sense that the ignoring of the substance of life in its case involves "abstraction not merely from the identity of agents, but . . . from their separateness,"[15] whereas the Kantian view "emphasizes something like the separateness of agents"—"*who* acts in a given situation makes a difference, and in particular I have a particular responsibility for *my* actions"[16] —while it nevertheless abstracts from the identity of agents. It is this abstracting from the identity of agents that makes the conceptions of the individual in these received traditions faulty. It is a serious question, for Williams, whether even "the honourable instincts of Kantianism to defend the individuality of individuals against the agglomerative indifference of Utilitarianism can in fact be effective granted the impoverished and abstract character of persons as moral agents which the Kantian view seems to impose."[17]

But my aim here is not to question the charge that Williams levels at the received traditions in moral theory. It is rather to understand his own account of the "individuality of individuals," for it is this account that suggests a reading for the idea of the importance of life that might ground the maxim of self-realization discussed above.

Briefly, Williams' view is that one's "individuality" or the "substance" of one's life—and hence the *importance* of one's life—is provided by *character*, and character is viewed as *constituted* by one's "pattern of interests, desires, and projects" (including commitments, attachments to other persons, and the like). One way of expressing Williams' point is to say that he "particularizes" individual identity so that, in effect, "I" *am* (for the purposes of the understanding of morality) my character. And among the elements of one's character are to be found some *categorical desires* that "propel one on" and that "constitute the conditions of there being" a future for one at all, plus "a *ground* project or set of projects which are closely related to [one's] existence and which to a significant degree give a meaning to [one's] life."[18]

There is much in Williams' vocabulary here that would repay careful sorting out. But for my purposes now only the direction of the main point is needed. If, for the purposes of moral theory, I *am* my character, and my character *is* a certain pattern of interests, desires, projects, commitments, and attachments, then the latter pattern of elements gives my life "substance"—my life has, in virtue of them, *importance*—and the development, cultivation, maintenance, realization, and, in general, flourishing of those elements is, as it were, *my* essential business. So, as Williams puts it, "the correct perspective on one's life is *from now*"[19] in contrast to some "external view on one's life" that loses one's "individuality" in its abstraction. Indeed, without the importance-constituting elements of character "there will not be enough substance or conviction in a man's life to compel his allegiance to life itself."[20] On this account, then, the "abstracting from identity" that occurs in even the separate-individual-respecting Kantian view is no minor "technical error"; it in fact represents a loss to the individual of the meaning of life, or, more exactly, it portrays the individual in such a way as to leave out of account the "individuality" that gives life meaning.

5 / Is One's Life Important?

My response to the account of the importance of one's life I have drawn from Williams' writings is in three parts. The first of these may be evident from my earlier discussion of Sandel's work (6.4 and 6.5), so I will not elaborate it at any length. It will be enough to say that I do not agree that moral theory profits from Williams' identifying the *individual* with *character* any more than it does from Sandel's identifying the *self* with *community*. It seems to me that "I" can distance myself from the elements of my character (my desires, projects, interests, commitments, attachments) so as to evaluate (and perhaps criticize and ultimately change) them, just as much as "the self" can distance itself from its communitarian features so as to evaluate (and perhaps criticize and then change) them. I think the quasi-reduction of the person to his or her character that Williams suggests is in fact distinctly unhelpful to moral theory insofar as it makes a gratuitous metaphysical mystery of something that certainly occurs, albeit with practical difficulty and psychological stress in some cases, namely, alterations or changes in one's character made *via* one's own agency, that is, self-willed change in the "substance" of one's life.

The second part of my response is to note what I take to be an objectionable implication of Williams' view. In fact, in the enthusiasm of the critique of the "abstraction from identity" characteristic of the Kantian (and utilitarian) view Williams is carried to the claims, reported above, that "the correct perspective on one's life is *from now*" and that the Kantian conception of the individual is a "misrepresentation." Now, if "correct" here means *correct* (and not merely "often to be preferred"), and "misrepresentation" means *mistaken* representation, then Williams' view has the effect, not of emphasizing or playing up the importance of the "perspective from now" over the Kantian "impartial point of view," but of *eliminating* the latter. That is to say, if Williams is correct about how the individual is to be understood, it appears that the classical notion of "impartiality" or "disinterestedness," variously interpreted but regularly counted as a feature of "the moral point of view" in the literature of ethics, is either *not possible* for us or *without relevance* to our moral lives. We are left not with, say, "conflicts" between possible "points of view" on our lives, each of which has a certain plausibility, but rather with *only* (or perhaps "substantially" only) the standpoint that Williams calls the "perspective from now." But this is surely to carry a critical point too far. It seems plain enough that we *are*, in fact, capable of perspectives other than the "perspective from now," and if this is so then what it is in the fact that we are capable of the "perspective from now" that makes these other perspectives lack relevance for our moral lives is not yet clear. Thomas Nagel writes:

> Conflicts between personal and impersonal claims are ubiquitous. They cannot, in my view, be resolved by subsuming either of these points of view under the other, or both under a third. Nor can we simply abandon any of them. There is no reason why we should. The capacity to view the world simultaneously from the point of view of one's life extended through time, from the point of view of everyone at once, and finally from the detached viewpoint often described as the view *sub specie aeternitatis* is one of the marks of humanity. This complex capacity is an obstacle to simplification.[21]

Against the background of this point about the plurality of perspectives available to us, Williams' view itself, as it stands, seems a kind of simplification. Even if the "perspective from now" is not only important to us but ineliminable for us, it would not follow that, say, the perspective *sub specie aeternitatis* is impossible, irrelevant, or even ineffective regarding our moral thinking.[22]

The third part of my response to Williams' view is that, even if one accepts Williams' characterization of the importance of one's life, nothing is thereby shown or settled regarding the *content* of one's character. Insofar as Williams wishes to respond to the conceptions of the individual associated with utilitarian and Kantian moral theory by developing a view involving a particularized conception of the individual that recognizes the individuality of character, the direction of such a line of thought already raises the question: when

5. Is One's Life Important?

is one's character (that pattern of desires, interests, commitments, projects—perhaps especially ground projects) *acceptable*? Given my interest in the credentials of shared-fate individualism, I am inclined to speculate that Williams' view—for all its playing up of the correctness of the "perspective on one's life . . . *from now*," and for all its playing down, and perhaps even elimination, of the "external" or "impartial" perspective—*allows* for shared-fate individualism *in the form of* an "element of character." Indeed, Williams seems to make this allowance in the process of making a last rejection of the impartial perspective in this final passage from the essay "Persons, Character, and Morality": "Life has to have substance if anything is to have sense, *including adherence to the impartial system*; but if it has substance, then it cannot grant supreme importance to the impartial system, and that system's hold on it will be, at the limit, insecure."[23]

On this account, then, Williams' view rejects shared-fate individualism in a form whereby it is, or is logically associated with, the impartial perspective construed as in competition with the "perspective from now" as a perspective for one's life; but it does *not* reject shared-fate individualism in a form whereby it is an "element" (for example, a policy covering projects accompanied by appropriate attitudes and commitments) *in* one's character. However, if this is accurate as an observation about how Williams' view works,[24] it should be observed further that Williams himself does not argue for shared-fate individualism as a to-be-recommended element of character for, say, the competent individual in today's world. In this situation, given an interpretation of Williams' view that allows a place to shared-fate individualism as a policy-element of character, but does not find a positive argument for shared-fate individualism as such a policy-element, I am inclined to conclude that Williams' characterization of the importance of one's life does *not* provide a reason for saying that shared-fate individualism is not what morality requires of competent individuals in today's world. In fact, shared-fate individualism need not reject, or even conflict with, Williams' "perspective from now"; rather, it may *order* the elements of character emphasized by that latter perspective in such a way that a "condition of legitimacy" is placed upon the pursuit of self-realization. This ordering of elements is allowed by the account of individuality-as-character that Williams offers, though that account does not itself call for that particular ordering of elements. There is nothing, on this interpretation of Williams' view, that renders the "importance of one's life" a defense against shared-fate individualism.

6 / Reconciliation and the Human Condition

The burden of the discussion above (sections 4 and 5) and earlier (7.2, 7.3, and 7.4) has been to argue that certain "considerations"—including those of "established liberty" and "the importance of one's life"—do not show that shared-fate individualism is not what is required by morality in today's world. I believe that a similar response could be made to other considerations that might be thought to "defend against" shared-fate individualism, though I will not carry a critical project of that sort forward here.[25] Instead I wish to finish by exploring briefly some other features of shared-fate individualism. Earlier (2.6 and 7.1) I indicated that I do not think that certain standard forms of independent justificatory argument are available for shared-fate individualism. But, still, there are some words to be said that have a place on the "positive" (rather than "defensive") side of the case for the shared-fate conception of individual responsibility.

Suppose we consider again the idea of one's individuality—the make-up of character in one's own case—containing or including what Williams described as "adherence to the impartial system." This is to say (in the context of this discussion) that, if such an idea applies to me, my "perspective from now" on my life gives a central place to shared-fate individualism and the facts about the human condition that seem naturally to prompt it. It is important to emphasize that this is not the situation in which I "give up" the "perspective from now" on my life in favor of an "external," "impartial," or "impersonal" perspective. Rather, this is the situation in which (as Nagel suggests about Williams' view):

6. Reconciliation and the Human Condition

since an agent lives his life from where he is, even if he manages to achieve an impersonal view of his situation, whatever insights result from this detachment need to be made a part of a personal view before they can influence decision and action. The pursuit of what seems impersonally best may be an important aspect of individual life, but its place in that life must be determined from a personal standpoint, because life is always the life of a particular person, and cannot be lived *sub specie aeternitatis*.[26]

The question then arises: what does or could influence the "place" in my life of what Nagel here calls "the pursuit of what seems impersonally best"? (We may loosely identify, for the purposes of this discussion, Nagel's notion of "what seems impersonally best" with my conception of "shared-fate individualism.") What is it that does or could bring it about that the pursuit of what seems impersonally best is an "important aspect of individual life"—indeed, so important as to make one attempt to render one's life in compliance with the condition of legitimacy that is part of shared-fate individualism?

Considerations of two different kinds come to mind. But none of them is of the order of an "independent argument" for shared-fate individualism; such considerations are not *justificatory* of anything in any usual sense. In a broad way they are moral-psychological in character, which means that they have to do with the emotional and motivational side of our nature as moral agents. But whatever may be the apt classification of them, they certainly bear on the concern for a "conception of the individual" appropriate to moral theory that marks Bernard Williams' work. More exactly, they bear on one's conception of oneself insofar as one is prepared to make room in that conception for the shared-fate conviction that my discussion as a whole has been about.

The first consideration is that the very recognition of ourselves as "in life together" with other human beings may tend in fact (not as a matter of logical or conceptual necessity) to carry with it the development of a certain sensitivity to the fate of others. It is (perhaps) this fact that lies at the base of the doctrine of natural sympathy in classical utilitarianism and that enables utilitarianism to have its own distinctive (and optimistic) account of the possibility of "moral progress" for humankind.[27] The following passage from Thomas Nagel's lectures "The Limits of Objectivity"[28] suggests the point I have in mind:

> I suspect that if we try to develop a system of reasons which harmonizes personal and impersonal claims, then even if it is acknowledged that each of us must live in part from his own point of view, there will be a tendency for the personal components to be altered. As the claims of objectivity are recognized, they may come to form a larger and larger part of each individual's conception of himself, and will influence the range of personal aims and ambitions, and the idea of his particular relations to others. I do not think it is utopian to look forward to the gradual development of a greater universality of moral respect, an internalization of moral objectivity analogous to the gradual internalization of scientific progress that seems to be a feature of modern culture.

The second consideration begins from what might be called "the problem of living with oneself" once one recognizes the crude facts of destitution and gross inequality in life prospects in the human condition in today's world. As noted above (8.2), Hume thought that a "requisite to happiness" is one's ability to make "a satisfactory review of one's conduct," and W. D. Falk reflects this point when he speaks of one's interest in a form of life that "requires that one should be able to bear before oneself the survey of one's own actions." Perhaps the distinctive, and, indeed, most familiar, response to the "review" or "survey" that finds in one's life an indifference to the fate of others is the feeling of *having cheated*. Perhaps very quickly one moves from this feeling to feelings of anger or indignation at finding oneself "stuck" in a human condition as cosmically unfair as ours is. (See 1.6.) But in any case my point here is not one about a label for one's feelings when one's review of one's life reveals indifference to others. It is enough, for present purposes, that these

6. Reconciliation and the Human Condition [187]

feelings are troubled and disturbing ones. The recognition of one's indifference to others is not "borne before oneself" easily. The point I wish to suggest as I conclude my discussion is that the adoption of shared-fate individualism affords a mode of *reconciliation* with the human condition in today's world that other general conceptions of individual responsibility may not. To understand one's life, morally, as subject to the condition of legitimacy of shared-fate individualism, and thus to place service before self-realization in relevant life decisions, is, so I suggest, to make one's peace with a human condition that is *given* to one as something that is *not* what it ought to be but that *can* be ameliorated. As a matter of personal policy for the governance of the human resources that constitute one's life, the adoption of shared-fate individualism makes the moral pain generated by the recognition of the facts of the human condition in today's world endurable. It does not *eliminate* that pain, of course; but it makes that pain bearable in the sense that goes with *doing what one can* about a *bad* situation that *can* be bettered, rather than avoiding that situation, or ignoring it, or pretending not to notice it.

In *A Theory of Justice* Rawls speaks of the power of the conception of justice as fairness that he develops: "should it be truly effective and publicly recognized as such, [it] seems more likely than its rivals to transform our perspective on the social world and to reconcile us to the dispositions of the natural order and the conditions of human life."[29] Rawls' conception of justice, of course, is meant to apply to the basic structure of society. My thought is that, apart from the importance of the reconciliation afforded by the conception of justice for the basic structure of a "national community" of the sort Rawls has in mind,[30] individuals (*as* individuals, not as citizens of this or that national community) stand in need of reconciliation with the human condition as it is in today's world. Shared-fate individualism, as a conception of responsibility for individuals (construed as members of the moral community, apart from their membership in particular national communities), responds to that need for reconciliation. At a minimum, if one attempts to satisfy the strenuous condition of legitimacy involved in shared-fate individualism — a condition made strenuous by the contingent facts of the human condition in today's world—then one's survey of one's life need not find that one has ignored the fate of those who are one's equals in the moral community of humankind. One conducts one's life with the sense that one has recognized the human lot for what it is, and then, since the situation thus acknowledged *is* ameliorable, one makes the effort to be of help to one's fellow human beings. One's making such an effort is not an undertaking whose sense depends in any calculative way upon one's chances for success being great or small. In the context of many of our long-term serious life decisions, our policy resolutions must typically be made without much in the way of "data" about how our efforts will fare. In such cases one resolves to do what one can (which may turn out to be a great deal[31]) about a bad situation that is ameliorable. *When* we do what we can to ameliorate the hard facts of the human condition, rather than (in one way or other) turn away from those facts, we are to that extent better able, morally, to live with ourselves. We can then tolerate the review or survey of our lives. In that way shared-fate individualism helps us reconcile ourselves to the human condition in our time.[32] It may be that the circumstances that now call for projects of service from responsible competent individuals will give way over time, and then, in improved circumstances, projects of self-realization may flourish among individuals in the human community. But that is to speak of a prospective "human condition"—one that is different from the human condition in our time.

7 / On One's Own Importance

Nothing I have said in defense or support of shared-fate individualism suggests either that one should not understand the importance of one's life in the manner of the conception of individuality discussed briefly above (8.4) or that one's own individuality thus understood[33] is not important. My view is that the human condition in our time is deeply flawed. I doubt that it takes special concepts or complicated theories to arrive at this view. The form of moral life we already share, so I believe, finds the human condition in our time

7. On One's Own Importance [189]

to be painfully different from what it ought to be.[34] The fact that we are creatures of the form of moral life we have, with its general interpretation of (all) persons as equal members of the moral community, makes attention to the destitution and gross inequality in the human condition quickly become unbearable. But these facts of the human condition are not only painful to contemplate; they are also contingent in logical character; the human condition as we know it *can* be ameliorated. That is, it can, through human effort, be "changed for the better," which is to say that it can be brought more nearly in line with our conception of what the situation in the moral community ought to be. It is when we recognize the cruelties of the human condition for the contingent facts they are, and we also take the prospect of amelioration seriously, that shared-fate individualism is seen to be a moral orientation to the human condition that in its own way *acknowledges* the importance of the life of the individual. It says, in effect, that each and every life is important—*so* important, in fact, that in the circumstances of today's world "putting oneself first" as a matter of personal policy *would* be to deny the importance of many—perhaps a great many—individual lives. (Cf. 2.5.)

Again, the central idea in shared-fate individualism is that morality requires of competent individuals in circumstances like those that characterize today's world that they place the value of service to others over the value of self-realization in deliberations in relevant serious life decisions. Doubtless some will find this idea to be objectionably overwhelming in its implications. Since the cruelties in the human condition as we know it cannot in fact be ameliorated *easily* or *soon*, this idea projects a picture in which "we" (competent individuals) are called upon to make a *great* sacrifice. And the notion that the burden of making that great sacrifice falls on "us" (competent individuals) may seem entirely arbitrary[35]—the "luck of the draw" in some silly cosmic lottery. One may then be inclined to dismiss shared-fate individualism as impossibly extreme—despite the fact that the human condition as we know it *is* both cruel and ameliorable.

But even if one is impatient with the central idea in shared-fate

8. On the Importance of One's Life

individualism in the way I just described, what follows for the question of personal policy for individual lives is not clear. It does *not* follow, so far as I can see, that one may after all legitimately "put oneself first" in the relevant serious life decisions. Of course, if the human condition is interpreted as something that *must* be constituted in the way we find it to be, then competent individuals might somehow be relieved of the pressure to put service to others before self-realization. "Putting oneself first" might then make sense as a policy reflecting resignation, and its intelligibility would rest on (what we call) the cruelties of the human condition being logically or metaphysically necessary such that "there is nothing one can do" about them. That is, in this case the facts we call "cruel" are not, after all, ameliorable. But *our* human condition (so I believe) is not that one—or, more carefully put, that human condition (the one whose cruelties are "necessary") is not the one I have "assumed" in this discussion. And, given a flawed human condition that is ameliorable, I do not see that the idea of putting-oneself-first can gain a foothold in a conception of individual responsibility that draws directly upon the form of moral life we share. Some observers might point out that individuals, or many of them, conduct their lives in such a way that the idea of putting-oneself-first "fits" both what they actually do and what their attitudes are toward their own lives. But the truth of any such observation about many people's actions and attitudes does not itself settle anything insofar as we are attempting to ascertain "what morality requires" of competent individuals in today's world.

A more moderate form of impatience with the central idea in shared-fate individualism might ensue in what I earlier called "liberal individualism" (2.5–2.7), which, in the present context, is the recommendation that in relevant serious life decisions one may "put oneself first" so long as one then implements one's decisions in such a way that one's courses of action are at least of some service to others. This recommendation might be thought of as following upon a reaction to shared-fate individualism not as "impossibly extreme" but rather as "unreasonably extreme." It finds shared-fate individualism to be not batty but merely "excessive" in its call for sacrifice. It attempts to accommodate the human condition as shared-fate individualism views it, but also to make room for, as it were, the moral legitimacy of the self-realizationist aspirations of competent individuals who happen to be in fortunate circumstances.

My worry about liberal individualism (see 2.6) is that it represents not so much "what morality requires," given the human condition in today's world, as a *compromise* with "what morality requires." The best practical antidote for the thought that the ordering of values involved in shared-fate individualism (service before self-realization) yields demands that are excessive continues to be further attention to the cruel contingent facts of the human condition. It is not puzzling to suppose that the form of moral life we have may, in difficult circumstances, make demands upon persons that would be excessive in circumstances that are not difficult. Indeed, what *would* be puzzling is our having a form of moral life that does *not* shift and adjust its requirements (and permissions) according to differences in the circumstances of those who share in it. Once one genuinely attends to the cruel facts about the human condition in our time, the liberal-individualist response cannot but seem (I believe) to be a moral shortfall.[36] I do not myself see the implausibility in the general idea that there may be certain situations in which *heavy sacrifice* on the part of relevantly able individuals is not *heroic* but simply *required*.[37] It is this general idea that shared-fate individualism finds applicable to the human condition in our time. It may be unfortunate that the circumstances in the human community today are such that this general idea is applicable. But it is no aid to clarity about individual responsibility to ignore those circumstances, or be indifferent to them, or pretend that they are other than what they are. Shared-fate individualism avoids all these obstacles to clarity.

8 / Feasibility and Reasonableness

John Rawls writes:

> [T]he feasibility of moral conceptions is settled largely by psychological and social theory, and by the theory of the corresponding well-ordered societies. The reasonableness of these

conceptions, given that they are feasible, is then settled by their content: that is, by the kind of society their principles direct us to strive for, and by the kind of person they encourage us to be.[38]

These two factors—feasibility and reasonableness—seem to me quite relevant to the assessment of the moral conception I call "shared-fate individualism." I view my discussion above as belonging to the theory of individual responsibility, though there are obviously many points in it to which the theory of the "well-ordered society" is relevant. The discussion contained little about feasibility insofar as that notion takes us into "psychological and social theory." I suppose some might see shared-fate individualism as a view that "smothers the self" or is "too much for individuals to bear"; others might see it as a sort of "bleeding heart-ism" whose appeal is chiefly to sentiment; in either case it might be considered to be less than "psychologically healthy." Now, I cannot here enter into a discussion of the notion of psychological health. Perhaps it is enough to acknowledge that the social and psychological aspects of the feasibility of shared-fate individualism are legitimate subjects for inquiry, but also to note again my thought that as a moral conception shared-fate individualism affords the possibility of a *reconciliation* to the human condition in our time that might itself be a contribution to, rather than a disruption of, the psychological health of individuals. In any case, shared-fate individualism urges one to order the values of service and self-realization in a certain way in the context of relevant serious life decisions, and it does this with the facts of the human condition in mind and under the "premise" that *all* human beings are equal members of the human community. There is nothing *personal* in such a view that asks one either to think of oneself as "worthless" as over against others or as a "controller" of the lives of others. These latter notions seem to me to pose threats of familiar sorts to psychological health, but they do not, so far as I can see, have any special association with shared-fate individualism.

Is shared-fate individualism "reasonable" in respect of "the kind of society" it directs us to strive for and "the kind of person" it

8. Feasibility and Reasonableness

encourages us to be? I think so. It is not a strange, new, technical, complicated, or artificial view. It draws directly upon major elements in the form of moral life we share. It directs us to strive (hard) for that form of society—the moral community—in which all persons are positioned to cultivate their fortunate natural gifts for their own sake. And it encourages us to be the kind of person who regards each and every individual life as *so* important as to require, in relevant circumstances, that we contribute (perhaps greatly) to the effort to bring about a "human condition" in which each and every individual life can flourish. I have expressed my reservations about the availability of an independent or "ultimate" justification for the shared-fate conception of individual responsibility. But—many (if not all) things considered—it nevertheless seems to be reasonable.

NOTES

Preface

1. The terms "basic structure" and "well-ordered" are from John Rawls, *A Theory of Justice* (Cambridge, Mass.: Belknap Press of Harvard University Press, 1971).
2. Rawls appears to hold that the choice of the latter conception is posterior to the choice of the former, though he views both choices as resulting from deliberations in the "original position." See *A Theory of Justice*, pp. 334, 339–40. I do not want to say that a conception of justice for the basic structure of society is *irrelevant* to a conception of responsibility for individuals. But I am especially concerned, in this discussion, with individual responsibility *when* no general basic structure is operating (though in principle one could be operating) to speak to faults in the community of the sort I mentioned. That is the situation in the human community in our time.

1. Challenges to Individual Responsibility

1. "Socrates: . . . and on what subject should even a man of slight intelligence be more serious?—namely, what kind of life one should live" (Plato, *Gorgias*, 500c).
2. The metaphor of shared fate is a guiding theme of John Rawls' development of the conception of justice as fairness for the basic structure of society in *A Theory of Justice* (Cambridge, Mass.: Belknap Press of Harvard University Press, 1971).
3. I do not suggest that the facts I now list are somehow "new" or "recent." And, obviously, my list is not exhaustive of the facts about the human condition in today's world that are troubling.
4. From an Associated Press report in the Cleveland *Plain Dealer*, Dec. 15, 1978, p. 6-C.
5. In this paragraph I follow John Rawls' discussion of "primary goods," and I link the notion of destitution to the lack of what Rawls calls "natural" primary goods. Cf. *A Theory of Justice*, p. 62.

6. Amartya Sen writes in *Poverty and Famines* (Oxford: Clarendon Press, 1981) that "the approach of relative deprivation . . . cannot really be the only basis for the concept of poverty. A famine, for example, will be readily accepted as a case of acute poverty no matter what the relative pattern within the society happens to be. Indeed, there is an irreducible core of *absolute* deprivation in our idea of poverty, which translates reports of starvation, malnutrition and visible hardship into a diagnosis of poverty without having to ascertain first the relative picture. Thus the approach of relative deprivation supplements rather than supplants the analysis of poverty in terms of absolute dispossession" (p. 17). Cf. Peter Singer, *Practical Ethics* (Cambridge, Eng.: Cambridge University Press, 1979), ch. 8 ("Rich and Poor"), pp. 158-59.

7. See Nick Eberstadt, "Myths of the Food Crisis," *New York Review of Books* 23 (Feb. 19, 1976): "With all the talk about starvation, it is seldom if ever mentioned how extremely difficult it is to die from it. . . . Conditions must be fantastically adverse for people to succumb to death from hunger. . . . To say that one dies from starvation is to say that the body wards off tuberculosis, diptheria, small pox, dysentery, and whatever else while its defenses progressively break down; it is a very unlikely situation." Eberstadt adds that "when someone is in danger of starving to death, he or she is facing conditions none of us in the rich world can understand or even imagine" (p. 34).

8. William Aiken and Hugh La Follette, eds., *World Hunger and Moral Obligation* (Englewood Cliffs, N.J.: Prentice-Hall, 1977), "Introduction," p. 1. Eberstadt, "Myths of the Food Crisis," sets the population of those so malnourished as to face death by starvation at about seventy million people.

Jean Mayer—a nutritionist and Vice Chairman of the President's Commission on World Hunger—provides the following characterization of death from starvation: "The first and most obvious effect of starvation is the wasting of the body's fat deposits. The stomach and intestines, heart and lungs are affected next. The liver shrinks drastically. The lining of the intestines becomes thin and smooth, losing some of its capacity to absorb nutrients, and diarrhea results. Starvation is a self-accelerating process, especially in children: because of intestinal damage, the food that is available is poorly absorbed, and undernutrition increases correspondingly. The damaged stomach lining stops secreting hydrochloric acid, which is necessary for digestion. Blood pressure and pulse rate drop. Early effects of starvation are cessation of menstruation in women and impotence and loss of libido in men. (In effect, the birth rate drops to zero.) Hair grows dull

Notes to Chapter 1 [197]

and bristling, and in children abnormal hair grows on the forearms and back. The skin acquires the consistency of paper and shows irreversible dusty brown splotches that will be the permanent marks of starvation—if the victim survives. The diseases that accompany famine—typhoid, cholera, small-pox, tuberculosis, malaria—are rampant. The weakened body is open to any infection. The psychological state deteriorates rapidly; the individual becomes listless and apathetic, but self-centered and mentally restless—and obsessed with food. Murder is not uncommon. Even cannibalism may be seen. As calorie requirements decline with the loss of weight, drop in blood pressure and pulse rate and slowing of activity, a perilous physical equilibrium may be created that can endure for several weeks or even months. At the end, there is constant diarrhea. Death may come from cardiovascular collapse or from disease and infection. Death from starvation occurs first and overwhelmingly in small children, then in older children and the elderly. (In a famine, anyone over 45 is "old.") Pregnant women not infrequently abort; lactating mothers always stop producing milk and the babies die. Adolescents are more likely to survive, although they are highly susceptible to tuberculosis. Adult men are least affected. Physiologically, young men are the most resistant to starvation, and armed men rarely starve—particularly since they can always justify requisitioning any remaining food by the nobility of their cause" ("Ban Starvation, a Military Weapon Against Children," Cleveland *Plain Dealer*, November 14, 1978, p. 5-B).

9. An informative and thorough study of the legal system of South Africa is John Dugard's *Human Rights and the South African Legal Order* (Princeton, N.J.: Princeton University Press, 1978).

10. Barrington Moore, Jr. has remarked: "Poverty is after all the starting line from which humanity has departed. If we define poverty very roughly as an insufficient and irregular supply of food, combined with shelter inadequate for protection against severe physical discomfort, the starting line is barely two centuries behind us for the bulk of the population in even the most economically advanced countries" (*Injustice: The Social Bases of Obedience and Revolt* [White Plains, N.Y.: Sharpe, 1978], p. 467).

11. Even where the welfare state has been relatively successful at the elimination of the extreme deprivation I have referred to, other "forms of destitution" may remain or arise. In *On Britain* (London: British Broadcasting Corp., 1982) Rolf Dahrendorf writes: "Today's poor are positively prosperous by comparison to the poor of 1945, let alone those of 1930, or indeed of 1913. But what has taken place is something different and much

more worrying: the emergence of what Americans call an 'underclass'. . . . Members of the underclass . . . have got used to scrounging, to petty theft and sometimes not so petty robbery, to hanging about in fleeting groups and gangs. . . . [T]hey document the inability of 'society', that is, of the rest of us, to find a place for some. . . . The underclass documents where a society draws the boundary between in and out. The fact that large numbers are, as it were, 'rotting away' below this line, is bound to leave traces. . . . In the United States it is estimated that the underclass comprises between five and fifteen per cent of the population. Even if one assumes the lower figure for Britain, it is a significant element of deprivation and rejection" (p. 53).

12. Norman E. Bowie and Robert L. Simon, *The Individual and the Political Order* (Englewood Cliffs, N.J.: Prentice-Hall, 1977), p. 211.

13. David Braybrooke argues, in effect, that the inflation of wants into needs that occurs in affluent societies is a threat to individual liberty ("Let Needs Diminish That Preferences May Prosper," in Nicholas Rescher, ed., *Studies in Moral Philosophy* (American Philosophical Quarterly Monograph no. 1; Oxford: Blackwell, 1968).

14. Cf. Rawls' references to the position of the "worst-off representative individual" in *A Theory of Justice*, pp. 64–65. Perhaps it is not possible to avoid a certain arbitrariness in the definitions of "representative individuals." Cf. *ibid.*, p. 98.

15. Cf. Rawls' use of the notion of "average citizen" in *ibid.*, p. 98.

16. "Men are not devils dominated by a wish to exterminate each other. . . . But if men are not devils, neither are they angels; and the fact that they are a mean between these two extremes is something which makes a system of mutual forbearances both necessary and possible" (H. L. A. Hart, *The Concept of Law* [Oxford: Clarendon Press, 1961], pp. 191–92). For a classical utilitarian discussion of the natural sentiments of self-love and sympathy for others, see John Stuart Mill's *Utilitarianism* (1863).

17. A most helpful discussion of Rawls' treatment of such questions is H. L. A. Hart's "Rawls on Liberty and Its Priority," *University of Chicago Law Review* 40 (Spring, 1973), reprinted in Norman Daniels, ed., *Reading Rawls* (New York: Basic Books, 1975). See, too, Brian Barry, *The Liberal Theory of Justice* (Oxford: Clarendon Press, 1973), esp. ch. 7, and Robert Paul Wolff, *Understanding Rawls* (Princeton, N.J.: Princeton University Press, 1977), ch. 9.

18. Rawls, *A Theory of Justice*, p. 61.

Notes to Chapter 1 [199]

19. Cf. Thomas Nagel, "Equal Treatment and Compensatory Discrimination," *Philosophy and Public Affairs* 2 (Summer, 1973), reprinted in Marshall Cohen, Thomas Nagel, and Thomas Scanlon, eds., *Equality and Preferential Treatment* (Princeton, N.J.: Princeton University Press, 1977) and also, as "The Policy of Preference," in Nagel's *Mortal Questions* (Cambridge, Eng.: Cambridge University Press, 1979).

20. I say "relatively free" here to acknowledge that even in societies with considerable individual liberty, there can be, as many theorists have argued, liberty-diminishing and liberty-cheapening economic and political factors that "there is no doubt" have "a distorting effect on the goals and purposes" of persons (Peter Singer, "Famine, Affluence, and Morality," in Aiken and La Follette, eds., *World Hunger and Moral Obligation*, p. 32).

21. John Stuart Mill's *On Liberty* (1859) is the classic defense of the view that such paternalistic practices should not be legal ones.

22. Cf. John Rawls, "The Basic Liberties and Their Priority," in Sterling M. McMurrin, ed., *The Tanner Lectures on Human Value*, vol. 3 (Salt Lake City: University of Utah Press, and Cambridge, Eng.: Cambridge University Press, 1982).

23. "[T]he United States has provided more assistance than any other nation—$7.1 billion last year [1980]. . . . But increasingly the money is targeted to support security and political interests rather than to alleviate economic hardships . . . and it is not the poorest nations that receive the bulk of the aid." In fact, "U.S. aid has been declining in recent years as a percentage of the nation's wealth. . . . Congressional Budget Office figures show that by 1978, the share had declined to 0.23% of GNP and it has remained there since." "Only Finland, Italy and Switzerland among the 17 industrial democracies gave less, and Japan's share was equal to that of the United States. Norway and Sweden were at the top with a 0.90% share" (Associated Press report, Cleveland *Plain Dealer*, Oct. 23, 1981, p. 11-A).

24. Joseph M. Moran, Michael D. Morgan, and James H. Wiersma, *An Introduction to Environmental Sciences* (Boston: Little, Brown, 1973), pp. 360–61. The data given are said to be "from Dr. Henry Leiper," but no further information is provided in the reference.

25. Eberstadt, "Myths of the Food Crisis," p. 32.

26. *Ibid.*, p. 33.

27. "Conceptually, malnutrition is a deviation from an ideal, and few things in this world are perfect. . . . [I]f you wish to assume that anyone who does not receive daily a sufficient and proper balance of proteins,

carbohydrates, fats, minerals, and vitamins is malnourished, you can say that almost everyone in the poor world and most in the rich world suffer from malnutrition" (*ibid.*).

28. *Ibid.*, p. 37. In Peter G. Brown and Henry Shue, eds., *Food Policy* (New York: Free Press, 1977), the editors write: "There is more than enough food for every human being in the world to be adequately fed. By some more equal distributions of food, including distributions which were still far from strictly equal, the amount of food now produced would provide an adequate diet for the current world population. Indeed, instead of an overall shortage of food, there are unjustifiable inequalities in the distribution of food among nations, within nations, and, where the allotment to each family is meager, within families. . . . Generally, the difference in per capita food consumption between the wealthy nations and the poor nations is not only immense but expanding, with the poor nations failing even to keep up. . . . [T]he basic cause of the 'world food shortage' is the high degree of inequality in the distribution of wealth and income both among and within nations. The food needed now is being produced now, but the poor who need it most are not producing it themselves and do not have the money to buy it. In short, there is no 'world food shortage,' but, most tragically, there is a shortage of food in many places in the world" ("Introduction," p. 2). Cf. Sen, *Poverty and Famines*, pp. 7–8.

29. Why, exactly, do human beings typically experience sorrow at the suffering of others? This is an important question that I cannot explore in detail here. According to the theory of the natural sentiments within classical utilitarianism (see note 16 above), we are supposed to be creatures of both "self-love" and "natural sympathy," the latter construed as an elemental regard for the plight and fate of others. This (contingent) fact of our nature is offered to explain our not being indifferent to pain and suffering in others. Pain and suffering in others, then, are not "neutral" facts to us. They move us emotionally—even if we fail to "do something" about what thus moves us. In *The Possibility of Altruism* (Oxford: Clarendon Press, 1970), Thomas Nagel writes: "Sympathy is not, in general, just a feeling of discomfort produced by the recognition of distress in others, which in turn motivates one to relieve their distress. Rather, it is the pained awareness of their distress *as something to be relieved*" (p. 80, n. 1). But *sorrow* then is perhaps different from *sympathy*, or perhaps "involved in" but not "equivalent to" sympathy. For sorrow *per se* does not, I think, construe its object "as something to be relieved," though it may, for reasons, *come to have* the latter construal associated with it.

Notes to Chapter 2 [201]

30. Jean-Jacques Rousseau, *A Discourse on the Origin of Inequality* (1755), in *The Social Contract and Discourses*, trans. and intro. G. D. H. Cole (New York: Everyman, 1950), pp. 271–72.

2. Career Choice

1. Immanuel Kant, *Lectures on Ethics* (New York: Harper Torchbooks, 1963), pp. 160 and 174.
2. I do not offer a full account of the idea of self-realization here. The ordinary wide understanding of this notion is sufficient for the issues I discuss in this chapter. Kant perhaps conveys this understanding when he speaks of "broadening and improving [one's] fortunate natural gifts." Kant thought of self-realizing as a duty. Cf. Immanuel Kant, *Foundations of the Metaphysics of Morals* (1785), sec. 2. Further discussion of the idea of self-realization occurs below (8.2–4). Later in this chapter I offer an interpretation of the idea of service to others.
3. John Stuart Mill, *On Liberty* (1859), ch. 1.
4. Cf. Mill's references to Humboldt early in ch. 3 of *On Liberty*. Self-realization, construed as the "individuality of power and development," is spoken of as having "intrinsic worth" or "deserving . . . regard on its own account."
5. Jane Addams, *Democracy and Social Ethics* (New York: Macmillan, 1902), p. 3.
6. I do not know that Jane Addams herself would have insisted that service to others should prevail over considerations of self-realization in individuals' deliberations about careers. It appears that she thought that service to others is natural in a sense that implies that one who ignores it over time stifles the personality: "Nothing so deadens the sympathies and shrivels the power of enjoyment, as the persistent keeping away from the great opportunities for helpfulness and a continual ignoring of the starvation struggle which makes up the life of at least half the race" ("The Subjective Necessity for Social Settlements," in Addams, *Twenty Years at Hull-House* [New York: Macmillan, 1910], p. 116). It is worth adding that Addams was quite aware of the hazards of service to others, including do-goodism that misfires, inappropriate methods of aid, and unjustified paternalism. Cf. ch. 2 ("Charitable Effort") in *Democracy and Social Ethics*.
7. Plato, *Gorgias*, 500c. See 1.1, note 1.

8. Marx claimed that one of the cruelest features of capitalist society is that it forces its members into narrow, repetitive modes of activity and in that way blocks the realization of the many talents and capacities to be found in any human being. For Marx, the ideal social circumstances for human beings would be those in which "nobody has one exclusive sphere of activity but each can become accomplished in any branch he wishes"; in those circumstances it would be possible for me "to do one thing today and another tomorrow, to hunt in the morning, fish in the afternoon, rear cattle in the evening, criticise after dinner, just as I have a mind, without ever becoming hunter, fisherman, shepherd or critic" (*The German Ideology*, in *The Marx-Engels Reader*, ed. Robert C. Tucker [New York: Norton, 1972], p. 124).

9. The more nearly just a society is, the more secure is individual liberty in it. But even if individual liberty is quite secure, a society may be beset by economic troubles, or technological failures, or natural disasters. These facts, clearly, can affect the range of opportunities for careers available to its members.

10. Arthur Miller's play *The Death of a Salesman* (New York: Viking Press, 1949) makes these points vivid.

11. Cf. Thomas Nagel's use of the term "radical inequality" in "Poverty and Food: Why Charity Is Not Enough," in Peter G. Brown and Henry Shue, eds., *Food Policy* (New York: Free Press, 1977). Cf., too, Henry Shue's use of the term "degrading inequality," in *Basic Rights* (Princeton, N.J.: Princeton University Press, 1980), esp. ch. 5 ("Affluence and Responsibility").

12. In *Twenty Years at Hull-House* ("Earliest Impressions," p. 14), Jane Addams records that already at age eight her "mind was busy . . . with the old question eternally suggested by the inequalities of the human lot."

13. They are also all anti-paternalist in their recommendations for the political order.

14. Such views need not uncritically regard just any self-realizationist projects as legitimate. They may recognize other values, and certain qualifications on projects may be imposed. But this is a separate problem, which these forms of individualism would address rather than treat as irrelevant, since in general they wish to honor rather than reject the claims of individual self-realization. See H. J. McCloskey, "Liberalism," *Philosophy* 49 (Jan., 1974): 26. See, too, the critique of liberalism in Vinit Haksar, *Equality, Liberty, and Perfectionism* (New York: Oxford University Press, 1979).

Notes to Chapter 2

15. While I mentioned above (1.1, note 2) that the shared-fate theme is central to John Rawls' *A Theory of Justice* (Cambridge, Mass.: Belknap Press of Harvard University Press, 1971), it is not always clear to me how, for Rawls, it is to be interpreted, as I will indicate later.

16. Robert Nozick, *Anarchy, State, and Utopia* (New York: Basic Books, 1974), p. 33 (emphasis mine).

17. Cf. this passage from *Anarchy, State, and Utopia*: "There are particular rights over particular things held by particular persons, and particular rights to reach agreements with others, *if* you and they together can acquire the means of reaching agreements. . . . No rights exist in conflict with this substructure of particular rights" (p. 238).

18. In this section I begin to use the phrase "our form of moral life." It occurs often in the discussion that follows. I do not mean anything especially technical, Wittgensteinian, or meta-ethical by such words. For the purposes of my discussion, "form of moral life" refers to a set or group of attitudes or values that may be given different interpretations and different orderings. When they are interpreted and ordered, we then have what I call "moral conceptions," and I think of these conceptions as useful (when people choose to pay attention to them) in decision-making, and hence in the structuring of individual lives. "Shared-fate individualism," "separate-life individualism," and "liberal individualism" are examples of moral conceptions that are relevant to some (as I refer to them) "serious life decisions." They all contain the same values, but they interpret and order them differently. When I speak of a form of moral life as "our" form of moral life, I make a claim that I suppose is empirical, but minimally controversial. Thus, I assume that what in this section I call certain "basic moral attitudes" would be recognized by readers as part of their own moral-psychological make-up. Also, for the purposes of this discussion (but outside this discussion as well), I consider these basic attitudes to be objects of respect. These "assumptions" do not seem to me either controversial or interesting. (I of course recognize that philosophically they can be quarreled with.) The posterior matter—the matter of how the basic attitudes are to be given interpretation, and how they are to be ordered—is the main subject-area for my discussion. My discussion as a whole attempts to support shared-fate individualism, but I make no such simple claim as that it is "our" view. Indeed, it strikes me initially in the way it strikes others, namely, as extreme. Further reflection suggests (as I put it at the end of my discussions in Chapters 7 and 8) that it is feasible and reasonable.

19. What Rawls calls the "basic structure" in *A Theory of Justice*. See,

too, Rawls' paper "The Basic Structure as Subject," *American Philosophical Quarterly* 14 (April, 1977), and its expansion (under the same title) in A. I. Goldman and Jaegwon Kim, eds., *Values and Morals* (Dordrecht, Holland: Reidel, 1978).

20. Still broader communities are imaginable, I suppose, depending on what one chooses to include under the concept of "equal moral person" and on what one thinks about creatures (if any) that are found one day in non-Earth locations. My discussion takes no stand on these questions, or the question of the moral status of non-human animals.

21. In a discussion of abortion, Judith Jarvis Thomson writes that "you have your own life to lead" (p. 20) and that "surely we do not have any . . . 'special responsibility' for a person unless we have assumed it, explicitly or implicitly" (p. 21). Also: "nobody is morally *required* to make large sacrifices, of health, of all other interests and concerns, of all other duties and commitments, for nine years, or even for nine months, in order to keep another person alive" (pp. 17–18) and "it is not morally required of anyone that he give long stretches of his life—nine years or nine months—to sustaining the life of a person who has no special right to demand it" (p. 19) ("A Defense of Abortion," in Marshall Cohen, Thomas Nagel, and Thomas Scanlon, eds., *The Rights and Wrongs of Abortion* [Princeton, N.J.: Princeton University Press, 1974]). My sketch of separate-life individualism applies the point that large sacrifices are not morally required to the problem of career choice; I do not know that Thomson would agree with this application of the point.

22. Rawls, "The Basic Structure as Subject," *American Philosophical Quarterly*, p. 160. Cf. "A Well-Ordered Society," in Peter Laslett and James Fishkin, eds., *Philosophy, Politics, and Society* (5th ser.; New Haven, Conn.: Yale University Press, 1979), p. 9.

23. Rawls, *A Theory of Justice*, p. 566. Cf. p. 290: "What men want is meaningful work in free association with others, these associations regulating their relations to one another within a framework of just institutions."

24. Rawls, "The Basic Structure as Subject," *American Philosophical Quarterly*, p. 160 (emphasis mine). Cf. the expansion in Goldman and Kim, eds., *Values and Morals*, p. 53. The relevant contrasting claim is made by Nozick in *Anarchy, State, and Utopia*, p. 159: "The system of entitlements is defensible when constituted by the individual aims of individual transactions. No overarching aim is needed, no distributional pattern is required."

25. Cf. Rawls' remark in *A Theory of Justice*: "It is only when social

Notes to Chapter 2

conditions do not allow the effective establishment of [the basic equal liberties] that one can acknowledge their restriction. The denial of equal liberty can be accepted only if it is necessary to enhance the quality of civilization so that in due course the equal freedoms can be enjoyed by all" (p. 542).

26. Rawls has remarked that the "reasonableness" of moral conceptions is "settled by their content: that is, by the kind of society their principles direct us to strive for, and by the kind of person they encourage us to be" ("The Independence of Moral Theory," *Proceedings and Addresses of the American Philosophical Association* 48 [1974-75]: 15). I return to this criterion at the end of my discussion (8.8).

27. See the discussion of "the strains of commitment" in Rawls' *A Theory of Justice*, pp. 145, 176-77, 423.

28. It has been suggested to me that health may require that one be caught up in one's work to some extent.

29. Shared-fate individualism views the period covered by the crash program in affirmative-action terms, that is, as a transitional period in which a sacrifice is demanded in order that we may reach a point at which effective equal membership in the moral community is realized.

30. In *Utilitarianism* (1863), ch. 5, John Stuart Mill wrote: "It is part of the notion of duty in every one of its forms that a person may rightfully be compelled to fulfill it." We might ask: if morality requires the shared-fate perspective, must the state enforce the requirement? Not necessarily. It might be unwise or impractical for the state to enforce such a requirement. But that does not prevent its being a requirement of morality for individuals. There are other sources of compulsion, including conscience and integrity. Cf. Brian Barry's remark: "we can agree that it should not be legally required to give blood or contribute to the common good without agreeing that people should not feel bad about failing to do so" ("And Who is My Neighbor?" *Yale Law Journal* 88 [Jan., 1979]: 655). For a discussion of the difficulties in implementing the idea that persons' talents should be "pooled," that is, treated as part of a common fund in which all share equally, see Anthony T. Kronman, "Talent Pooling," in J. Roland Pennock and John W. Chapman, eds., *Nomos XXIII: Human Rights* (New York: New York University Press, 1981).

31. "Moral duties are pitched at a point where the conformity of the ordinary man can reasonably be expected" (A. M. Honoré, "Law, Morals, and Rescue," in Joel Feinberg and Hyman Gross, eds., *Philosophy of Law* [2nd ed.; Belmont, Calif.: Wadsworth, 1980], p. 441). Cf. Jan Narveson,

"Aesthetics, Charity, Utility, and Distributive Justice," *The Monist*, 56 (October, 1972): pp. 549–51. See, too, James D. Wallace, *Virtues and Vices* (Ithaca, N.Y.: Cornell University Press, 1978), ch. 5 ("Benevolence"), esp. pp. 147–49.

32. For useful discussions of these rights, see Henry Shue, *Basic Rights*, and Rodney Peffer, "A Defense of Rights to Well-Being," *Philosophy and Public Affairs* 8 (Fall, 1978).

33. A reference to the Rawlsian form of contractualism. But I do not know how far Rawls would agree with my endorsement of the shared-fate perspective for career choice. On the whole, Rawls' theory is concerned with principles for society's "basic structure" rather than for individuals—though principles of both sorts are "those that would be acknowledged in the original position" (*A Theory of Justice*, p. 115). "Natural duties" (among them the duty to aid others) are recognized, though they are said to allow of "exemptions" when they bring "excessive risk or loss" to individuals (pp. 114–17). In general, Rawls views the "choice of principles for individuals" as posterior to the selection of principles for institutions (p. 334). This means, I think, that the framework provided by the basic structure of society affects what is to count as "excessive risk or loss" to individuals. But what are the principles for individuals when no general basic structure is operating (but one could be operating) to ameliorate the life-prospects of the worst-off—as is the situation for individuals in the "world community" today? In that case the passage from Rawls' text that I quoted in note 25 above seems at least to suggest what I am calling the shared-fate perspective.

34. For a discussion arguing "that we neither need nor should introduce a higher morality of aspiration (and with it . . . a lower morality of duty)," see Elizabeth M. Pybus, " 'Saints and Heroes,' " *Philosophy* 57 (1982).

35. A moral-psychological account of this matter might emphasize what could be called "the problem of living with oneself." In *An Enquiry Concerning the Principles of Morals* (1777) David Hume writes that a "requisite to happiness" is one's ability to make "a satisfactory review of one's conduct" (sect. 9, pt. 2). W. D. Falk speaks of our "stake in the kind of self-preservation which requires that one should be able to bear before oneself the survey of one's own actions" ("Morality, Self, and Others," in Hector-Neri Castañeda and George Nakhnikian, eds., *Morality and the Language of Conduct* [Detroit: Wayne State University Press, 1963], pp. 63–64). These are suggestive themes. Some might find the human condition in today's world such that they could not *bear* to put their own

self-realization before relief for the destitution of others. It would seem too much like cheating. I return to these ideas in Chapter 8, especially sections 2, 6, 7, and 8.

3. Membership in the Moral Community

1. In Chapter 8 below.
2. It is convenient to use the vocabulary of "interests" in this part of my discussion since that is the language of the view I challenge below. I do not suggest that self-responsibility reduces to self-interestedness, or other-responsibility to other-interestedness, so that persons are somehow typically in tension with each other and only contingently "convergent" with each other. The shared-fate individualism that I favor is in any case hardly "individualistic" and is in its own way a "communitarian" moral conception. I argue later (6.4) that this can be so without "constituting" the self with "community" in a metaphysical fashion. But in the present chapter a preliminary logical point is at stake: namely, that the notion of other-responsibility (under some interpretation) can be conceptually a part of the idea of moral agency—and would be under certain conditions. Other parts of my views about "community" and "individuality" are given in Chapter 5 (especially sections 8 and 9), Chapter 7 (especially sections 3–6), and Chapter 8 (especially sections 4–8).
3. P. F. Strawson, "Social Morality and Individual Ideal," *Philosophy*, 36 (1961): 10.
4. This appears to fit with Kurt Baier's remarks that "a moral order . . . differs from a merely conventional one in that it purports to satisfy a condition which gives all those living under it adequate independent reason to regard its directives as overriding reasons" ("The Social Source of Reason," *Proceedings and Addresses of the American Philosophical Association* 51 (Aug., 1978): 722.
5. Strawson, "Social Morality and Individual Ideal," p. 10.
6. *Ibid*.
7. *Ibid*.
8. Strawson proposes to give an account of morality "which at least begins to square with what we nowadays vaguely understand by the word." It is this latter aim that leads him to give the account he does of what it is for a set of demands to be a system of moral demands, such that (MI) is a conceptual truth. See *ibid.*, pp. 9–10.

9. A parallel claim of ambiguity might be possible in the case of the general characterization of "being (A) but not (I)," but I do not pursue this idea here.

10. See the interesting discussion of "psychopaths" in Herbert Fingarette, *On Responsibility* (New York: Basic Books, 1967), ch. 2 ("Acceptance of Responsibility").

11. Cf. the conception of "equal concern and respect" in Ronald Dworkin, *Taking Rights Seriously* (Cambridge, Mass.: Harvard University Press, 1978), ch. 9 ("Reverse Discrimination"). See, too, Dworkin's essay "Liberalism," in Stuart Hampshire, ed., *Public and Private Morality* (Cambridge, Eng.: Cambridge University Press, 1978).

12. Cf. H. L. A. Hart's discussion of the conditions of the existence of a legal system, in *The Concept of Law* (Oxford: Clarendon Press, 1961), pp. 60, 86–88, esp. pp. 113–14 and 197–98. "In an extreme case . . . only officials might accept and use the system's criteria of legal validity. The society in which this was so might be deplorably sheeplike; the sheep might end in the slaughter-house. But there is little reason for thinking that it could not exist or for denying it the title of a legal system" (p. 114). I assume that what Hart depicts in this "extreme case" would not retain the title of "moral community."

4. Participation and Policy

1. Arnold S. Kaufman, "Wants, Needs, and Liberalism," *Inquiry* 14 (Autumn, 1971): 192.

2. *Ibid.*, p. 197.

3. *Ibid.*, p. 201.

4. This is the trouble Kaufman sees in the classical liberal's preferred solution; though there are dangers in "forcing people to be free, they are less than those inherent in uncritically accepting the modes of socialization that happen to prevail" (*ibid.*, pp. 201–2).

5. Peter Bachrach, "Interest, Participation, and Democratic Theory," in J. Roland Pennock and John W. Chapman, eds., *Nomos XVI: Participation in Politics* (New York: Lieber-Atherton, 1975), p. 40. See, too, Arnold S. Kaufman, *The Radical Liberal* (New York: Atherton, 1968), p. 56: "A political process is not just a means of implementing political programs. The process itself has an impact on participants that may speed or retard achievement of the values liberals cherish. The central claim of John

Dewey's philosophy was that the democratic process could enrich the lives of men not only by what it does *for* them but by what it does *to* them."

6. M. B. E. Smith, "The Value of Participation," in Pennock and Chapman, eds., *Nomos XVI*, p. 130.

7. *Ibid.*, pp. 129–30.

8. *Ibid.*, pp. 133–34.

9. Cf. John Rawls, *A Theory of Justice* (Cambridge, Mass.: Belknap Press of Harvard University Press, 1971), pp. 85–86.

10. "Living adults share, we must believe, the same public interest. For them, however, the public interest is mixed with, and is often at odds with, their private and special interests. Put this way, we can say, I suggest, that the public interest may be presumed to be what men would choose if they saw clearly, thought rationally, acted disinterestedly and benevolently" (Walter Lippman, *Essays in the Public Philosophy* [Boston, Mass.: Little, Brown, 1955], p. 42).

11. Whether any given proponent of the value of participation in political life, for example, someone who favors what is termed "participatory democracy," holds the strong form of the participation view may be unclear. Someone might *favor* participation in politics for a variety of reasons, such as that it facilitates communication between persons in different positions in society, that it is self-educative, that it is reflective of autonomy and is hence "humanizing," and so forth, but nevertheless think of it as (merely) tending to produce acceptable policies. But I will deal with the participation view in its strong form, on the ground that it has greater philosophical interest. In any event Rousseau, I believe, held the strong form of the view in *Social Contract* (1762); and Rousseau is regularly cited as a main historical influence by those who favor participation in political decision-making. For a general discussion of "theorists of participatory democracy," see Carole Pateman, *Participation and Democratic Theory* (Cambridge, Eng.: Cambridge University Press, 1970), esp. ch. 2.

12. Rousseau, *Social Contract*, bk. 2, ch. 3.

13. *Ibid.*

14. Cf. David Lyons, "Nature and Soundness of the Contract and Coherence Arguments," in Norman Daniels, ed., *Reading Rawls* (New York: Basic Books, 1975), p. 156.

15. Thomas Hobbes, *Leviathan* (1651), pt. 1, ch. 4.

16. Rawls, *A Theory of Justice*, esp. pp. 136–42.

17. *Ibid.*, pp. 19–20.

18. *Ibid.*, p. 15.

19. Robert Nozick's remarks in *Anarchy, State, and Utopia* (New York: Basic Books, 1974), p. 132, are suggestive, but what follows in my text does not duplicate them exactly.

20. See Rousseau, *Social Contract*, bk. 4, ch. 1.

21. It may be that the notion of a desire for "primary goods," that is, "things which it is supposed a rational man wants whatever else he wants," which Rawls ascribes to the parties in his original position, would be a useful analyzing concept for this idea of "best." See *A Theory of Justice*, pp. 62, 90–95, esp. p. 92.

22. I am being led here somewhat by Brian Barry's discussion of Rousseau's views in "The Public Interest," in Anthony Quinton, ed., *Political Philosophy* (Oxford: Oxford University Press, 1967).

23. It should be clear that I am treating (strong) participation as a structured activity that proceeds according to rules or operating instructions, though I do not assume that what these rules are, in detail, is built into the idea of (strong) participation itself.

24. See Hobbes, *Leviathan*, pt. 1, ch. 4.

25. Ibid. In Chapter 5 I discuss in some detail a "motivation problem" for the acceptability of public policy. That discussion fills out somewhat the "condition" merely stated here.

26. Rousseau, *Social Contract*, bk. 2, ch. 2.

27. There are problems here that I must leave undiscussed. I am not sure, for example, whether procedural moral acceptability requires of procedures culminating in a last vote that all such votes be equal. In contexts in which the policy problem before the agreement group is one of compensatory justice, it may be that acceptability allows (or requires) votes with different weights.

28. Cf. Rousseau's confidence in majority voting under certain conditions in *Social Contract*, bk. 4, chs. 1 and 2.

29. Rawls, *A Theory of Justice*, p. 121.

30. Immanuel Kant, *Foundations of the Metaphysics of Morals* (1785), sec. 2.

31. See on this topic, Peter Singer, *Democracy and Disobedience* (Oxford: Clarendon Press, 1973), esp. the sections from part 1 titled "Fairness and Compromise," "The Problems of Minorities," and "Participation." Also, I should note that I have not considered whether there might be cases in which it is right to pursue the special interests of individuals even when this conflicts with pursuing the real interests of members of the community. Cf. Barry, "The Public Interest," pp. 124–25.

Notes to Chapter 5

32. Cf. Lyons, "Nature and Soundness," pp. 157–60.
33. It should be noted that none of this is to suggest that problems that are open to solution by accepted independent criteria of right ought never to be dealt with otherwise. For "accepted independent criteria of right" may not be *the* criteria of right.
34. I am grateful to Warner Wick for pressing these questions and for very helpful discussion of them in correspondence.
35. A comprehensive and useful work on the history of the theory of the social contract is J. W. Gough, *The Social Contract* (2nd ed.; Oxford: Clarendon Press, 1957).

5. Future Generations, Public Policy, and the Motivation Problem

1. My thoughts on what it is to be an "independent policy-maker for a free society" put together features from (for example) the position of the Supreme Court justice, the tenured professor with academic freedom and research time, and the Rawlsian parties to the original position. But the position of the independent policy-maker in a free society is not identical with any of these. In rough terms, the independent policy-maker is the "participant" in an "agreement group" engaged in the "(strong) participation" discussed in Chapter 4, but the "free society" here is not necessarily the "moral community."
2. Here again I think of the words of A. M. Honoré: "Moral duties are pitched at a point where the conformity of the ordinary man can reasonably be expected" ("Law, Morals, and Rescue," in Joel Feinberg and Hyman Gross, eds., *Philosophy of Law* [2nd ed.; Belmont, Calif.: Wadsworth, 1980], p. 441).
3. The phrase is Robert L. Heilbroner's, in *An Inquiry Into the Human Prospect* (New York: Norton, 1975, 1974), p. 114.
4. This is the theme of Christopher Lasch's *The Culture of Narcissism* (New York: Norton, 1979).
5. This supposition is not meant to deny either that morality requires other things as well, for example, policies that address destitution among *current* people, or even that these latter policies are more urgent or important than policies regarding our legacy for the world of the future. The "motivation problem" I discuss is independent of this priority issue. See, too, the last paragraph of section 2 below.

6. See David Hume, *An Enquiry Concerning the Principles of Morals* (1777), end of sec. 9.

7. See John Rawls, *A Theory of Justice* (Cambridge, Mass.: The Belknap Press of Harvard University Press, 1971), pp. 145, 176–77, 423, for discussion of "the strains of commitment." "The general facts of human psychology and the principles of moral learning are relevant matters for the parties to examine. If a conception of justice is unlikely to generate its own support, or lacks stability, this fact must not be overlooked. . . . [T]hey will not enter into agreements they know they cannot keep, or can do so only with great difficulty. Along with other considerations, they count the strains of commitment" (p. 145). By way of examples of what is meant, Rawls argues that agreements that have the parties acquiescing in a loss of freedom over a lifetime for the sake of the greater good of others "exceed the capacity of human nature" (p. 176), and that the parties "cannot agree to a conception of justice if the consequences of applying it may lead to self-reproach should the least happy possibilities be realized. They should strive to be free from such regrets" (p. 423). Rawls adds, though, that if the only possible candidate conceptions of justice all involved risks that similarly exceed the capacity of human nature, then "the problem of the strains of commitment would have to be waived" (p. 177).

8. Perhaps, though, it is difficult to feel much toward persons in large numbers. Sidgwick remarks that "one cannot easily sympathize with each individual in a multitude" (*The Methods of Ethics* [7th ed., 1907; New York: Dover, 1966], p. 251).

9. Heilbroner, *An Inquiry Into the Human Prospect*, pp. 114–15 (Heilbroner's italics).

10. *Ibid.*, pp. 131, 132, 135–36.

11. Heilbroner's pessimistic motivational claim may be controversial, of course. Cf. Joel Feinberg's remarks: "I shall assume . . . that it is psychologically possible for us to care about our remote descendants, that many of us do in fact care, and indeed that we ought to care" ("The Rights of Animals and Unborn Generations," in Richard A. Wasserstrom, ed., *Today's Moral Problems* [2nd ed.; New York: Macmillan, 1979], p. 581).

12. *Ibid.*, p. 598.

13. The equal-opportunity maxim is discussed by Brian Barry in "Circumstances of Justice and Future Generations," in R. I. Sikora and Brian Barry, eds., *Obligations to Future Generations* (Philadelphia: Temple University Press, 1978), pp. 242–44; the custody maxim is endorsed though not discussed by Barry in "Justice Between Generations," in P. M. S.

Notes to Chapter 5

Hacker and Joseph Raz, eds., *Law, Morality, and Society* (Oxford: Clarendon Press, 1977), p. 284. (Barry remarks at the end of the latter essay that these maxims might form the minimum content of the "new ethic" that some theorists call for regarding our obligations to future people.) The equal-opportunity maxim is characterized as a "global extension" of a principle for families that have wealth to pass on, namely, "Keep the capital intact" ("Circumstances of Justice and Future Generations," pp. 243–44). One might ask: why don't our intuitions pick out a "global extension" of the principle that immigrants to a new nation promising great opportunity and material improvement have been known to follow regarding their own level of sacrifice for their children, namely, "Your lot better than mine." I can think of two things that bear on why the immigrants' principle does not seem right for the world of the future, even though they do not settle this matter: (1) the facelessness and impersonality of future people such that their fate does not arouse our ambition, or even our concern, in the way the fate of our own children may; (2) the sense we have — perhaps itself a recent development among us — that our resources are now strained, so that we could not do better than pass the world along "intact" without excessive sacrifice. Barry discusses the appropriateness of "equal-opportunity justice" for future generations further in "Intergenerational Justice in Energy Policy," in Douglas MacLean and Peter G. Brown, eds., *Energy and the Future* (Totowa, N.J.: Rowman and Littlefield, 1983). Cf. 6.3 below.

14. Immanuel Kant, *Foundations of the Metaphysics of Morals* (1785), sec. 2: "if reason of itself does not sufficiently determine the will . . . , in a word, if the will is not of itself in complete accord with reason (the actual case of men), then the actions which are recognized as objectively necessary are subjectively contingent, and the determination of such a will according to objective laws is constraint. That is, the relation of objective laws to a will which is not completely good is conceived as the determination of the will of a rational being by principles of reason to which this will is not by nature necessarily obedient."

15. For example, Kant's theory of the categorical imperative, or Mill's utilitarianism.

16. Hume, *Enquiry*, sec. 9.

17. In considering our duty to respond to the needs of others "out of our superfluity," Sidgwick notes that "we are commonly prompted to fulfill it by the specific emotion of Pity or Compassion. Here . . . there seems a doubt how far it is good to foster and encourage this emotion. . . . On the

one hand, the emotional impulse tends to make the action of relieving need not only easier to the agent, but more graceful and pleasing: on the other hand, it is generally recognized that mistaken pity is more likely to lead us astray than—e.g.—mistaken gratitude: as it is more liable to interfere dangerously with the infliction of penalties required for the maintenance of social order, or with the operation of motives to industry and thrift, necessary for economic well-being" (*The Methods of Ethics*, p. 262).

18. Cf. Kant, *Foundations*, sec. 2: "Humanity might indeed exist if no one contributed to the happiness of others, provided he did not intentionally detract from it; but this harmony with humanity as an end in itself is only negative rather than positive if everyone does not also endeavor, so far as he can, to further the ends of others. For the ends of any person, who is an end in himself, must as far as possible also be my end, if that conception of an end in itself is to have its full effect on me." Of course, I speak here of benevolence as part of our emotional make-up. It may be, as Rawls suggests, that benevolence *in effect* can be achieved in other ways; see *A Theory of Justice*, p. 148.

19. Sidgwick, *The Methods of Ethics*, p. 262.

20. Cf. H. L. A. Hart, *The Concept of Law* (Oxford: Clarendon Press, 1961), pp. 189–95: "it is a truth of some importance that for the adequate description not only of law but of many other social institutions, a place must be reserved, besides definitions and ordinary statements of fact, for a third category of statements: those the truth of which is contingent on human beings and the world they live in retaining the salient characteristics which they have" (p. 195).

21. In "Harm and Self-Interest," in P. M. S. Hacker and Joseph Raz, eds., *Law, Morality, and Society* (Oxford: Clarendon Press, 1977), Joel Feinberg urges that we "think of all harm as done to interests themselves, and interpret talk of harm done to men and women as convenient elliptical references to, and identification of, the interest that was thwarted or set back" (p. 301). In "The Rights of Animals and Unborn Generations," Feinberg remarks about future people that "the fact of their interest-ownership is crystal clear, and that is all that is necessary to certify the coherence of present talk about their rights" (p. 599). Also: "philosophers have not helped matters by arguing that animals and future generations are not the kinds of beings who can have rights now, that they don't presently qualify for membership, even 'auxiliary membership,' in our moral community. I have tried in this essay to dispel the conceptual confusions that make such conclusions possible. To acknowledge their rights is the very

Notes to Chapter 5

least we can do for members of endangered species (including our own). But that is something" (p. 600).

22. Again, following Feinberg, in "The Rights of Animals and Unborn Generations": "It is important to reemphasize here that the questions of whether fetuses [in our case, future people] do or ought to have rights are substantive questions of law and morals open to argument and decision. The prior question of whether fetuses [in our case, future people] are the kind of beings that can have rights, however, is a conceptual, not a moral question, amenable only to what is called 'logical analysis,' and irrelevant to moral judgment. The correct answer to the conceptual question, I believe, is that unborn children [in our case, future people] are among the sorts of beings of whom possession of rights can meaningfully be predicated, even though they are (temporarily) incapable of having interests, because their future interests can be protected now, and it does make sense to protect a potential interest even before it has grown into actuality" (p. 587). One must add, though, that how far our protection of the interests of future people is effective depends "on the behavior of the intervening generations, whom we have no way of binding" (Barry, "Justice Between Generations," p. 276).

23. "[W]e acquire attachments to persons and institutions according to how we perceive our good to be affected by them. The basic idea is one of reciprocity, a tendency to answer in kind. Now this tendency is a deep psychological fact. Without it our nature would be very different and fruitful social cooperation fragile if not impossible" (Rawls, *A Theory of Justice*, pp. 494–95).

24. Perhaps it is already known that these are not thought of highly as motivational bases relative to the world of the present either. As Barrington Moore, Jr. puts it: "By itself, love, sympathetic identification, empathy, or whatever one chooses to call this elusive emotion or series of emotions, is nowhere near enough to hold together any large human society and make it run. Under certain conditions it can be very powerful. But it won't get food and water into the cities and garbage off the streets" (*Injustice: The Social Bases of Obedience and Revolt* [White Plains, N.Y.: Sharpe, 1978], p. 99).

25. Following the advice in the quotation from Feinberg at the beginning of note 21 above.

26. Cf. Rawls, *A Theory of Justice*: "Individuals in their role as citizens with a full understanding of the content of the principles of justice may be moved to act upon them largely because of their bonds to particular persons and an attachment to their own society" (p. 475).

27. For helpful studies of the moral emotions, see Herbert Morris, *On Guilt and Innocence* (Berkeley: University of California Press, 1976).
28. How this arousal works, that is, what its mechanisms are, I do not know. Its characterization is a problem for psychology.
29. Apparently, we are positioned so as to have unilateral power over future people. Some might argue that since we have power over the fate of future people, but they have no power over our fate, we can have no *obligations* to them. But I do not hold that obligations require reciprocal power relations. Nor do I think that the absence of reciprocation *qua* exchange of ideas and interpretations of ends eliminates the possibility of morality requiring something of us relative to future people. Cf. Barry, "Justice Between Generations," pp. 269-70.
30. Rawls, *A Theory of Justice*, p. 475.
31. It may be that this "appropriate conception of what morality requires" is what Rawls calls "the conception of justice as fairness"; but it is not my aim here to make a case for this claim. In Chapter 7 I discuss the compatibility of shared-fate individualism as a moral conception for individual responsibility with the Rawlsian conception of justice as fairness for the basic structure of society.
32. Cf. 4.5 above.
33. Feinberg, "The Rights of Animals and Unborn Generations," p. 599.
34. Rawls, *A Theory of Justice*, p. 491.
35. It is not clear to me whether the form of motivation I call "extended shared-fate motivation" is what Rawls calls "the sense of justice." Perhaps there is a certain ambiguity in Rawls' work on this point. Much of his discussion is conducted under the assumption that the subject of justice is the basic structure of the nation state: "The relevant systems here, of course, are the basic structures of the well-ordered societies corresponding to the different conceptions of justice.... Now I assume that the boundaries of these schemes are given by the notion of a self-contained national community" (*A Theory of Justice*, p. 457). But the shared-fate motivation requisite to the nation-state is hardly "extended" at all when contrasted with the extended shared-fate motivation needed to support policies implementing what morality requires for the world of the future. The latter, I have suggested, is linked to the idea of a community *without* "boundaries" in any familiar sense. In certain parts of Rawls' discussion, though, it seems clear that his sense of justice is something like the more "extreme" extended shared-fate motivation that I have in mind. (Cf., e.g., p. 587.) Cf. Barry, "Circumstances of Justice and Future Generations," esp. pp. 235-37.

36. Cf. David Gauthier, "The Social Contract as Ideology," *Philosophy and Public Affairs* 6 (Winter, 1977).

37. Here I should note that my discussion is limited. I have not, for example, canvassed all the forms of motivation that might operate in behalf of what Ernest Partridge has called "self-transcendence" ("Why Care About the Future?" in Partridge, ed., *Responsibilities to Future Generations* [Buffalo, N.Y.: Prometheus Press, 1981]). It is not part of my view in any case that ordinary people are locked into their present lives in a narrow way. We do make provision for our children, our reputations, and the projects we care about, well into the future. But the special problem for my imagined "independent policy-makers for a free society," sketched at the beginning of the chapter, should be recalled. It is not at all clear to me that, in the circumstances there imagined, the familiar motivational bases of "ordinary" self-transcendence are "available and reliable" to support policies of serious sacrifice as these may be required by morality for the world of the future. And, as I have suggested (though with little elaboration), the form of motivation that might be directly serviceable in this connection, namely, extended shared-fate motivation, is hardly *cultivated* by our current social institutions and moral ideology.

6. Public Policy and the Interpretation of Persons

1. This phrase, again, is from A. M. Honoré, "Law, Morals, and Rescue," in Joel Feinberg and Hyman Gross, eds., *Philosophy of Law* (2nd ed.; Belmont, Calif.: Wadsworth, 1980), p. 441.

2. David Hume, *An Enquiry Concerning the Principles of Morals* (1777), end of sec. 9.

3. The "framework" for persons' pursuits of interests is ultimately the subject at issue between John Rawls in *A Theory of Justice* (Cambridge, Mass.: The Belknap Press of Harvard University Press, 1971) and Robert Nozick in *Anarchy, State, and Utopia* (New York: Basic Books, 1974).

4. "Unusual," of course, need not mean "new." It may simply mean "not hitherto attended to."

5. I am not sure what to say about Derek Parfit's point that differences in our policies now make for different persons in the future. In some remarks toward the end of "Energy Policy and the Further Future: The Identity Problem," in Douglas MacLean and Peter G. Brown, eds., *Energy and the Future* (Totowa, N.J.: Rowman and Littlefield, 1983), Parfit seems

(to me) to say that the claims as I express them here "are not seriously misleading" (p. 175).

6. The phrase "alterations of lifeways" is from Robert L. Heilbroner, *An Inquiry Into the Human Prospect* (New York: Norton, 1975, 1974), pp. 135–36. Cf. 5.3 above.

7. By (FG) I have in mind Brian Barry's "equal opportunity" approach to the problem of our legacy for members of future generations. See his "Circumstances of Justice and Future Generations" in R. I. Sikora and Brian Barry, eds., *Obligations to Future Generations* (Philadelphia: Temple University Press, 1978), and his "Intergenerational Justice in Energy Policy," in MacLean and Brown, eds., *Energy and the Future*. Cf. 5.4, note 13. The latter paper has a discussion of the compatibility of *inter*generational and *intra*generational justice. Barry does not propose (D), but he comes close to it.

8. For the point that distance is not a factor relevant to the duties of aid, see Peter Singer's "Famine, Affluence, and Morality," *Philosophy and Public Affairs* 1 (1972). In "Energy Policy and the Further Future: The Social Discount Rate," in MacLean and Brown, eds., *Energy and the Future*, Derek Parfit claims that "a mere difference in timing is itself morally neutral" (p. 31). For the point that the "circumstances of justice" are not a set of necessary conditions for the application of the concept of justice, see Brian Barry's "Circumstances of Justice and Future Generations."

9. What prompts my interest in this subject is Rawls' very brief discussion of the "strains of commitment" in *A Theory of Justice* (pp. 145, 176–77, 423). I do not know that Rawls would agree with the account I develop in what follows, or the points I use it to suggest.

10. Barry, "Intergenerational Justice in Energy Policy," pp. 20–21.

11. Rawls, *A Theory of Justice*, p. 587. I offer further discussion of the idea of the "moral point of view" in 8.4–7.

12. Here what I say reminds me of the view expressed in "The Fragmentation of Value" (and other essays) in Thomas Nagel's *Mortal Questions* (Cambridge, Eng.: Cambridge University Press, 1979), a view very fully developed in Nagel's *The View from Nowhere* (New York: Oxford University Press, 1986). I touch again on Nagel's view in the discussion in 8.4–7.

13. Michael J. Sandel, *Liberalism and the Limits of Justice* (Cambridge, Eng.: Cambridge University Press, 1982). A helpful short overview of Sandel's views is provided in his essay "Morality and the Liberal Ideal," *New Republic*, May 7, 1984.

Notes to Chapter 6 [219]

14. Sandel, *Liberalism and the Limits of Justice*, p. 62.
15. Michael Walzer, *Spheres of Justice* (New York: Basic Books, 1983).
16. Cf. Alasdair MacIntyre's remarks about "community" and "shared understanding" in "Justice as a Virtue: Changing Conceptions," ch. 17 of *After Virtue* (Notre Dame, Ind.: University of Notre Dame Press, 1981), esp. pp. 232–33.
17. Even though the works by Sandel and Walzer are very different, and neither refers to the other (though Walzer reviewed Sandel's book in the *New Republic*, Dec. 13, 1982, and Sandel Walzer's in *The New York Times Book Review*, April 24, 1983), my thought is that their views might be connectable in a certain way. In broad terms I think Walzer's view of justice for society can incorporate among its premises (were they to be formulated) a "communitarian" conception of self of the sort Sandel proposes and faults the Rawlsian view for lacking. I am less certain whether the connection could proceed in the other direction, that is, whether Sandel's (only partly worked-out) communitarian conception of self directly suggests the relativistic "plural justice" that Walzer recommends for society. Some considerations that bear on the latter uncertainty are indicated toward the end of the discussion of this section.
18. Sandel, *Liberalism and the Limits of Justice*, p. 1.
19. Ibid.
20. Ibid., p. 18.
21. Ibid., p. 3.
22. Ibid., p. 9 (emphasis mine).
23. Ibid., p. 49.
24. Ibid., p. 50.
25. Ibid., p. 53.
26. Ibid., p. 54.
27. Ibid., p. 55.
28. Ibid., p. 62.
29. Ibid. (emphasis mine).
30. Ibid.
31. Ibid., p. 150.
32. Ibid., p. 92.
33. Cf. John Rawls, "The Independence of Moral Theory," *Proceedings and Addresses of the American Philosophical Association* 48 (1974–75): esp. sec. 4.
34. The avoidance need not be complete. Rawls notes that "it is neither possible, nor desirable, to enable everyone to advance their final ends no

matter what those ends are, for some may desire, for example, the oppression of others as an end in itself. Nevertheless, a sufficiently wide range of ends can be accommodated to secure ways of life fully worthy of human endeavour" ("Social Unity and Primary Goods," in Amartya Sen and Bernard Williams, eds., *Utilitarianism and Beyond* [Cambridge, Eng.: Cambridge University Press, 1982]). For a full discussion of how far a defensible liberalism requires "perfectionist considerations," see Vinit Haksar, *Equality, Liberty, and Perfectionism* (New York: Clarendon Press, 1979). My review of Haksar's book is in *Nous* 17 (May, 1983).

35. Sandel, *Liberalism and the Limits of Justice*, p. 150.
36. Ibid., p. 144.
37. I should note at this point that I am assuming that the Rawlsian conception of the self with which Sandel figures his community-constitutive conception competes is *not* the one that Rawls often refers to as a "conception of person," which is *part* of the conception of justice. (See, Rawls, "Social Unity and Primary Goods," esp. secs. 2-5 and 8, and also Rawls' 1980 Dewey Lectures, titled "Kantian Constructivism in Moral Theory," *Journal of Philosophy* 77 [Sept., 1980].) The latter conception is hardly a conception of the self as "pure" and "unadulterated." It is, in fact, a conception of a person equipped with "moral personality" and certain "specified highest-order interests" developed with a certain sort of "community" already in mind. As Rawls says in the Dewey Lectures, "we are not trying to find a conception of justice suitable for all societies regardless of their particular social or historical circumstances. We want to settle a fundamental disagreement over the just form of basic institutions *within a democratic society under modern conditions*. . . . In addressing the public culture of a democratic society, Kantian constructivism hopes to invoke a conception of the person *implicitly affirmed in that culture*, or else one that would prove acceptable to citizens once it was properly presented and explained" (p. 518, my emphasis). Rather than let these remarks render Sandel's critique otiose, I assume, again, that the Rawlsian conception of self that Sandel wishes to criticize is not this "community-constitutive" one, but one that is somehow *still deeper* in the Rawlsian theory.
38. Sandel, *Liberalism and the Limits of Justice*, p. 143.
39. In "The Independence of Moral Theory" Rawls notes that "what sorts of persons we are is shaped by how we think of ourselves and this in turn is influenced by the social forms we live under" (p. 20).
40. Sandel, *Liberalism and the Limits of Justice*, p. 160.

Notes to Chapter 7

41. *Ibid.*, pp. 160–61.
42. *Ibid.*, p. 161.

7. The Weight of Established Liberty

1. Cf. the use of the notion of "mode of self-understanding" by Michael J. Sandel in *Liberalism and the Limits of Justice* (Cambridge, Eng.: Cambridge University Press, 1982), e.g., p. 150. Cf., too, Sandel's vocabulary of "constitutive convention," p. 181. These notions were discussed briefly in 6.4 above.
2. John Stuart Mill, *Utilitarianism* (1863), ch. 4.
3. John Rawls, *A Theory of Justice* (Cambridge, Mass.: Belknap Press of Harvard University Press, 1971), p. 178.
4. John Rawls, "Fairness to Goodness," *Philosophical Review* 84 (Oct., 1975): 550.
5. Shared-fate individualism, as a conception of individual responsibility, is also consistent with Robert Nozick's libertarianism, that is, his "entitlement" conception of justice for the basic structure of society, as seems suggested in part 3 of *Anarchy, State, and Utopia* (New York: Basic Books, 1974). Cf. Peter Singer, *Practical Ethics* (Cambridge, Eng.: Cambridge University Press, 1979), ch. 8 ("Rich and Poor"), p. 173. For Rawls' view that "it seems simpler to adopt all principles for individuals after those for the basic structure," see *A Theory of Justice*, secs. 18 and 19; cf. sec. 51, esp. pp. 339–40.
6. It may also be that utilitarianism fails to recognize the morally relevant way in which one's projects (including one's career) help constitute one's personal identity for practical purposes, and thus brings to something like the career-choice problem a view of moral agency that is inadequate from the outset. Cf. Bernard Williams, "A Critique of Utilitarianism," in J. J. C. Smart and Bernard Williams, *Utilitarianism, For and Against* (Cambridge, Eng.: Cambridge University Press, 1973), esp. sec. 5 ("Integrity"), and "Persons, Character, and Morality" and "Moral Luck" in Williams' *Moral Luck* (Cambridge, Eng.: Cambridge University Press, 1981).
7. For an extended discussion of the problems of world poverty and hunger that gives detailed attention to the workings of different kinds of moral theory, see Onora O'Neill, *Faces of Hunger* (London: Allen and Unwin, 1986). This fine book is not limited to individual responsibility in

the way mine is (it speaks "not only to individuals but to influential institutions and collectivities"), and it responds to political questions as well. It argues for "a (maverick) Kantian theory of obligation" over "currently popular consequentialist and rights theories" (p. 7).

8. On the last of these subjects, a useful general discussion is William K. Frankena's "The Philosophy of Vocation," *Thought* 51 (Dec., 1976).

9. Even these examples might be controversial to some extent, or with respect to some aspects of the "life decisions" involved in them. It is not *incoherent*, I suppose, to think of something like shared-fate individualism as applying to decisions concerning whether to have or adopt children, or even to decisions concerning sexuality. Erik H. Erikson, in *Gandhi's Truth* (New York: Norton, 1969), remarks about Gandhi's own sexual renunciation: "He gave up sexual intimacy for a wider communal intimacy and not just because sexuality seemed immoral in any Calvinist sense" (p. 192). (My thanks to Thomas R. Frieden for the reference and discussion of this interesting point.)

10. Cf. the discussion of the "open texture" of rules in H. L. A. Hart, *The Concept of Law* (Oxford: Clarendon Press, 1961), ch. 7.

11. Cf. Feinberg's distinction between "conceptual" and "moral" questions in "The Rights of Animals and Unborn Generations," in Richard A. Wasserstrom, ed., *Today's Moral Problems* (2nd ed.; New York: Macmillan, 1979), p. 587.

12. I refer, of course, to Rawls' theory of justice, as presented in *A Theory of Justice* and subsequent essays.

13. *Ibid.*, p. 106.

14. *Ibid.*, p. 542.

15. Alexander M. Bickel, "Citizen or Person? What Is Not Granted Cannot Be Taken Away," in Bickel, *The Morality of Consent* (New Haven, Conn.: Yale University Press, 1975), p. 34.

16. Rawls, *A Theory of Justice* and a subsequent essay, "The Basic Structure as Subject," *American Philosophical Quarterly* 14 (April, 1977).

17. Rawls, *A Theory of Justice*, p. 7. Cf. "The Basic Structure as Subject," p. 159.

18. Rawls, *A Theory of Justice*, p. 457.

19. *Ibid.*, p. 139 (emphasis mine). Rawls adds that the original position "is not to be thought of as a general assembly which includes at one moment everyone who will live at some time; or, much less, as an assembly of everyone who could live at some time. It is not a gathering of all actual or possible persons" (p. 139).

Notes to Chapter 7

20. *Ibid.*, pp. 377-78.
21. Brian Barry, *The Liberal Theory of Justice* (Oxford: Clarendon Press, 1973), p. 133 (emphasis mine). Regarding the original position populated by nation-state representatives, Barry adds: "As far as economic relations are concerned, I can see no reason within Rawls' theory why the representatives of different countries should not, meeting under the conditions specified, agree on some sort of international maximin. One way of presenting the case for this conclusion would be to say: suppose that you were an embryo with a random chance of being any child conceived in the world in a certain period of twenty-four hours, what kind of world would you prefer? One, like the present one, which gives you about a fifty-fifty chance of being born in a society with widespread malnutrition and a high mortality rate and about a one-in-four chance of being born in a rich country, or a world in which the gap between the best and the worst prospects had been reduced? Surely, it would be rational to opt for the second kind of world; and this conclusion is reinforced if we accept Rawls' view that an element in rationality is playing safe when taking big decisions" (pp. 132-33).
22. Rawls, *A Theory of Justice*, p. 19 (emphasis mine).
23. *Ibid.*, pp. 179-80.
24. *Ibid.*, p. 252. Cf. sec. 40 ("The Kantian Interpretation of Justice as Fairness"), pp. 251-57.
25. *Ibid.*, pp. 114-15 (emphasis mine). Rawls adds here: "This feature in particular suggests the propriety of the adjective 'natural.' One aim of the law of nations is to assure the recognition of these duties in the conduct of states. This is especially important in constraining the means used in war, assuming that, in certain circumstances anyway, wars of self-defense are justified" (p. 115). On p. 339 Rawls indicates that a "sufficient ground" for adopting the "duty of mutual aid" is "its pervasive effect on the quality of everyday life": its chief value "is not measured by the help we actually receive but rather by the sense of confidence and trust in other men's good intentions and the knowledge that they are there if we need them. Indeed, it is only necessary to imagine what a society would be like if it were publicly known that this duty was rejected."
26. *Ibid.*, p. 115. The last phrase here represents what Rawls calls "the exemption which the natural duties allow" (p. 117). *Why* the natural duties are construed as having such exemptions is not explained or argued for in *A Theory of Justice*. Perhaps the explanation involves making logical room for acts of supererogation. Consider these remarks from *A Theory of Jus-*

tice: acts of supererogation "are acts of benevolence and mercy, or heroism and self-sacrifice. It is good to do these actions but it is not one's duty or obligation. Supererogatory acts are not required, though normally they would be were it not for the loss or risk involved for the agent himself. A person who does a supererogatory act does not invoke the exemption which the natural duties allow. For while we have a natural duty to bring about a great good, say, if we can do so relatively easily, we are released from this duty when the cost to ourselves is considerable" (p. 117). What counts as a "considerable" cost, loss, or risk is, of course, controversial. Cf. Peter Singer's essay "Famine, Affluence, and Morality," *Philosophy and Public Affairs* 1 (1972), and the development of it in ch. 8 ("Rich and Poor") of his *Practical Ethics*. I discuss this matter further in 8.7.

27. Rawls, *A Theory of Justice*, pp. 128-29 (emphasis mine).
28. Ibid., p. 140.
29. Rawls, "The Basic Structure as Subject." For an approach that "relativizes" the idea of justice to particular communities (which differ from one another), see Michael Walzer, *Spheres of Justice* (New York: Basic Books, 1983). See 6.4 above.
30. Rawls, *A Theory of Justice*, p. 542.
31. H. L. A. Hart, "Rawls on Liberty and Its Priority," in Norman Daniels, ed., *Reading Rawls* (New York: Basic Books, 1975), p. 250.
32. For the view that the Hobbesian characterization of the current situation of nations-among-nations is not apt, see Charles Beitz, *Political Theory and International Relations* (Princeton, N.J.: Princeton University Press, 1979).
33. See George Sher, "Justifying Reverse Discrimination in Employment," in Marshall Cohen, Thomas Nagel, and Thomas Scanlon, eds., *Equality and Preferential Treatment* (Princeton, N.J.: Princeton University Press, 1977).
34. "[M]y view is that the aid should be of whatever type is most effective" (Peter Singer, in a "postscript" to a reprinting of "Famine, Affluence, and Morality" in William Aiken and Hugh La Follette, eds., *World Hunger and Moral Obligation* [Englewood Cliffs, N.J.: Prentice-Hall, 1977], p. 35).
35. *Sacrifice*, perhaps, from the long-range view of the parties to the original position, but *abolition*, in practical effect, for current real persons and their children.
36. Cf. Rawls, *A Theory of Justice*, pp. 440-46, 543-48.
37. At the end of a helpful review essay ("Liberalism and Global Jus-

Notes to Chapter 8

tice: Hoffman and Nardin on Morality in International Affairs," *Philosophy and Public Affairs* 15 [Winter, 1986]) Thomas W. Pogge remarks that the "projected global institutional structure, featuring procedural practices supportive of personal autonomy, must be effective and able to maintain itself in our world under modern conditions. And it must be within reach from where we are, via a realistic transitional path not involving unacceptable moral costs." My conclusion is gloomy, relative to these words, in the sense that I do not see that a world community operating in line with the liberal conception of justice is much "within reach from where we are." I might of course be wrong in my estimate of the entrenched character of the nation-state system. Pogge adds that a "promising strategy" in this matter "requires a thorough understanding of social regularities and of the present international regime," and it may be that my understanding of these latter items is less than thorough.

8. On the Importance of One's Life

1. The phrase is W. D. Falk's, in "Morality, Self, and Others," in Hector-Neri Castañeda and George Nakhnikian, eds., *Morality and the Language of Conduct* (Detroit: Wayne State University Press, 1963), p. 64.
2. Ibid., p. 49.
3. Ibid., pp. 49–50.
4. Cf. Christopher Lasch, *The Culture of Narcissism* (New York: Norton, 1979). For a delightful discussion of current self-help books and "the continuing American dialectic of self-indulgence and blame," see Jacob Epstein's essay "Help!" *New York Review of Books* 27 (Feb. 21, 1980).
5. Falk, "Morality, Self, and Others," p. 51.
6. Immanuel Kant, "Duties to Oneself," in *Lectures on Ethics* (New York: Harper Torchbooks, 1963), p. 121.
7. Falk, "Morality, Self, and Others," pp. 63–64.
8. David Hume, *An Enquiry Concerning the Principles of Morals* (1777), in *Hume's Enquiries*, ed. L. A. Selby-Bigge (Oxford: Clarendon Press, 1962), p. 283.
9. Cf. Bernard Williams, "Moral Luck," in Williams, *Moral Luck* (Cambridge, Eng.: Cambridge University Press, 1981), and Thomas Nagel, "Moral Luck," in Nagel, *Mortal Questions* (Cambridge, Eng.: Cambridge University Press, 1979).

10. Cf. Vinit Haksar, *Equality, Liberty, and Perfectionism* (New York: Oxford University Press, 1979).

11. John Rawls, *A Theory of Justice* (Cambridge, Mass.: Belknap Press of Harvard University Press, 1971), p. 15. Cf. p. 104.

12. Robert Nozick, *Anarchy, State, and Utopia* (New York: Basic Books, 1974), ch. 7, sec. 2.

13. Henry Sidgwick, *The Methods of Ethics* (7th ed., 1907; New York: Dover, 1966), p. 498.

14. Williams, *Moral Luck*, p. 5.

15. Ibid., p. 4.

16. Ibid.

17. Ibid., pp. 4-5.

18. Ibid., pp. 1-2.

19. Ibid., p. 13.

20. Ibid., p. 18.

21. Thomas Nagel, "The Fragmentation of Value," in *Mortal Questions*, p. 134.

22. Rawls writes that "we want to live with others on terms that everyone would recognize as fair from a perspective that all would accept as reasonable. The ideal of persons cooperating on this basis exercises a natural attraction upon our affections" (*A Theory of Justice*, p. 478). I do not see that Williams' "perspective from now"—*my* perspective—could meet the standard of being a perspective that "all would accept as reasonable."

23. Williams, *Moral Luck*, p. 18 (emphasis mine).

24. I believe my observation here about how Williams' view works fits with his discussion in *Ethics and the Limits of Philosophy* (Cambridge, Mass.: Harvard University Press, 1985), pp. 66-70, esp. pp. 68-69.

25. One reason for thinking that shared-fate individualism may in principle be able to overcome criticisms that attempt to show that it is not what is required by morality in today's world is suggested by Nagel's view in "The Fragmentation of Value." Nagel argues that morality is *not unitary*, but in fact includes values of irreducibly different *types*. These types of value have "fundamentally different kinds of sources" in what Nagel calls (for example, in the quoted passage in the previous section) the "perspectives" or "points of view" that we as human beings are capable of. The point is that conflicting arguments over a moral issue may involve considerations that are "relevant" to the issue but of different types and thus belong to different perspectives. Nagel then adds: "When faced with con-

Notes to Chapter 8

flicting and incommensurable claims we still have to do something. . . . Briefly, I contend that there can be good judgment without total justification, either explicit or implicit. The fact that one cannot say why a certain decision is the correct one, given a particular balance of conflicting reasons, does not mean that the claim to correctness is meaningless. Provided one has taken the process of practical justification as far as it will go in the course of arriving at the conflict, one may be able to proceed without further justification, but without irrationality either" (pp. 134–35). In the context of my discussion I interpret this to mean that insofar as shared-fate individualism is a reflection of one of the battery of perspectives (contributory sources of moral value) we are capable of, then one's maintaining it in the face of candidate criticisms of it may be defensible in at least the sense that the criticisms will not, or cannot, show that shared-fate individualism is irrational. That is, it is not *mistaken* to "stay with" shared-fate individualism in the face of considerations grounded in other perspectives. One may follow shared-fate individualism while agreeing that the considerations grounded in other perspectives apply.

26. Thomas Nagel, "Subjective and Objective," in *Mortal Questions*, p. 205. Nagel adds (n. 10) that Williams "presses the claims not only of the view from within one's own life but of the view from the present time."

27. Cf. John Stuart Mill, *Utilitarianism* (1863), ch. 3.

28. Thomas Nagel, "The Limits of Objectivity," in Sterling M. McMurrin, ed., *The Tanner Lectures on Human Values*, vol. 1 (Salt Lake City: University of Utah Press, and Cambridge, Eng.: Cambridge University Press, 1980), pp. 137–38. Cf. Nagel's *The View from Nowhere* (New York: Oxford University Press, 1986), p. 187.

29. Rawls, *A Theory of Justice*, p. 512.

30. On the point of importance, Rawls writes that "the public realization of justice is a value of community" and that "the collective activity of justice is the preeminent form of human flourishing" (*A Theory of Justice*, p. 529). For the "national community" stipulation, see p. 457.

31. But this is *not* to say that the resolution is not justified if it "turns out" that doing what one can is not a great deal. I do not wish to view this as a case of "retrospective justification" of the sort Williams explores in "Moral Luck."

32. Perhaps these remarks help respond to the worry that my account may in general exaggerate the conflict between self-realization and service-to-others. After all, a person may serve others as a by-product of his or her

self-realizationist efforts even if he or she neither intends nor is motivated to serve others; and, conversely, persons who intend or are motivated to serve others may have their projects misfire and end up harming others. To what extent is it necessary to the amelioration of the faults in the human condition that individuals act in line with the particular ordering of values involved in shared-fate individualism? My thought here is that it is not enough to leave the prospect of the amelioration of destitution to the contingency of a fortuitous coincidence between the self-realizationist aims of competent individuals, or the fortunate by-products of their self-realizationist activities, and that relief—even though, as I say in the text, we may not, on the shared-fate approach I recommend, be confident about the success of our efforts to serve. From the standpoint of a theory that means to recommend a moral conception for responsible individuals (not from the standpoint of a theory concerned with, say, morally principled economic policies within nation-states), something more nearly targeted on the problem seems to me called for. I think shared-fate individualism, which *is* targeted on the problem, would help "get the job done" and would also speak to the moral-psychological consideration of "reconciliation" that I discuss in this section. It is not part of my view that the general adoption of shared-fate individualism on the part of competent individuals would be easy to accomplish. On the contrary, in many places in this discussion I have expressed my pessimism on this point. But I think that shared-fate individualism can be, as I put it, "required by morality," even if there are grounds for such pessimism about achieving its general adoption.

33. But without the quasi-reduction of the person to his or her character that Williams proposes. See 8.5.

34. For a discussion of the idea that "existing morality" affords more efficacious arguments in support of an extensive duty to relieve suffering than does "unfamiliar moral theory," see Susan James, "The Duty to Relieve Suffering," *Ethics* 93 (Oct., 1982).

35. Cf. James D. Wallace, *Virtues and Vices* (Ithaca, N.Y.: Cornell University Press, 1978), ch. 5, sec. 4, esp. pp. 148–49.

36. Susan Wolf's view, in "Moral Saints," *Journal of Philosophy* 79 (Aug., 1982), has the effect of making room for "putting oneself first" without claiming that to do so is "what morality requires." It is thus different in its make-up from both of the views discussed above as forms of "impatience" with shared-fate individualism. Wolf calls attention to the "point of view of individual perfection," which yields judgments of a type that is "neither moral nor egoistic" (p. 436). This point of view "provides

us with reasons that are independent of moral reasons for wanting ourselves and others to develop our characters and live our lives in certain ways" (p. 437). Insofar as the perspective of individual perfection might be suggestive of an interpretation of the idea of putting-oneself-first, Wolf's view leads us to "call into question the assumption that it is always better to be morally better" (p. 438). I gather that, on Wolf's account, individual-perfection values are not *moral* values. But the substance of her view is nevertheless an assertion of the propriety and importance of the former values. However, toward the end of her essay she writes: "This is not to say that moral value should not be an important, even the most important, kind of value we attend to in evaluating and improving ourselves and our world. It is to say that our values cannot be fully comprehended on the model of a hierarchical system with morality at the top" (p. 438). Now, one may agree with this last negative point about the "organization" of our values, *and* (as I understand Wolf's account) claim—without, as it were, failure of rationality—that shared-fate individualism conveys "what morality requires." Beyond that, I think one may *also* cite the cruel facts about the human condition in our time, and their character as ameliorable, in support of the judgment that moral value (as interpreted *via* shared-fate individualism) should be considered (in our time) "the most important kind of value for us to attend to," without necessarily being in conflict with the major claims in Wolf's account.

37. My remark here is in disagreement with the following passage from Rawls' *A Theory of Justice*: "Neither concern for others nor for self has priority, for all are equal; and the balance between persons is given by the principles of justice. And where this balance moves to one side, as with the moralities of supererogation, it does so from the election of self, which freely takes on the larger part" (p. 485). My thought is that in certain cases the balance may "move to one side" (giving priority to concern for others), but *not* thereby move from the morality of duty to "the moralities of supererogation." Cf. Elizabeth M. Pybus, " 'Saints and Heroes,' " *Philosophy* 57 (1982).

38. John Rawls, "The Independence of Moral Theory," *Proceedings and Addresses of the American Philosophical Association* 48 (1974–75): 15.

WORKS CITED

Addams, Jane. *Democracy and Social Ethics.* New York: Macmillan, 1902.
———. *Twenty Years at Hull-House.* New York: Macmillan, 1910.
Aiken, William, and Hugh La Follette, eds. *World Hunger and Moral Obligation.* Englewood Cliffs, N.J.: Prentice-Hall, 1977.
Bachrach, Peter. "Interest, Participation, and Democratic Theory." In J. Roland Pennock and John W. Chapman, eds., *Nomos XVI: Participation in Politics.* New York: Lieber-Atherton, 1975.
Baier, Kurt. "The Social Source of Reason." *Proceedings and Addresses of the American Philosophical Association* 51 (Aug., 1978).
Barry, Brian. "The Public Interest." *Proceedings of the Aristotelian Society* supp. 38 (1964). Reprinted in Anthony Quinton, ed., *Political Philosophy* (London: Oxford University Press, 1967).
———. *The Liberal Theory of Justice.* Oxford: Clarendon Press, 1973.
———. "Justice Between Generations." In P. M. S. Hacker and Joseph Raz, eds., *Law, Morality, and Society.* Oxford: Clarendon Press, 1977.
———. "Circumstances of Justice and Future Generations." In R. I. Sikora and Brian Barry, eds., *Obligations to Future Generations.* Philadelphia: Temple University Press, 1978.
———. "And Who Is My Neighbor?" *Yale Law Journal* 88 (Jan., 1979). A review of Charles Fried, *Right and Wrong* (Cambridge, Mass.: Harvard University Press, 1978).
———. "Intergenerational Justice in Energy Policy." In Douglas MacLean and Peter G. Brown, eds., *Energy and the Future.* Totowa, N.J.: Rowman and Littlefield, 1983.
Beitz, Charles. *Political Theory and International Relations.* Princeton, N.J.: Princeton University Press, 1979.
Bickel, Alexander M. "Citizen or Person? What Is Not Granted Cannot Be Taken Away." In Bickel, *The Morality of Consent.* New Haven, Conn.: Yale University Press, 1975.
Braybrooke, David. "Let Needs Diminish That Preferences May Prosper." In Nicholas Rescher, ed., *Studies in Moral Philosophy.* American Philosophical Quarterly Monograph no. 1. Oxford: Blackwell, 1968.

Bowie, Norman E., and Robert L. Simon. *The Individual and the Political Order.* Englewood Cliffs, N.J.: Prentice-Hall, 1977.
Brown, Peter G., and Henry Shue, eds. *Food Policy.* New York: Free Press, 1977.
Care, Norman S. "Participation and Policy." *Ethics* 88 (July, 1978).
———. "Future Generations, Public Policy, and the Motivation Problem." *Environmental Ethics* 4 (Fall, 1982).
———. Review of Vinit Haksar, *Equality, Liberty, and Perfectionism. Nous* 17 (May, 1983).
———. "Career Choice." *Ethics* 94 (Jan., 1984).
———. Review of Michael J. Sandel, *Liberalism and the Limits of Justice. Nous* 19 (Sept., 1985).
Dahrendorf, Rolf. *On Britain.* London: British Broadcasting Corp., 1982.
Dugard, John. *Human Rights and the South African Legal Order.* Princeton, N.J.: Princeton University Press, 1978.
Dworkin, Ronald. "Liberalism." In Stuart Hampshire, ed., *Public and Private Morality.* Cambridge, Eng.: Cambridge University Press, 1978.
———. *Taking Rights Seriously.* Cambridge, Mass.: Harvard University Press, 1978.
Eberstadt, Nick. "Myths of the Food Crisis." *New York Review of Books* 23 (Feb. 19, 1976).
Epstein, Jacob. "Help!" *New York Review of Books* 27 (Feb. 21, 1980).
Erikson, Erik H. *Gandhi's Truth.* New York: Norton, 1969.
Falk, W. D. "Morality, Self, and Others." In Hector-Neri Castañeda and George Nakhnikian, eds., *Morality and the Language of Conduct.* Detroit: Wayne State University Press, 1963.
Feinberg, Joel. "The Rights of Animals and Unborn Generations." In William T. Blackstone, ed., *Philosophy and Environmental Crisis.* Athens: University of Georgia Press, 1974. Reprinted in Richard A. Wasserstrom, ed., *Today's Moral Problems* (2nd ed.; New York: Macmillan, 1979).
———. "Harm and Self-Interest." In P. M. S. Hacker and Joseph Raz, eds., *Law, Morality, and Society.* Oxford: Clarendon Press, 1977.
Fingarette, Herbert. *On Responsibility.* New York: Basic Books, 1967.
Frankena, William K. "The Philosophy of Vocation." *Thought* 51 (Dec., 1976).
Gauthier, David. "The Social Contract as Ideology." *Philosophy and Public Affairs* 6 (Winter, 1977).

Works Cited

Gough, J. W. *The Social Contract*. 2nd ed. Oxford: Clarendon Press, 1957.
Haksar, Vinit. *Equality, Liberty, and Perfectionism*. New York: Oxford University Press, 1979.
Hart, H. L. A. *The Concept of Law*. Oxford: Clarendon Press, 1961.
———. "Rawls on Liberty and Its Priority." *University of Chicago Law Review* 40 (Spring, 1973). Reprinted in Norman Daniels, ed., *Reading Rawls* (New York: Basic Books, 1975).
Heilbroner, Robert L. *An Inquiry Into the Human Prospect*. New York: Norton, 1975, 1974.
Hobbes, Thomas. *Leviathan* (1651), ed. and intro. Michael Oakeshott. Oxford: Blackwell, 1957.
Honoré, A. M. "Law, Morals, and Rescue." In James M. Ratcliffe, ed., *The Good Samaritan and the Law*. New York: Doubleday, 1966. Reprinted in Joel Feinberg and Hyman Gross, eds., *Philosophy of Law* (2nd ed.; Belmont, Calif.: Wadsworth, 1980).
Hume, David. *An Enquiry Concerning the Principles of Morals* (1777). In *Hume's Enquiries*, ed. L. A. Selby-Bigge. Oxford: Clarendon Press, 1962.
James, Susan. "The Duty to Relieve Suffering." *Ethics* 93 (Oct., 1982).
Kant, Immanuel. *Foundations of the Metaphysics of Morals* (1785), trans. and intro. Lewis White Beck. Indianapolis: Bobbs-Merrill, 1959.
———. *Lectures on Ethics*. New York: Harper Torchbooks, 1963.
Kaufman, Arnold S. *The Radical Liberal*. New York: Atherton, 1968.
———. "Wants, Needs, and Liberalism." *Inquiry* 14 (Autumn, 1971).
Kronman, Anthony T. "Talent Pooling." In J. Roland Pennock and John W. Chapman, eds., *Nomos XXIII: Human Rights*. New York: New York University Press, 1981.
Lasch, Christopher. *The Culture of Narcissism*. New York: Norton, 1979.
Lippman, Walter. *Essays in the Public Philosophy*. Boston: Little, Brown, 1955.
Lyons, David. "Nature and Soundness of the Contract and Coherence Arguments." In Norman Daniels, ed., *Reading Rawls*. New York: Basic Books, 1975.
McCloskey, H. J. "Liberalism." *Philosophy* 49 (Jan., 1974).
MacIntyre, Alasdair. *After Virtue*. Notre Dame, Ind.: University of Notre Dame Press, 1981.
Marx, Karl. *The German Ideology*. In *The Marx-Engels Reader*, ed. Robert C. Tucker. New York: Norton, 1972.

Mayer, Jean. "Ban Starvation, a Military Weapon Against Children." Cleveland *Plain Dealer*, Nov. 14, 1978. Originally published in the Washington *Post*.

Mill, John Stuart. *On Liberty* (1859), ed. Elizabeth Rapaport. Indianapolis: Hackett, 1978.

———. *Utilitarianism* (1863), ed. George Sher. Indianapolis: Hackett, 1979.

Miller, Arthur. *The Death of a Salesman*. New York: Viking Press, 1949.

Moore, Barrington, Jr. *Injustice: The Social Bases of Obedience and Revolt*. White Plains, N.Y.: Sharpe, 1978.

Moran, Joseph M., Michael D. Morgan, and James H. Wiersma. *An Introduction to Environmental Sciences*. Boston: Little, Brown, 1973.

Morris, Herbert. *On Guilt and Innocence*. Berkeley: University of California Press, 1976.

Nagel, Thomas. *The Possibility of Altruism*. Oxford: Clarendon Press, 1970.

———. "Equal Treatment and Compensatory Discrimination." *Philosophy and Public Affairs* 2 (Summer, 1973). Reprinted in Marshall Cohen, Thomas Nagel, and Thomas Scanlon, eds., *Equality and Preferential Treatment* (Princeton, N.J.: Princeton University Press, 1977). Also reprinted as "The Policy of Preference" in Nagel, *Mortal Questions* (Cambridge, Eng.: Cambridge University Press, 1979).

———. "Poverty and Food: Why Charity Is Not Enough." In Peter G. Brown and Henry Shue, eds., *Food Policy*. New York: Free Press, 1977.

———. *Mortal Questions*. Cambridge, Eng.: Cambridge University Press, 1979. See esp. "Moral Luck," "The Fragmentation of Value," and "Subjective and Objective."

———. "The Limits of Objectivity." In Sterling M. McMurrin, ed., *The Tanner Lectures on Human Values*, vol. 1. Salt Lake City: University of Utah Press, and Cambridge, Eng.: Cambridge University Press, 1980.

———. *The View from Nowhere*. New York: Oxford University Press, 1986.

Narveson, Jan. "Aesthetics, Charity, Utility, and Distributive Justice." *The Monist* 56 (Oct., 1972).

Nozick, Robert. *Anarchy, State, and Utopia*. New York: Basic Books, 1974.

Works Cited

O'Neill, Onora. *Faces of Hunger*. London: Allen and Unwin, 1986.
Parfit, Derek. "Energy Policy and the Further Future: The Social Discount Rate" and "Energy Policy and the Further Future: The Identity Problem." Both in Douglas MacLean and Peter G. Brown, eds., *Energy and the Future*. Totowa, N.J.: Rowman and Littlefield, 1983.
Partridge, Ernest. "Why Care About the Future?" In Partridge, ed., *Responsibilities to Future Generations*. Buffalo, N.Y.: Prometheus Press, 1981.
Pateman, Carole. *Participation and Democratic Theory*. Cambridge, Eng.: Cambridge University Press, 1970.
Peffer, Rodney. "A Defense of Rights to Well-Being." *Philosophy and Public Affairs* 8 (Fall, 1978).
Plato. *Gorgias*. In *The Dialogues of Plato*, trans. Benjamin Jowett, intro. Raphael Demos. New York: Random House, 1937.
Pogge, Thomas W. "Liberalism and Global Justice: Hoffman and Nardin on Morality in International Affairs." *Philosophy and Public Affairs* 15 (Winter, 1986).
Pybus, Elizabeth M. "'Saints and Heroes.'" *Philosophy* 57 (1982).
Rawls, John. *A Theory of Justice*. Cambridge, Mass.: Belknap Press of Harvard University Press, 1971.
———. "The Independence of Moral Theory." *Proceedings and Addresses of the American Philosophical Association* 48 (1974–75).
———. "Fairness to Goodness." *Philosophical Review* 84 (Oct., 1975).
———. "The Basic Structure as Subject." *American Philosophical Quarterly* 14 (April, 1977). Also (slightly expanded) in A. I. Goldman and Jaegwon Kim, eds., *Values and Morals* (Dordrecht, Holland: Reidel, 1978).
———. "A Well-Ordered Society." In Peter Laslett and James Fishkin, eds., *Philosophy, Politics, and Society*. 5th ser. New Haven, Conn.: Yale University Press, 1979.
———. "Kantian Constructivism in Moral Theory" (1980 Dewey Lectures). *Journal of Philosophy* 77 (Sept., 1980).
———. "The Basic Liberties and Their Priority." In Sterling M. McMurrin, ed., *The Tanner Lectures on Human Values*, vol. 3. Salt Lake City: University of Utah Press, and Cambridge, Eng.: Cambridge University Press, 1982.
———. "Social Unity and Primary Goods." In Amartya Sen and Bernard Williams, eds., *Utilitarianism and Beyond*. Cambridge, Eng.: Cambridge University Press, 1982.

Rousseau, Jean-Jacques. *A Discourse on the Origin of Inequality* (1755). In *The Social Contract and Discourses*, trans. and intro. G. D. H. Cole. New York: Everyman, 1950.

———. *The Social Contract* (1762). In *The Social Contract and Discourses*, trans. and intro. G. D. H. Cole. New York: Everyman, 1950.

Sandel, Michael J. *Liberalism and the Limits of Justice*. Cambridge, Eng.: Cambridge University Press, 1982.

———. Review of Michael Walzer, *Spheres of Justice*. *New York Times Book Review*, April 24, 1983.

———. "Morality and the Liberal Ideal." *New Republic*, May 7, 1984.

Sen, Amartya. *Poverty and Famines*. Oxford: Clarendon Press, 1981.

Sher, George. "Justifying Reverse Discrimination in Employment." *Philosophy and Public Affairs* 4 (Winter, 1975). Reprinted in Marshall Cohen, Thomas Nagel, and Thomas Scanlon, eds., *Equality and Preferential Treatment*. Princeton, N.J.: Princeton University Press, 1977.

Shue, Henry. *Basic Rights*. Princeton, N.J.: Princeton University Press, 1980.

Sidgwick, Henry. *The Methods of Ethics*. 7th ed. (1907). New York: Dover, 1966.

Singer, Peter. "Famine, Affluence, and Morality." *Philosophy and Public Affairs* 1 (1972). Reprinted in William Aiken and Hugh La Follette, eds., *World Hunger and Moral Obligation* (Englewood Cliffs, N.J.: Prentice-Hall, 1977).

———. *Democracy and Disobedience*. Oxford: Clarendon Press, 1973.

———. *Practical Ethics*. Cambridge, Eng.: Cambridge University Press, 1979.

Smith, M. B. E. "The Value of Participation." In J. Roland Pennock and John W. Chapman, eds., *Nomos XVI: Participation in Politics*. New York: Lieber-Atherton, 1975.

Strawson, P. F. "Social Morality and Individual Ideal." *Philosophy* 36 (1961).

Thomson, Judith Jarvis. "A Defense of Abortion." *Philosophy and Public Affairs* 1 (Fall, 1971). Reprinted in Marshall Cohen, Thomas Nagel, and Thomas Scanlon, eds., *The Rights and Wrongs of Abortion* (Princeton, N.J.: Princeton University Press, 1974).

Wallace, James D. *Virtues and Vices*. Ithaca, N.Y.: Cornell University Press, 1978.

Works Cited

Walzer, Michael. "From Contract to Community." *New Republic*, Dec. 13, 1982. Review of Michael J. Sandel, *Liberalism and the Limits of Justice*.
———. *Spheres of Justice*. New York: Basic Books, 1983.
Williams, Bernard. "A Critique of Utilitarianism." In J. J. C. Smart and Bernard Williams, *Utilitarianism, For and Against*. Cambridge, Eng.: Cambridge University Press, 1973.
———. *Moral Luck*. Cambridge, Eng.: Cambridge University Press, 1981. See esp. "Persons, Character, and Morality" and "Moral Luck."
———. *Ethics and the Limits of Philosophy*. Cambridge, Mass.: Harvard University Press, 1985.
Wolf, Susan. "Moral Saints." *Journal of Philosophy* 79 (Aug., 1982).
Wolff, Robert Paul. *Understanding Rawls*. Princeton, N.J.: Princeton University Press, 1977.

INDEX

Acceptance of terms, as condition of (strong) participation, 79
Addams, Jane, 28–29, 201 n. 6, 202 n. 12
Affluent society, 14–15, 129, 161
Agreement group, 73, 76, 77, 83, 85, 88, 90–92, 211 n. 1
Aiken, William, 196 n. 8
Amelioration of the human condition, 18–19, 25, 37, 45, 161, 162–63, 187–91, 228 n. 32, 229 n. 36
Anti-paternalism, 202 n. 13
Autonomy, 70, 131–32

Bachrach, Peter, 208 n. 5
Baier, Kurt, 207 n. 4
Barry, Brian, 102, 127, 153, 198 n. 17, 205 n. 30, 210 nn. 22, 31, 212–13 n. 13, 215 n. 22, 216 nn. 29, 35, 218 nn. 7, 8, 223 n. 21
Basic structure of society, 37, 150, 151–56, 203 n. 19, 222 nn. 16, 17, 18. *See also* Conception of justice for society
Beitz, Charles, 224 n. 32
Benevolence, 104, 214 n. 18
Bickel, Alexander M., 150, 222 n. 15
Bowie, Norman E., 198 n. 12
Braybrooke, David, 198 n. 13
Brown, Peter G., 200 n. 28

Career choice: common opinion of, 28–29; problem of, 26–48; risks of, 33–34; and society's degree of justice, 32–33
Careers, 27, 29–32. *See also* Service to others
Character, 179–84. *See also* Individuality
Claims of established liberty against shared-fate individualism, 148–67
Claims of one's own life against shared-fate individualism, 168–93
Community, idea of, in critique of liberalism, 130–40
Community bonding, and reciprocation, 109–15
Community self-interestedness, as condition of (strong) participation, 81–82
Competent individual, 29, 31–33, 76, 118, 122, 144–45, 150, 169, 189–90, 228 n. 32
Conception of justice for society, 86, 143–44, 148, 187, 192, 210 n. 29, 216 n. 31, 228 n. 32
Conception of responsibility for individuals, 143–44, 148, 187, 192, 216 n. 31, 228 n. 32
Concern for generations to come, 99–116
Condition of legitimacy in shared-

Condition of legitimacy, *continued*
fate individualism, 40, 42, 147, 158, 164–65, 183–85, 187–88
Constraints of morality, and (strong) participation, 84
Count all votes, as condition of (strong) participation, 83

Dahrendorf, Rolf, 197 n. 11
Democratic theory, 69–70
Destitution, 11–14, 119–20; as distribution problem, 21–22, 200 n. 8; as issue of rights as well as needs, 162–63; and racism and sexism, 161–62
Dilemma, posed by liberal and shared-fate individualism, 43–44, 47–48
Disinterestedness, as condition of (strong) participation, 79–80, 87, 91
Dugard, John, 197 n. 9
Duties of aid, 122, 123–24, 128, 218 n. 8
Dworkin, Ronald, 208 n. 11

Eberstadt, Nick, 196 nn. 7, 8
Egoism, 54, 55–60, 98
Enforcement of morality by state, 205 n. 30
Epstein, Jacob, 225 n. 4
Equal moral persons, 37, 42, 44, 63–64, 149, 153–56, 160–61, 165, 188–89, 192, 204 n. 20, 205 n. 29, 208 n. 11
Equal opportunity, and future generations, 102, 120, 212–13 n. 13, 218 n. 7
Erikson, Eric H., 222 n. 9

Established liberty. *See* Claims of established liberty against shared-fate individualism
Extended shared-fate motivation, 111–16, 217 n. 37

Falk, W. D., 170–71, 186, 206 n. 35, 225 n. 1
Fatalism, 24–25
Feinberg, Joel, 102, 113, 212 n. 11, 214–15 n. 21, 215 nn. 22, 25, 222 n. 11
Fingarette, Herbert, 208 n. 10
Foreign aid, individual and national, 165–67
Form of moral life, 36, 43, 57, 59, 188–91, 193, 203 n. 18
Framework of society, 38, 118, 204 n. 24, 217 n. 3
Frankena, William K., 222 n. 8
Freedom of the person, 17, 161
Frieden, Thomas R., 222 n. 9
Future people, 13, 106–16, 119, 161

Gauthier, David, 217 n. 36
Gough, J. W., 211 n. 35
Guilt, 22–23, 24, 109–11

Haksar, Vinit, 202 n. 14, 219–20 n. 34, 226 n. 10
Hart, H. L. A., 198 nn. 16, 17, 208 n. 12, 214 n. 20, 222 n. 10, 224 n. 31
Heilbroner, Robert L., 100, 115–16, 211 n. 3, 212 n. 11, 218 n. 6
Hobbes, Thomas, 79, 82–84, 92, 160

Index

Honoré, A. M., 205 n. 31, 211 n. 2, 217 n. 1
Human condition, 24–25, 39, 129, 186–93, 228–29 n. 36; cosmic unfairness of, 24, 186; as flawed, 188–91
Hume, David, 98, 103, 118, 171, 186, 206 n. 35

Impartiality, 81–82, 92, 184–85
Importance of one's life, 178–80, 184
Incentive question, 10. See also Motivation
Independent policy makers for a free society, 96–98, 116, 211 n. 1, 217 n. 37
Indignation, 23, 24
Individualism, 35
Individuality, 28, 178–80, 182–84, 188
Individual liberty, 16–18, 158–60, 161, 166, 202 n. 9, 224 n. 35. See also Claims of established liberty against shared-fate individualism
Individual responsibility: course of, in different circumstances, 46; idea of, 3–11; as more demanding than public policy, 121, 126; theory of, distinct from theory for basic structure of society, 143–44, 148, 187, 216 n. 31, 228 n. 32
Inequality in levels of life, 14–18
Information, equal and full, as condition of (strong) participation, 82, 87, 91
Interests: collision of, 65; and future people, 106–9; perceived and real, 69–72, 79, 85, 87, 88, 105, 210 n 31; and procedural moral acceptability, 74; pursuit of individual conceptions of, 120

James, Susan, 228 n. 34
Joint agreement, as condition of (strong) participation, 80–81, 83
Justice, liberal theory of: Sandel's critique of, 130–40; and shared-fate individualism, 141–67

Kant, Immanuel, 87, 103, 112, 130, 144–45, 153, 171, 179–82, 201 n. 2, 213 nn. 14, 15, 214 n. 18
Kaufman, Arnold S., 208 nn. 1, 4, 5
Kronman, Anthony T., 205 n. 30

La Follette, Hugh, 196 n. 8
Lasch, Christopher, 211 n. 4, 225 n. 4
Liberal conception of justice. See Justice, liberal theory of
Liberal individualism, 38–41, 45, 190–91. See also Conception of responsibility for individuals; Moral conceptions
Libertarianism, 144–45, 221 n. 5
Lippman, Walter, 209 n. 10
Locke, John, 92, 150
Love, 107–9
Lyons, David, 209 n. 14, 211 n. 32

McCloskey, H. J., 202 n. 14
MacIntyre, Alasdair, 219 n. 16
Malnutrition, 13, 21, 199–200 n. 27

[241]

Marx, Karl, 144–45, 174, 202 n. 8
Mayer, Jean, 196 n. 8
Meaning of life, 179–80
Members of future generations. *See* Future people
Members of moral community, 49–67, 128–29, 131, 173
Mill, John Stuart, 28, 143, 198 n. 16, 199 n. 21, 201 n. 4, 205 n. 30, 213 n. 15, 227 n. 27
Miller, Arthur, 202 n. 10
Moore, Barrington, Jr., 197 n. 10, 215 n. 24
Moral absolutes, personal, 172–73
Moral agency, interpretation of, 51–53, 57–58. *See also* Members of moral community
Moral attitudes, basic, 35, 203 n. 18
Moral causes, seriousness of, 162
Moral community, 22, 65–67, 112–15, 175, 193, 211 n. 1, 216 n. 35. *See also* Members of moral community
Moral conceptions, 24, 35–36, 203 n. 18, 216 n. 31. *See also* Conception of justice for society; Conception of responsibility for individuals; Justice, liberal theory of; Liberal individualism; Separate-life individualism; Shared-fate individualism
Moral-emotional reaction to destitution, 21–25, 200 n. 29
Moral point of view, 162, 178–91, 218 n. 11. *See also* Perspectives
Moral psychology, 21, 185, 203 n. 18, 206 n. 35

Moral requirements, 124–25. *See also* Supererogation
Moral sensibility, 47, 104–6
Moral standing of individual lives, 34–41, 46, 142–43, 146
Morris, Herbert, 216 n. 27
Motivation: and coercion, 116; idea of, 103–6; problem of, 10, 95–116, 210 n. 25, 211 n. 5

Nagel, Thomas, 182, 184–85, 186, 199 n. 19, 200 n. 29, 202 n. 11, 218 n. 12, 225 n. 9, 226 n. 25, 227 nn. 26, 28
Narveson, Jan, 205 n. 31
Nation-state system, 165–67
Non-coercion, as condition of (strong) participation, 77–78, 87, 91
Non-riskiness, as condition of (strong) participation, 82–83
Nozick, Robert, 145, 177, 203 n. 17, 204 n. 24, 210 n. 19, 217 n. 3, 221 n. 5

O'Neill, Onora, 221 n. 7
Ordering problem for self-responsibility and other-responsibility, 10–12
Ordinary persons, as distinct from members of moral community, 121–40, 167, 172. *See also* Members of moral community
Other-responsibility. *See* Responsibility for others

Parfit, Derek, 217–18 n. 5, 218 n. 8

Index   [243]

Participation: conditions of (strong), 77–84; criticism of, 71–72; difficulties with (strong), 84–90, 93; (strong), as an ideal, 87–90; strong and weak forms of, 72–76, 209 n. 11, 211 n. 1
Particularity, of persons, 107–9, 110–15, 139–40. *See also* Individuality
Partridge, Ernest, 217 n. 37
Pateman, Carole, 209 n. 11
Peffer, Rodney, 206 n. 32
Personal relations, 179
Perspectives, 181–85; "from now," 180, 181–84, 184–85, 226 n. 22; impartial, external, 183–84; of individual perfection, 228–29 n. 36; *sub specie aeternitatis*, 127–28, 218 n. 11
Pessimism, 24–25
Plato, 195 n. 1
Plurality voting, 85–86
Pogge, Thomas W., 224–25 n. 37
Policies, 6–10, 62–63, 73, 145; general features of, 6–10; moral acceptability of, 68–94, 96–99, 101; public, 117–26. *See also* Procedural moral acceptability
Politics of accommodation, 94
Possibility, as condition of (strong) participation, 83
Pragmatism, 92
Problem of living with oneself, 186, 206 n. 35. *See also* Reconciliation with human condition
Procedural moral acceptability, 73–74, 77–94, 210 n. 27. *See also* Participation

Pure procedural justice. *See* Procedural moral acceptability
Pybus, Elizabeth M., 206 n. 34, 229 n. 37

Racism, 162–63
Rationality, as condition of (strong) participation, 78
Rawls, John, 17, 112–13, 127–28, 130–40, 141–67, 177, 187, 191–92, 195 n. 2, 198 nn. 14, 15, 199 n. 22, 203 n. 15, 203–4 n. 19, 204 nn. 22, 23, 24, 204–5 n. 25, 205 nn. 26, 27, 206 n. 33, 209 n. 9, 214 n. 18, 215 nn. 23, 26, 216 n. 31, 219 n. 33, 219–20 n. 34, 220 nn. 37, 39, 223 n. 24, 224 n. 36, 226 n. 22, 229 n. 37; equal moral persons, Kantian interpretation of, 153–54; justice across generations, 155; natural duties, 154–55, 165, 223 n. 25, 223–24 n. 26; original position, 76, 79–80, 86, 151–53, 156, 166, 211 n. 1, 222 n. 19; perspective *sub specie aeternitatis*, 127–28, 218 n. 11; primary goods, 12, 195 n. 5, 210 n. 21; Sandel's critique of, 130–40; sense of justice, 114, 216 n. 35; strains of commitment, 212 n. 7, 218 n. 9; subject of justice, 150, 151–56; veil of ignorance, 79–80, 152, 155. *See also* Basic structure of society; Conception of justice for society
Reciprocation, and community bonding, 109–15

Reconciliation with human condition, 187–88, 192–93
Representation, 85
Representative reasonably well-off individual in affluent free society, 14–18, 122, 125
Resignation, 25, 190
Responsibility for oneself, 3–6, 52–53, 169–78
Responsibility for others, 3–6, 52–60, 60–65. *See also* Shared-fate individualism
Rousseau, Jean-Jacques, 71–78, 81–82, 83, 84, 86, 95, 209 n. 11, 210 nn. 20, 28

Sacrifice, 96–98, 102–3, 124, 191
Sandel, Michael J., 130–40, 181, 218 n. 13, 219 n. 17, 220 n. 37, 221 n. 1
Selection problem for a conception of individual responsibility, 41–43, 141–48
Self, idea of, 130–40; as constituted by community, 134–40; in deontological liberalism, 132–34, 136, 139
Self-realization, 4, 27, 28–29, 37, 38–39, 43–44, 47, 97, 173–82, 187–93, 201 n. 2, 202 n. 14, 227–28 n. 32
Self-respect, 171, 173
Self-responsibility. *See* Responsibility for oneself
Sen, Amartya, 196 n. 6, 200 n. 28
Sense of common humanity. *See* Extended shared-fate motivation
Separate-life individualism, 37–41, 43. *See also* Conception of responsibility for individuals; Moral conceptions
Serious life decisions, 145, 169, 187–90, 192, 203 n. 18, 222 n. 9
Service to others, 27, 28–29, 34, 37–40, 187–93, 227–28 n. 32
Settlement view, 70–72, 94, 120, 123
Sexism, 162–63
Shared-fate individualism, 29, 38–48, 129, 140–48, 148–67, 169, 189–91, 191–93, 203 n. 18. *See also* Conception of responsibility for individuals; Moral conceptions
Sher, George, 224 n. 33
Shue, Henry, 200 n. 28, 206 n. 32
Sidgwick, Henry, 104, 178, 212 n. 8, 213–14 n. 17
Simon, Robert L., 198 n. 12
Singer, Peter, 196 n. 6, 199 n. 20, 210 n. 31, 218 n. 8, 221 n. 5, 224 nn. 26, 34
Smith, M. B. E., 209 nn. 6, 7, 8
Social-contract theory, 91–92, 206 n. 33
Socrates, 30, 195 n. 1
Sorrow, 22, 24, 200 n. 29
Starvation, 13, 196–97 n. 8
Strawson, P. F., 53–54, 55, 58, 207 n. 8
Supererogation, 45–48, 126, 140, 223–24 n. 26, 229 n. 37
Sympathy, natural, 105, 186

Thomson, Judith Jarvis, 204 n. 21

Universality, as condition of (strong) participation, 81

Index

Utilitarianism, 143–45, 179–82, 185–86, 221 n. 6

Voice, as condition of (strong) participation, 83–84

Wallace, James D., 205–6 n. 31, 228 n. 35
Walzer, Michael, 130–31, 219 n. 17, 224 n. 29

Welfare state, 37, 197 n. 11
Wick, Warner, 211 n. 34
Williams, Bernard, 179–85, 221 n. 6, 225 n. 9, 226 nn. 22, 24, 227 n. 31, 228 n. 33
Wolf, Susan, 228 n. 36
Wolff, Robert Paul, 198 n. 17
World community, 19–21, 37, 119–20, 124, 149, 151, 153, 156–67